R 970.00497021 STU

Stuart, Paul, 1943-

Nations within a nation

CENTRAL

D0143042

NATIONS
WITHIN A NATION

NATIONS WITHIN A NATION

Historical Statistics
of
American Indians

PAUL STUART

GREENWOOD PRESS
New York • Westport, Connecticut • London

Library of Congress Cataloging-in-Publication Data

Stuart, Paul, 1943-
  Nations within a nation.

  Bibliography: p.
  Includes index.
  1. Indians of North America—History—Statistics.
I. Title.
E77.S924   1987   973'.0497'021   86-33618
ISBN 0-313-23813-8 (lib. bdg. : alk. paper)

British Library Cataloguing in Publication Data is available.

Copyright © 1987 by Paul Stuart

All rights reserved. No portion of this book may be
reproduced, by any process or technique, without the
express written consent of the publisher.

Library of Congress Catalog Card Number: 86-33618
ISBN: 0-313-23813-8

First published in 1987

Greenwood Press, Inc.
88 Post Road West, Westport, Connecticut 06881

Printed in the United States of America

♾™

The paper used in this book complies with the
Permanent Paper Standard issued by the National
Information Standards Organization (Z39.48-1984).

10 9 8 7 6 5 4 3 2

For Lisa and Caitlin

Contents

Preface

As with any scholarly effort, my debts to individuals and institutions are enormous. This work could not have been completed without support from many colleagues, librarians, and institutions. Since my attempt has been to compile data from a variety of sources, I have also relied heavily upon those who gathered the data.

Michael Sherraden and Norman Pollock were the first to suggest the possibility and usefulness of a volume of American Indian historical statistics. Both of these scholars provided suggestions and encouragement at an early stage of the effort. The George Warren Brown School of Social Work, Washington University, provided me with student assistance at an early stage.

The University of Wisconsin–Eau Claire provided me with a supportive environment. My colleagues in the Department of Social Work cheerfully put up with disruptions in my schedule, diversion of clerical time and resources, and my lack of responsiveness to their needs so that I could complete this work. My debt to all of them and in particular to the chairperson of the department, Dr. David J. Johnson, is enormous. Leonard E. Gibbs was generous in his provision of moral support.

The University of Wisconsin–Eau Claire materially supported the completion of this work by providing release time from teaching duties and financial support during the 1983–1984 academic year. The University of Wisconsin System American Ethnic Studies Coordinating Committee also provided financial support for this project. I am very grateful to the Faculty Research Committee at the University of Wisconsin–Eau Claire and the American Ethnic Studies Coordinating Committee for their support. Dean Lee E. Grugel of the School of Arts and Sciences and Dean Ronald N. Satz of the School of Graduate Studies, both historians, have been unfailingly supportive of my research efforts.

Colleagues and scholars eased the way at various points and provided needed encouragement. Among many, I would single out my mentor, Allan G. Bogue of the University of Wisconsin–Madison, who has always been generous with encouragement; Kenneth R. Philp of the University of Texas at Arlington; Fred Nicklason of the University of Maryland; and Ronald N. Satz of the University of Wisconsin–Eau Claire. Ronald Satz was particularly helpful in guiding me to sources of data on the removal period of the early nineteenth century.

Without libraries and librarians, no work of this nature could be contemplated, let alone completed. At the William D. McIntyre Library at the University of Wisconsin–Eau Claire, Leslie A. Foster and her able assistant, Bebeanna B. Buck, were models of informed government publications librarians. Also at the William D. McIntyre Library, Kathleen Henning, interlibrary loan librarian, cheerfully obtained copies of many difficult-to-find items from other libraries. Other institutions also provided invaluable support. The Government Publications Department at the O. Merideth Wilson Library, University of Minnesota–Minneapolis, and the Government Documents Department at the State Historical Society of Wisconsin were both excellent places to work.

The unsung heroes of any publication, particularly one that includes as many tables as this one does, are the clerical staff who must cope with difficult-to-read notations, the uncertainties and hedging of the author, and still prepare a manuscript that is free of errors. Carol Modl, Program Assistant of the Department of Social Work, supervised the typing of the manuscript and did much of the typing herself, particularly of the final version. Most of the tables and first drafts of chapters were typed by Diana Sigler, who spent the greater part of a Wisconsin summer looking at tables on the screen of a word processor. Judy Schoepp and Kathleen Josifek also contributed materially to the completion of the project. To all of these able co-workers, I extend my grateful thanks.

Anyone who attempts to write a book learns very quickly how important the support of friends and family are. My daughters, Lisa and Caitlin, have been a constant source of joy and inspiration. To them, I dedicate this book, with pride and affection.

NATIONS
WITHIN A NATION

1

Introduction, Scope, and Purpose

In this volume, an attempt has been made to gather a variety of statistics pertaining to American Indian groups in the United States. Topics such as land holdings, population, migration, vital statistics, federal government activity, health care and education, occupations, and the use of natural resources were covered. It was the intention to provide in one volume data relating to a variety of topics along with suggestions for locating additional sources of data and for further reading. It would be impossible to include in one volume all of the available statistical data on American Indians. Consequently, the data that have been gathered will be a beginning point for most investigations; it is hoped that the additional sources and suggestions for further reading will enable the reader to pursue topics on his or her own.

Historical statistics pertaining to American Indians present the investigator with a bewildering inconsistency. They are found in a variety of locations and reflect differing units of measurement and categories of analysis. Every effort was made to reduce inconsistencies and to give the reader an idea of the shortcomings of the statistical data that have been included. Accuracy is always a serious problem with statistical data, particularly with data pertaining to American Indian groups. In part, this is because of cultural differences between the government officials and others who gathered the data and the subjects of the data, the American Indian people themselves. Because of this cultural difference, those responsible for gathering data—government agents, census enumerators, and others—may not have known of the occurrence of events, or the occurrence of events may have been hidden from them. In addition, some of those responsible for gathering data had interests in distorting the data to serve their own purposes. For example, Indian agents in the nineteenth century had an interest in appearing to be successful at accomplishing the government's goals; some may have altered reports of school attendance or "progress in civilization." Contracts for the provision of goods were based upon the number of Indians located at any specific agency; some agents exaggerated the number of Indians living at the agency for that reason. For most of the sources of data reported in this book, various estimation procedures were used to fill in for incomplete data. Every effort has been made to indicate the limitations of the data. While providing any data based on estimation or approximation may be questioned, my approach has been to try to provide the best available data with an indication of its shortcomings. As suggested by Henry Dobyns in *Native American Historical Demography,* "one either uses such data as may be available and learns something, however inadequate, or abjures such data and learns nothing."[1]

Many readers will be struck by the relative absence of statistical data from the nineteenth century and the almost complete absence of data from the eighteenth century and earlier. This is not to suggest any evaluation as to the importance of various historical periods. It is an indication of the author's assessment of the quality of the available data. Many series of nineteenth-century data were rejected because of concerns about the accuracy of the available data. Even for those nineteenth-century statistics that are used, particular caution must be exercised. Statistical data-gathering procedures, including the sophistication of estimation procedures, as well as the general volume of statistical production, increased enormously during the twentieth century in Indian affairs, as in many other areas. Consequently, the reader will discern in this compilation a decided "tilt" toward twentieth-century topics. The emphasis on the twentieth century is not entirely fortuitous, however. In recent years, twentieth-century Indian history has become an increasingly exciting and stimulating field. In 1976, Vine Deloria, Jr., called for increased attention by historians to Indian affairs in the twentieth century. That call has been echoed by Francis Paul Prucha and others, and today there is a large and growing literature on Indian affiars in the recent past.[2] Historians of the twentieth century will need to make extensive use of statistical data, not only because it is more readily available, but also because of the increasing complexity of events, the increasing mobility of the Indian population, and the increasingly diverse environments of American Indians, who are found today in urban areas, on reservations, and in the historic Indian areas of Oklahoma and Alaska.

Major sources for the statistical data compiled herein include publications of the Bureau of the Census, and publications of federal government agencies such as the Bureau of Indian Affairs and the Indian

Health Service. Congressional investigations, the reports of such federal agencies as the Minerals Management Service, the Congress's Office of Technology Assessment, and data gathered by demographers and historians also have been used. In some cases, reservation or tribal-level data have been provided. However, it was not possible in one volume to provide as much tribal-level data as one would like. Consequently, in the discussions of sources of additional data that follow, an indication of where tribal-level data may be found is included.

American Indian communities in the twentieth century are, in a very real sense, "nations within a nation." American Indian communities have a unique political relationship to the United States, enjoying what has come to be called a "government to government" relationship with the federal government. They are sovereign entities, which enjoy some, if not all, of the attributes of sovereignty. They are also distinct cultural communities, identifying themselves as separate political and national communities within the United States. Thus, American Indian communities can be truly viewed as "nations within a nation."[3]

American Indians constitute a small but significant group within the United States. The population of the indigenous people of the United States is small in proportion to the total population. Of the eighteen Western hemisphere countries with significant indigenous populations, the United States, with 0.6 percent of the national population classified as indigenous, is among the Western hemisphere countries with the smallest porportions of native peoples. However, 1.4 million persons is a significant number and American Indians have been important in American history. They are also significant because Indian policy in the United States has been significant for Indian policy for other countries in the Western Hemisphere, particularly during the twentieth century. Cross-national contact between Indian and other indigenous groups may be increasing in the contemporary period. For some Western hemisphere countries, such as Bolivia, Ecuador, Guatemala, Mexico, and Peru, American Indian populations are significant proportions of the total (see Table 1.1 at end of chapter).

The indigenous population of the United States is made up of American Indians and two groups of Alaska Natives, Eskimos and Aleuts, with American Indians constituting the vast majority. The Eskimos and Aleuts, who are found primarily in Alaska, today number less than 100,000 (see Table 1.2). Canada is the Western hemisphere country that is most similar to the United States in Indian policy and in the status of its Indian people. At the 1981 census there were fewer than half a million indigenous people in Canada (see Table 1.3). However, because of its smaller total population, the natives of Canada accounted for 2 percent of the national population. There were nearly 300,000 "status Indians," those Indians recognized by the Canadian government, and smaller numbers of Metis (persons of mixed Indian and European descent), "nonstatus Indians," and Inuits (Eskimos).

The American Indian groups found in the United States are varied. The United States has 278 Indian tribes and about 200 Alaska Native villages.[4] An additional 100 or more tribes lack federal recognition.[5] Inadequacies in the available data and in the accessibility of what data are available have been pointed out repeatedly.[6] It is hoped that the publication of this book will contribute in a small way to a solution of the problem by making what data are available more accessible to scholars, policymakers, and tribal people.

Following are chapters on the Indian land base and climate; on the Indian population; on removal, relocation, and urbanization; on vital statistics; on government activity; on health care and education; on occupations, earnings, and income; and on the use of natural resources. Each chapter includes sections that provide suggestions for additional sources of statistical data and suggestions for further reading on the chapter topic. Following the text of each chapter are tables displaying selected statistical information available on the chapter's topic.

In addition to the specific suggestions at the end of each chapter, a general bibliography compiled by Francis Paul Prucha is an essential guide for persons seeking information on most aspects of Indian-White relations in the United States. Prucha published *A Bibliographical Guide to the History of Indian-White Relations in the United States* in 1977. This was followed by his *Indian-White Relations in the United States: A Bibliography of Works Published, 1975-1980* (1982). These two volumes provide an unparalleled guide to the published literature on American Indians in the United States and are the starting point for any serious scholarly investigation of American Indian history. The D'Arcy McNickle Center for the History of the American Indian, Newberry Library, 60 West Walton Street, Chicago, Illinois 60610, has announced plans to update the Prucha bibliographies with a series of annual bibliographies on Indian history. The center also publishes a series of critical bibliographies in American Indian history in cooperation with Indiana University Press.

NOTES

1. Henry F. Dobyns, *Native American Historical Demography: A Critical Bibliography* (Bloomington: Indiana University Press, 1976), p. 7.

2. Vine Deloria, Jr., "The Twentieth Century," in Daniel Tyler, ed., *Red Men and Hat-Wearers: Viewpoints in Indian History* (Boulder, Colorado: Pruett Publishing Company, 1976), pp. 155-166; and Francis Paul Prucha, "Federal Indian Policy in the Twentieth Century," *Western Historical Quarterly* 15 (January 1985): 5-18.

3. Vine Deloria, Jr., and Clifford Lytle provide an excellent discussion of the unique political status of American Indian communities in *The Nations Within: The Past and Future of American Indian Sovereignty* (New York: Pantheon, 1984).

4. Prucha, "Federal Indian Policy"; U.S. Bureau of the Census, *1980 Census of Population. Supplementary Report. American Indian Areas and Alaska Native Villages*, PC80-S1-13 (Washington, D.C.: U.S. Government Printing Office, 1984).

5. U.S. Congress, American Indian Policy Review Commission, *Report on Terminated and Nonfederally Recognized Tribes*, Final Report of Task Force 10 (Washington, D.C.: U.S. Government Printing Office, 1976); Susan D. Greenbaum, "In Search of Lost Tribes: Anthropology and the Federal Acknowledgement Process," *Human Organization* 44 (Winter 1985): 361-367.

6. See, for example, Stephen A. Langone, "A Statistical Profile of the Indian: The Lack of Numbers," in U.S. Congress, Joint Economic Committee, *Toward Economic Development for Native American Communities* vol. 1 (Washington, D.C.: U.S. Government Printing Office, 1969), pp. 1-18.

TABLES

Table 1.1
Estimated American Indian Population, 18 Western Hemisphere Countries, Late 1970s–Early 1980s

COUNTRY	INDIGENOUS POPULATION (in thousands)	% OF NATIONAL POPULATION
Argentina	398	1.5
Bolivia	3,526	59.2
Brazil	243	0.2
Canada	491	2.0
Chile	616	5.7
Columbia	547	2.2
Costa Rica	10	0.6
Ecuador	2,564	33.9
El Salvador[1]	100	2.3
Guatemala	3,739	59.7
Honduras[1]	107	3.2
Mexico	8,042	12.4
Nicaragua[1]	43	1.8
Panama	121	6.8
Paraguay	67	2.3
Peru	6,025	36.8
United States[2]	1,423	0.6
Venezuela	202	1.5

Notes:

  1. Unreliable estimate.
  2. Corrected count.

Source: James W. Wilkie and Adam Perkal, eds., Statistical Abstract of
         Latin America, vol. 24 (Los Angeles: UCLA Latin America Center
         Publications, University of California, 1985), p. 105; Statistics
         Canada, Canada Yearbook 1985 (Ottawa: Minister of Supply and
         Services, 1985), p. 61; U.S. Bureau of the Census, 1980 Census of
         Population. Supplementary Report. American Indian Areas and Alaska
         Native Villages, PC80-51-13 (Washington, D.C.: U.S. Government
         Printing Office, 1984), p. 2.

Table 1.2
American Indians and Alaska Natives in the United States at the 1980 Census

American Indians	1,366,676
Eskimos	42,162
Aleuts	14,205
Total American Indians and Alaska Natives	1,423,043

Note:

Corrected count.

Source: U.S. Bureau of the Census, 1980 Census of Population. Supplementary Report. American Indian Areas and Alaska Native Villages, PC 80-S1-13 (Washington, D.C.: U.S. Government Printing Office, 1984), p. 2.

Table 1.3
Native Peoples of Canada at the 1981 Census

Status Indians	292,700
Non-Status Indians	75,110
Metis	98,260
Inuit	25,390
Total Native Peoples	491,460

Note:

Excludes inmates of institutions. Based on 20% sample.

Source: Statistics Canada, Canada Year Book, 1985 (Ottawa: Minister of Supply and Services, 1985), p. 61.

2

Land Base and Climate

The possession and control of land is an essential element of nationhood. Prior to the arrival of Europeans in the sixteenth and seventeenth centuries, American Indian tribes controlled nearly two billion acres of land in what is now the United States. Indian tribes and individuals now own less than 3 percent of that total—around 52 million acres. Land passed from Indian to non-Indian control in a number of ways. Some was taken as a result of military defeats, while other losses of Indian land were the result of land sales, cessions, and fraudulent theft. By the time of the American Revolution, Indian title to most of the land along the Atlantic seaboard had been extinguished by the English and the other colonial powers. By 1858, the United States had acquired over 581 million acres from the Indians in more than 400 treaties at a cost of less than fifteen million dollars. The Indians reserved the lands not ceded or sold to the United States; these became the reservations of the last century and a half.

The reserved lands of the tribes were reduced during the next century, as white expansion into Indian country continued at a rapid rate. Since the goal of federal Indian policy during most of the nineteenth century was to assimilate American Indians into the mainstream of American life, and since experience seemed to show that individual Indian landowners would more readily part with their land than would corporate tribes, a major component of Indian land tenure during the nineteenth century and after was the allotment of Indian lands.

Allotment meant the division of tribal land holdings into individually held holdings, specified as 160 acres for the head of a family and half that much for his spouse and children in the General Allotment Act (Dawes

Act) of 1887. Indian lands were allotted throughout the late nineteenth and early twentieth centuries under treaties, the Dawes Act, and other special acts and agreements between the United States and Indian tribes. Table 2.1 shows Indian land holdings recognized by the United States between 1871 and 1933. These are divided into tribal lands, or lands owned in common by all tribal members, and allotted lands that had been granted to individual Indians. The figures in the "allotted" column in Table 2.1 show all lands allotted to Indians, including those held in trust for the Indian owner by the United States and those that had passed out of trust or had been alienated after 1910. Some of these alienated lands passed out of the control of the Indian allottee through land sales, condemnation proceedings for nonpayment of taxes, and for other reasons. Therefore, the amount of land indicated in Table 2.1 overstates the amount of land actually controlled by American Indians for the years after 1910.

Table 2.2 shows that by 1934 more than twenty-three million acres of the forty million acres of land allotted to Indians had passed out of trust status. Even with all allotted lands included, Indian land holdings declined to less than seventy million acres by 1933. Table 2.2 summarizes reductions in the size of reservations from their establishment to 1934. Indian reservations were established between 1794 and 1933 as the United States engaged in the treaty and agreement process with Indian tribes.

By adding the lands added up to 1934 to the original acreage of the reservations, it is possible to compute the maximum total tribal acreage, nearly 140 million acres by 1934. Allotments made between 1854 and 1932 reduced tribal holdings by some forty million acres. Twenty-three million acres of these lands had passed out of trust by 1934. The vast majority of these lands passed out of Indian ownership. For example, nearly four million acres of allotted lands were sold to non-Indians between 1903 and 1934. Indian lands were reduced for reasons other than allotment and the alienation of allotments. Thus, thirty-eight million acres, nearly as much land as was allotted, was ceded by tribes in treaties and agreements after the initial creation of the reservations. Some of this land was sold; other lands were exchanged for new land owned by the United States, while other lands were traded for improvements made by the United States on tribal lands.

The General Allotment Act provided that when a reservation was allotted, the "surplus," the land remaining on the reservation after each tribal member had received his or her allotment, could be open to settlement by non-Indians. By 1934, twenty-two million acres had been opened to settlement by non-Indians. The opening of the reservations to settlement, together with the sale of alienated allotments, has resulted in a "checkerboard" pattern of land tenure in which Indian-held tracts alternate with tracts of land held by non-Indians on many reservations. Total reductions through alienated allotments, land cessions, the opening of surplus lands, and miscellaneous reasons resulted in a total reduction in Indian land holdings of nearly eighty-eight billion acres by 1934. By the early 1930s, less than fifty million acres remained in Indian hands and in trust status.

Table 2.3 shows the annual sales of Indian allotted lands between 1903 and 1934 together with the proceeds in the average price per acre paid. The price paid per acre fluctuated as did the number of the acres sold annually, reflecting differences in the views of various administrations toward Indian land sales as well as general economic conditions, especially changes in the value placed upon farmlands. The highest prices per acre were realized in the years just before, during, and immediately after World War I. The average price per acre declined sharply in the late 1920s and early 1930s; after 1931, the number of acres sold per year declined as well.

Removals and the migration of Indian groups during the nineteenth century resulted by the early twentieth century in a number of landless Indians residing far from established reservations. For example, in Wisconsin, landless Winnebago and Pottawatomi Indians were found in a number of locations in the northern, central, and western parts of the state. An act of 1881 provided that Indians wishing to sever tribal relations could select allotments on the public lands much as non-Indian homesteaders could select homesteads under the 1862 Homestead Act. Like other allotments, the "public domain" allotment was to remain in trust for a period of time to enable the allottee to establish himself on the land. While public domain allotments never constituted a significant percentage of total Indian land holdings in the United States, their magnitude was at times significant. Table 2.4 shows the number of allotments from the public domain at the end of selected fiscal years between 1912 and 1926. Table 2.4 also shows, for the year 1953, the number of public domain allotments remaining in trust.

The Meriam Report of 1928 recommended ending the practice of allotting Indian lands and urged a halt to Indian land sales. The Indian New Deal of John Collier (1933-1945) attempted to reverse the attrition in the Indian land base by promoting a modest land purchase program. As a result of widespread allotment and alienation and sales of allotments, landlessness had become a significant problem on many Indian reservations by the early 1930s. Table 2.5 shows the results of the Collier program. While the number of acres of allotted lands declined during the 1930s and 1940s as a result of land sales and for other reasons, the decline was quite gradual up to 1945. Less than half a million acres of allotted lands passed out of trust during the Collier years. At the same time, land purchase programs and the restoration of previously ceded lands to reservation status added nearly eight million acres to tribal lands between 1933 and 1945. Tribal land holding has continued to increase gradually in the last forty years, while the acreage in allotment status has declined. The result has been stability in the total acreage of Indian land holdings despite reductions in the Indian land base during the termination era of the 1950s, when the federal government attempted to terminate the special status of Indian tribes, including the trust protection of Indian land. Today, Indian land holdings are more than fifty-two million acres in area.

Reservations, states, and regions display considerable variation around the general national patterns described above. Table 2.6 shows unallotted tribal lands by state or territory between 1895 and 1934. The decline is quite dramatic in some cases. In particular, Oklahoma, formerly Indian Territory, lost tribal land rapidly between 1895 and 1915. In states with smaller amounts of Indian land holdings, more stability was often experienced. However, tribal land holdings declined by fifty million acres during the forty years before 1934. Table 2.7 shows the reduction in tribal land holdings for reasons other than allotment up to 1934 by state. In some cases, land cessions played a significant part in reducing Indian land holdings. In Montana, 75 percent of the maximum total tribal acreage was lost as a result of land cessions. In other cases, as in Utah, the disposal of the surplus remaining after allotment was significant. Seventy-one percent of Utah's maximum total tribal acreage was sold as surplus lands to non-Indian settlers. An enormous variation exists between states in the loss of lands for reasons other than allotment; states show a wide variety of percentage of maximum total tribal acreage "remaining before allotment"—that is, not ceded.

Table 2.8 shows the effects of allotment on tribal land holding by showing the acreage allotted by state, the percentage of tribal acreage accounted for by allotments, and the acreage of allotments removed from trust status before 1934. In midwestern states such as Kansas and Oklahoma, nearly all of the tribal acreage remaining after cessions and distribution of the surplus was allotted. In southwestern states, such as New Mexico and Arizona, a much smaller proportion of tribal land was allotted. The acreage of allotted lands removed from trust similarly varies between states. In the midwestern states of Minnesota, Nebraska, Kansas, and Oklahoma, for example, a significant portion of allotments were alienated from trust status. On the other hand, New Mexico had no allotments alienated from trust status before 1934 and the acreage removed from trust in Arizona was negligible. These differences probably reflect differences in land conditions as well as in tribal abilities to resist allotment and alienation of allotments.

Table 2.9 shows, by state, the number of allotments and the acreage of allotments on the public lands in 1914 and 1953. While the overall acreage of public domain allotments is quite similar in the two years, an examination of the individual states reveals considerable variation. Thus, public domain allotments in Arizona increased substantially between 1914 and 1953, probably reflecting the use of public domain allotments to provide land for landless Navajos and others, while public domain allotments in other states declined considerably, reflecting the passing of allotments out of trust status, sales of allotments, and other factors.

Tables 2.10, 2.11, 2.12, 2.13, 2.14, and 2.15 show the acreage of tribal and individually owned Indian trust lands by state for various years between 1936 and 1983. As was the case in 1935, the bulk of tribally owned acreage was located in six states—Arizona, New Mexico, Utah, Wyoming, Oregon, and Montana—in each of these years. The bulk of allotted land was located in five states—Montana, South Dakota, Oklahoma, New Mexico, and North Dakota—in each year. These patterns have remained fairly constant since the 1930s as a result of restrictions on the sales of Indian lands combined with land purchase programs that have never been significant enough in terms of appropriations to affect significantly the distribution of Indian lands.

Table 2.16 shows the distribution of all lands in the United States in the year 1950, when Indian land holding reached its highest level in the twentieth century. In that year, Indian lands accounted for less than 3 percent of the total lands in the United States. Total lands under federal control, including Indian lands, accounted for nearly a quarter of all land in the United States.

Tables 2.17, 2.18, and 2.19 show the area and land status for selected reservations in 1920, 1974, and 1983. The acreage of tribally held and allotted lands is presented for selected reservations.

Climate and elevation are significant elements determining life and land use. Indian reservations present nearly as much variation in this regard as is found in the United States as a whole. Tables 2.20 through 2.25 present a variety of data on the climatic conditions of the Indian reservations that are described in Tables 2.17, 2.18, and 2.19. These data were gathered in the early twentieth century by the U.S. Weather Bureau and were compiled in the *Climatic Survey of the United States* in the early 1930s. This survey was judged preferable to later surveys since the number of stations reporting climatic data was much larger, resulting in better coverage of rural areas. In almost every case it was possible to find reservation reporting stations, rather than using reports from nearby off-reservation stations. The elevations of the reporting stations are given in Table 2.25.

Indian land holdings declined during most of the history of European contact with Indian people. Indian land holding reached a nadir in the 1920s and early 1930s; since the 1930s, after a brief increase during the

Collier years, Indian land holding has remained relatively stable, despite the sale of nearly a million acres during the termination era of the 1950s. Despite the stability of Indian land holdings in recent times, significant increases, which have been advocated since the 1930s, have not occurred. The lack of available land has been a significant problem for reservation economic development.

Land statistics are found in a variety of sources. The Bureau of Indian Affairs' *Annual Report on Indian Lands* is a significant source of data on Indian land holding in contemporary years. The nineteenth century *Annual Reports* of the Commissioner of Indian Affairs present land statistics in varying detail as do the Statistical Supplements to the *Annual Report* of the Commissioner of Indian Affairs in the 1930s and 1940s. Investigations and reports have included a variety of data on Indian land holding. Particularly valuable are the House Interior and Insular Affairs Committee's *Investigation of the Bureau of Indian Affairs* (1953), and the National Resource Board's *Report on Indian Land Tenure, Economic Status, and Population Trends* (1935).

Imre Sutton, *Indian Land Tenure: Bibliographical Essays and a Guide to the Literature* (1975) is a mine of information on land, land tenure, and land use. The Meriam Report (1928) includes a number of recommendations on land. Jay P. Kinney provides a history of Indian land tenure in *A Continent Lost—A Civilization Won* (1937). Wilcomb Washburn reviews the relationship between land and law in *Red Man's Land/White Man's Law* (1968). Kirke Kickingbird and Karen Duchenaux, in *One Hundred Million Acres* (1970), present a detailed plan for a significant addition to the Indian land base.

TABLES

Table 2.1
Indian Lands, 1871–1933 (Acres)

Year	Tribal Lands	Allotted*	Total
1871	111,761,558	10,231,725	121,993,283
1881	139,006,794	16,625,518	155,632,312
1887	119,375,930	17,018,965	136,394,895
1890	86,540,824	17,773,525	104,314,349
1900	52,455,827	25,409,546	77,865,373
1911	40,263,442	32,272,420	72,535,862
1920	35,501,661	37,158,655	72,660,316
1929	32,014,945	39,129,268	71,144,213
1933	29,481,685	40,106,736	69,588,421

Notes: *Includes alienated and non-trust allotments for 1911 and after.

Source: J.P. Kinney, A Continent Lost——A Civilization Won
(Baltimore: Johns Hopkins Press, 1937).

Table 2.2
Reductions in Size of Reservations from Establishment to 1934 (Acres)

Reservation Land Area (Reservations established between 1794 and 1933)

Original Acreage of Reservations	130,730,190
Lands Added Before 1934	9,106,312
Maximum Total Tribal Acreage	139,836,502

Allotments (Allotments made between 1854 and 1932)

Total Number of Allotments	246,569
Total Acreage of Allotments	40,848,172
Acreage of Alienated Allotments	23,225,472
Acreage of Allotments Remaining in Trust	17,622,700

Reductions other than Alienation of Allotments

Lands Ceded After Establishment of Reservations	38,299,109
Surplus Opened to Settlement	22,694,658
Miscellaneous Land Losses	3,475,217
Total Reductions other than Alienated Allotments	64,468,984
Total Reductions, including Alienated Allotments	87,694,456

Source: National Resources Board, Report on Land Planning, Part X: Indian Land Tenure, Economic Status and Population Trends (Washington: Government Printing Office, 1935), Tables VI-VII.

Table 2.3
Annual Sales of Allotted Lands, 1903–1934

Year	Number of Tracts	Acres	Proceeds	Average Price per Acre
1903	*	44,494	$ 757,173.25	$17.02
1904	1,236	122,222	2,057,464.50	16.83
1905	978	90,215	1,393,131.52	15.44
1906	643	64,448	981,430.87	15.23
1907	820	106,359	1,248,793.34	11.74
1908	860	99,294	1,461,827.75	14.72
1909	988	136,768	1,764,021.57	12.90
1910	1,393	212,016	3,201,955.88	15.10
1911	1,132	135,864	2,482,548.65	18.27
1912	716	78,043	1,458,165.77	18.68
1913	317	31,577	692,413.28	21.93
1914	947	90,768	1,552,835.30	17.11
1915	815	102,674	1,300,293.08	12.66
1916	907	90,721	1,663,852.72	18.34
1917	1,243	145,741	2,587,167.00	17.75
1918	1,100	123,342	2,716,033.00	22.02
1919	970	115,397	2,805,132.00	24.31
1920	2,206	302,841	7,574,374.00	25.01
1921	1,935	205,086	5,713,738.00	27.86
1922	1,006	104,814	2,232,833.00	21.30
1923	1,186	125,099	2,904,337.00	23.22
1924	1,155	140,363	2,666,108.00	18.99
1925	1,161	139,464	2,495,415.00	17.89
1926	1,203	126,051	3,569,345.00	28.32
1927	1,284	141,422	2,565,533.00	18.14
1928	1,268	151,413	2,338,774.00	15.45
1929	1,330	181,413	2,306,508.00	12.71
1930	886	108,515	1,607,795.00	14.82
1931	644	69,795	1,008,538.00	14.45
1932	565	71,684	666,524.00	9.30
1933	328	38,917	423,569.34	10.88
1934	232	33,445	474,345.28	14.18
TOTAL	31,454	3,730,265	$68,671,976.10	$18.41

Source: National Resources Board, <u>Report on Land Planning</u>, Part X: Indian <u>Land Tenure, Economic Status, and Population Trends</u> (Washington: Government Printing Office, 1935), p. 36.

Table 2.4
Allotments on the Public Domain at the End of Selected Fiscal
Years, 1912–1926, 1953

Fiscal Year	Number of Allotments	Area in Acres	% Increase (or decrease)
1912	*	889,277	–
1915	7,470	1,077,257	21%
1919	8,039	1,155,049	7%
1923	9,734	1,407,838	22%
1926	10,012	1,446,757	3%
1953	*	905,037	(37%)

Notes: * – not given

Source: Laurence F. Schmeckebier, The Office of Indian Affairs: Its
History, Activities, and Organization (Baltimore: The Johns
Hopkins Press, 1927), p. 147; U.S. House of Representatives,
Committee on Interior and Insular Affairs, Investigation of the
Bureau of Indian Affiars (Washington: Government Printing Office,
1953).

Table 2.5
Indian Trust Lands, 1933–1983 (Acres)

Year	Tribal Lands	Allotted	Total
1933	29,481,685	17,829,414	47,311,099
1939	35,402,440	17,594,376	52,996,816
1945	37,288,768	17,357,540	54,646,308
1953	42,785,935	14,674,763	57,460,698
1962	38,814,074	11,763,160	50,577,234
1974	40,772,934	10,244,481	51,017,415
1979	41,803,230	10,058,445	51,861,675
1983	42,385,031	10,226,180	52,611,211

Table 2.5
(Continued)

Source: J.P. Kinney, A Continent Lost—A Civilization Won (Baltimore: Johns Hopkins Press, 1937); Statistical Supplement to the Annual Report of the Commissioner of Indian Affairs, FY 1939 (Washington: Department of the Interior, 1939); Statistical Supplement to the Annual Report of the Commissioner of Indian Affairs, FY 1945 (Washington: Department of the Interior, 1945); Committee on Interior and Insular Affairs, U.S. House of Representatives, Investigation of the Bureau of Indian Affairs, House Report 2503, 82nd Congress, 2nd session (Washington: Government Printing Office, 1953); Bureau of Indian Affairs, U.S. Indian Population and Land (Washington: Department of the Interior, 1962); Bureau of Indian Affairs, Annual Report of Indian Lands, 1974 (Washington: Department of the Interior, 1974); BIA Profile: The Bureau of Indian Affairs and American Indians (Washington: Government Printing Office, 1981); Bureau of Indian Affairs, Annual Report of Indian Lands, 1983 (Washington: Department of the Interior, 1983).

Table 2.6
Unallotted Tribal Lands, by State or Territory, 1895–1934 (in Acres)

	1895	1905	1915	1920	1934
Arizona	14,098,597	16,917,560	16,343,588	18,571,285	18,398,470
California	432,859	410,319	430,136	433,511	404,517
Colorado	1,094,400	483,740	396,143	396,143	510,465
Florida	-	-	23,542	23,542	125,825
Idaho	1,896,861	948,440	54,841	54,841	344,906
Iowa	2,900	2,965	3,251	3,251	3,353
Kansas	32,674	12,587	-	-	80
Michigan	5,944	3,402	803	191	-
Minnesota	2,243,753	947,672	546,932	553,798	408,012
Montana	9,382,400	7,450,264	4,312,452	3,543,353	1,071,312
Nebraska	125,817	17,928	6,159	6,118	3,386
Nevada	954,135	954,135	686,219	726,312	609,318
New Mexico	1,797,085	1,699,485	3,870,517	4,024,049	4,817,493
New York	87,677	87,677	87,677	87,677	87,677
N. Carolina	65,211	98,211	63,211	63,211	62,930
N. Dakota	3,812,833	3,695,644	100,000	100,000	24,569
Oklahoma*	26,825,288	10,256,978	6,205	3,142	10,126
Oregon	1,625,931	1,274,554	1,208,804	1,190,790	1,295,425
S. Dakota	9,837,299	7,952,172	630,895	363,607	614,639
Utah	3,972,480	282,460	1,506,960	1,529,360	1,468,053
Washington	4,046,564	2,622,242	2,159,172	1,699,327	1,745,122
Wisconsin	416,751	328,918	288,116	270,925	262,055
Wyoming	1,810,000	1,754,960	608,637	1,857,228	2,019,603
TOTAL	84,571,459	58,202,323	33,334,261	35,501,661	34,287,336

*(includes Indian Territory)

Source: Commissioner of Indian Affairs, Annual Reports, 1895, 1905, 1915, 1920; National Resources Board, Report on Land Planning, Part X: Indian Land Tenure, Economic Status, and Population Trends (Washington: Government Printing Office, 1935).

Table 2.7

Reductions in Tribal Lands, Other Than by Allotment, to 1934, by State

State	Maximum Total Tribal	Cessions		Surplus Lands		Miscellaneous		Total Deductions (other than allotment)		Acreage Remaining	
	acres	acres	%	acres	%	acres	%	acres	%	acres	%
Arizona	18,714,433	-	-	12,160	*	44,249	*	56,409	*	18,658,024	99+%
California	470,219	-	-	-	-	2,940	1%	2,940	1%	467,279	99%
Colorado	584,744	-	-	-	-	-	-	-	-	584,744	100%
Florida	125,880	-	-	-	-	-	-	-	-	125,880	100%
Idaho	2,206,298	436,910	20%	242,101	11%	552,656	25%	1,231,667	56%	974,631	44%
Iowa	3,394	-	-	-	-	33	1%	33	1%	3,361	99%
Kansas	116,438	-	-	-	-	-	-	-	-	116,438	100%
Minnesota	2,180,403	-	-	119,013	5%	757,867	35%	876,880	40%	1,303,523	60%
Mississippi	5,908	-	-	-	-	-	-	-	-	5,908	100%
Montana	46,012,169	34,380,726	75%	3,870,897	8%	113,243	*	38,364,866	83%	7,647,303	17%
Nebraska	513,299	-	-	-	-	163,650	32%	163,650	32%	349,649	68%

	Total										
Nevada	698,396	-	-	-	-	-	-	-	-	698,396	100%
New Mexico	6,043,730	-	-	-	-	145,280	2%	145,280	2%	5,898,450	98%
New York	87,677	-	-	-	-	-	-	-	-	87,677	100%
N. Carolina	91,035	-	-	-	-	27,775	31%	27,775	31%	63,260	69%
N. Dakota	2,037,477	-	-	264,795	13%	417,050	20%	681,845	33%	1,355,632	67%
Oklahoma	29,668,760	4,000	*	9,735,162	33%	408,600	1%	10,147,762	34%	19,520,998	66%
Oregon	3,465,487	706,576	20%	-	-	785,259	23%	1,491,835	43%	1,973,652	57%
S. Dakota	12,341,601	1,270,897	10%	2,865,770	23%	56,154	*	4,192,821	34%	8,148,780	66%
Utah	5,449,142	-	-	3,859,463	71%	-	-	3,859,463	71%	1,589,679	29%
Washington	4,680,808	1,500,000	32%	224,870	5%	461	*	1,725,331	37%	2,955,477	63%
Wisconsin	570,704	-	-	-	-	-	-	-	-	570,704	100%
Wyoming	3,768,500	-	-	1,500,427	40%	-	-	1,500,427	40%	2,268,073	60%
TOTAL	139,836,502	38,299,109	27%	22,694,658	16%	3,475,217	2%	64,468,984	46%	75,367,518	54%

Notes: * - less than 1%

Source: National Resources Planning Board, Report on Land Planning, Part X: Indian Land Tenure, Economic Status, and Population Trends (Washington: Government Printing Office, 1935).

Table 2.8

Number and Acreage of Allotments, Acreage of Allotments Removed
from Trust Status, to 1934, by State

State	Acres Remaining (from Table 7)	# of Allotments	Acreage Allotted	Allotments as % of Remaining Acres	Acreage of Allotments Removed from Trust	% of Allotted Acres out of Trust
Arizona	18,658,024	7,110	242,986	1%	40	*
California	467,279	2,887	58,597	13%	15,341	26%
Colorado	584,744	375	72,851	12%	33,473	46%
Florida	125,880	-	-	-	-	-
Idaho	974,631	4,125	628,540	64%	172,843	27%
Iowa	3,361	-	-	-	-	-
Kansas	116,438	1,305	116,337	99.9%	81,617	70%
Minnesota	1,303,523	12,507	892,508	68%	760,110	85%
Mississippi	5,908	+	5,706	97%	-	-
Montana	7,647,303	21,744	6,527,048	85%	1,461,420	22%
Nebraska	349,649	4,529	345,403	99%	280,369	81%
Nevada	698,396	1,654	88,579	13%	1,804	2%
New Mexico	5,898,450	4,697	1,072,220	18%	-	-
New York	87,677	-	-	-	-	-
North Carolina	63,260	-	-	-	-	-
North Dakota	1,355,632	7,034	1,325,302	98%	348,159	26%
Oklahoma	19,520,998	119,449	19,488,396	99.9%	16,601,112	85%
Oregon	1,973,652	5,736	669,858	34%	169,543	25%
South Dakota	8,148,780	32,952	7,445,882	91%	2,834,178	38%
Utah	1,589,679	1,375	115,247	7%	29,619	26%
Washington	2,955,477	11,898	1,199,644	41%	242,562	20%
Wisconsin	570,704	4,789	307,287	54%	174,785	57%
Wyoming	2,268,073	2,403	245,781	11%	18,497	8%
TOTAL	75,367,518	246,569	40,848,172	54%	23,225,472	57%

Notes: * - less than 1%
        + - not given

Source: National Resources Board, Report on Land Planning, Part X: Indian Land Tenure, Economic Status and
         Population Trends (Washington: Government Printing Office, 1935).

Table 2.9
Allotments on the Public Domain, by State, 1914 and 1953 (Acres)

State	1914		1953
	# of Allotments	Acres	Acres
Alaska	–	–	6,047
Arizona	674	104,700	663,851
California	1,786	242,184	56,325
Colorado	8	1,201	9,079
Idaho	58	4,732	1,656
Michigan	51	3,615	2,143
Minnesota	41	3,119	2,157
Montana	1,604	254,145	–
Nevada	608	74,552	796
New Mexico	949	151,628	77,047
North Dakota	552	84,869	14,200
Oklahoma	16	1,070	400
Oregon	342	51,331	13,094
South Dakota	16	2,397	1,440
Utah	–	–	160
Washington	364	41,941	48,886
Wisconsin	67	4,676	7,756
TOTAL	7,136	1,026,161	905,037

Source: Commissioner of Indian Affairs, Annual Report, 1914-15 (Washington: Government Printing Office, 1915); U.S., House of Representatives, Committee on Interior and Insular Affairs, Investigation of the Bureau of Indian Affairs (Washington: Government Printing Office, 1953), pp. 68-74.

Table 2.10
Indian Lands, by State and Type, 1936 (Acres)

State	Tribal	Allotted	Total
Arizona	18,915,802	172,800	19,088,602
California	507,865	60,683	568,548
Colorado	396,143	39,440	435,583
Florida	26,741	—	26,741
Idaho	57,369	460,513	517,882
Iowa	3,480	—	3,480
Kansas	863	37,195	38,058
Michigan	683	12,952	13,635
Minnesota	565,003	177,854	742,857
Mississippi	2,609	—	2,609
Montana	958,758	5,096,050	6,054,808
Nebraska	7,317	60,630	67,947
Nevada	1,024,382	15,066	1,039,448
New Mexico	5,385,122	354,327	5,739,449
North Carolina	63,211	—	63,211
North Dakota	117,142	3,067,574	3,184,716
Oklahoma	78,543	2,803,160	2,881,703
Oregon	1,197,192	375,600	1,572,792
South Dakota	661,775	4,162,053	4,823,828
Texas	3,071	—	3,071
Utah	1,583,280	83,408	1,666,688
Washington	749,135	975,204	1,724,339
Wisconsin	273,574	146,178	419,752
Wyoming	525,000	194,789	719,789
TOTAL	33,104,050	18,295,476	51,399,526

Source: Jay P. Kinney, A Continent Lost — A Civilization Won
          (Baltimore: Johns Hopkins Press, 1937)

Table 2.11
Indian Lands, by State and Type, 1953 (Acres)

State	Tribal	Allotted	Total
Alaska	2,987,682	6,047	2,993,729
Arizona	22,986,732	834,726	23,821,458
California	481,230	112,144	593,374
Colorado	851,585	14,370	865,955
Florida	78,933	--	78,933
Idaho	239,884	436,490	676,374
Iowa	3,476	--	3,476
Kansas	1,717	33,860	35,577
Louisiana	262	160	422
Michigan	7,818	14,709	22,257
Minnesota	678,090	150,957	829,047
Mississippi	16,212	408	16,620
Montana	1,413,596	4,717,140	6,130,736
Nebraska	14,431	56,748	71,179
Nevada	1,254,158	82,152	1,336,310
New Mexico	3,054,796	93,186	3,147,982
North Carolina	56,115	--	56,115
North Dakota	235,086	1,309,305	1,544,391
Oklahoma	59,775	2,333,952	2,393,727
Oregon	1,321,483	349,701	1,671,184
South Carolina	4,249	--	4,249
South Dakota	2,010,109	2,850,374	4,860,483
Texas	4,181	--	4,181
Utah	1,049,628	77,837	1,127,465
Washington	1,772,677	916,082	2,688,759
Wisconsin	289,807	141,392	431,199
Wyoming	1,914,682	143,021	2,057,703
TOTAL	42,785,935	14,674,763	57,460,698

Source: U.S., House, Committee on Interior and Insular Affairs, Investigation of the Bureau of Indian Affairs (Washington: Government Printing Office, 1953), pp. 60-74.

Table 2.12
Indian Lands, by State and Type, 1962 (Acres)

State	Tribal	Allotted	Total
Alaska	87,636	9,311	96,947
Arizona	19,389,073	260,395	19,649,468
California	467,168	86,175	533,343
Colorado	746,420	5,131	751,551
Florida	78,974	--	78,974
Idaho	440,448	390,601	831,049
Iowa	4,105	--	4,105
Kansas	1,784	26,420	28,204
Louisiana	262	*	262
Michigan	7,816	9,427	17,243
Minnesota	670,525	55,194	725,719
Mississippi	16,270	209	16,479
Missouri	--	373	373
Montana	1,613,201	3,640,283	5,253,484
Nebraska	14,235	52,818	67,053
Nevada	1,062,316	80,260	1,142,576
New Mexico	5,886,887	649,138	6,536,025
North Carolina	56,414	--	56,414
North Dakota	130,075	736,176	866,251
Oklahoma	58,627	1,638,609	1,697,236
Oregon	496,062	195,615	691,677
South Dakota	1,933,166	2,920,546	4,853,712
Texas	--	11	11
Utah	2,045,157	70,292	2,115,449
Washington	1,827,842	722,465	2,550,307
Wisconsin	60,015	86,048	146,063
Wyoming	1,759,596	127,663	1,887,259
TOTAL	38,814,074	11,763,160	50,577,234

Note: * - less than 1 acre

Source: Bureau of Indian Affairs, U.S. Indian Population and Land, 1962, (Washington: U.S. Department of the Interior, 1962), p. 6.

Table 2.13
Indian Lands, by State and Type, 1974 (Acres)

State	Tribal	Allotted	Total
Alaska	86,741	19,375	106,116
Arizona	19,505,283	253,127	19,758,410
California	469,601	74,267	543,867
Colorado	777,525	4,206	781,731
Florida	79,014	--	79,014
Idaho	440,189	346,256	786,445
Iowa	4,133	--	4,133
Kansas	2,669	23,486	26,156
Louisiana	262	--	262
Michigan	7,939	9,242	17,181
Minnesota	683,420	51,198	734,618
Mississippi	17,381	1	17,381
Missouri	--	375	375
Montana	1,946,482	3,210,200	5,156,682
Nebraska	18,080	43,381	61,460
Nevada	1,064,622	78,808	1,143,430
New Mexico	6,468,353	680,802	7,149,155
North Carolina	56,444	--	56,444
North Dakota	181,062	662,554	843,616
Oklahoma	63,757	1,235,016	1,298,773
Oregon	612,369	148,710	761,080
South Dakota	2,231,155	2,638,497	4,869,652
Utah	2,233,675	42,399	2,276,073
Washington	1,958,767	540,013	2,498,780
Wisconsin	80,069	81,479	161,549
Wyoming	1,783,942	101,090	1,885,032
TOTAL	40,772,934	10,244,481	51,017,415

Source: Bureau of Indian Affairs, Annual Report of Indian Lands, 1974. (Washington: U.S. Department of the Interior, 1974).

Table 2.14
Indian Lands, by State and Type, 1979 (Acres)

State	Tribal	Allotted	Total
Alaska	86,741	299,400	386,141
Arizona	19,554,391	252,972	19,807,362
California	500,036	73,014	573,050
Colorado	752,017	3,878	755,895
Florida	79,014	--	79,014
Idaho	459,756	334,475	794,231
Iowa	4,164	--	4,164
Kansas	5,504	22,522	28,025
Louisiana	374	--	374
Michigan	12,039	9,247	21,286
Minnesota	712,125	50,750	762,876
Mississippi	17,478	19	17,496
Missouri	--	375	375
Montana	2,170,265	3,051,321	5,221,586
Nebraska	22,275	42,531	64,806
Nevada	1,067,674	78,388	1,146,062
New Mexico	6,462,826	677,845	7,140,671
North Carolina	56,461	--	56,461
North Dakota	200,683	650,481	851,164
Oklahoma	85,566	1,145,871	1,231,437
Oregon	615,692	141,293	756,984
South Dakota	2,572,817	2,516,505	5,089,323
Utah	2,249,068	34,525	2,283,594
Washington	1,996,018	497,219	2,493,237
Wisconsin	328,437	80,886	409,324
Wyoming	1,791,808	94,927	1,886,736
TOTAL	41,803,230	10,058,445	51,861,675

Source: U.S. Department of the Interior, BIA Profile: The Bureau of Indian
Affairs and American Indians (Washington: Government Printing Office,
1981), p. 71.

Table 2.15
Indian Lands, by State and Type, 1983 (Acres)

State	Tribal	Allotted	Total
Alaska	86,759	705,445	792,204
Arizona	19,556,806	252,407	19,809,213
Arkansas	--	*	*
California	501,388	67,839	569,227
Colorado	783,903	3,043	786,946
Florida	79,495	--	79,495
Idaho	462,395	330,104	792,499
Iowa	4,164	--	4,164
Kansas	7,355	22,298	29,653
Louisiana	416	--	416
Maine	221,633	--	221,633
Michigan	12,230	9,266	21,496
Minnesota	714,118	51,259	765,377
Mississippi	17,635	19	17,654
Missouri	--	374	374
Montana	2,256,358	2,966,353	5,222,711
Nebraska	23,389	41,146	64,535
Nevada	1,141,501	78,567	1,220,068
New Mexico	6,499,030	674,701	7,173,731
North Carolina	56,461	--	56,461
North Dakota	210,116	632,166	842,282
Oklahoma	87,635	1,111,766	1,199,401
Oregon	622,297	136,851	759,148
South Dakota	2,636,292	2,456,043	5,092,335
Utah	2,249,726	33,423	2,283,149
Washington	2,027,475	477,644	2,505,119
Wisconsin	333,615	81,141	414,756
Wyoming	1,792,841	94,325	1,887,166
TOTAL	42,385,031	10,226,180	52,611,211

* - Less than one acre

Source: Bureau of Indian Affairs, Office of Trust Responsibilities, Annual
Report of Indian Lands, September 30, 1983. (Washington: Department
of the Interior, 1983).

Table 2.16
Federal Lands, 1950

Agency or Bureau	Acres	Percent of Federal Lands	Percent of All Lands
Bureau of Land Management	179,556,897	39.5	9.43
Forest Service	160,061,408	35.2	8.40
Bureau of Indian Affairs	56,549,743	12.4	2.97
National Park Service	15,951,375	3.5	0.84
Department of the Air Force	11,738,806	2.6	0.62
Soil Conservation Service	7,412,639	1.6	*
Army, Military Lands	6,539,213	1.4	*
Bureau of Reclamation	5,729,680	1.3	*
Fish and Wildlife Service	4,359,669	1.0	*
Army, Civil Works Lands	2,481,211	0.5	*
Navy Department	2,345,496	0.5	*
All others	2,420,589	0.5	*
Total, Federal Lands	455,146,726	100.0	23.89
Total, All Lands	1,905,000,000	-	100.00

*Less than 0.5%

Source: U.S., House of Representatives, Committee on Public Lands, "Area, in
         Acres, of Lands in Federal Ownership," September 19, 1950, 81st
         Congress, 2nd Session, House Report No. 3116, Serial 11384; Bureau of
         Indian Affairs, Indian Land and Its Care (Lawrence, Kansas: The
         Haskell Press, 1953), p. 1.

Table 2.17
Area and Land Status, Selected Reservations, 1920 (Acres)

Reservation	Tribal	Allotted	Total
Blackfeet, MT	603,868	889,519	1,493,387
Cherokee, NC	63,211	–	63,211
Cheyenne River, SD	190,841	1,019,989	1,210,830
Crow, MT	1,771,030	542,183	2,313,213
Flathead, MT	–	228,408	228,408
Ft. Apache, AZ	1,681,920	–	1,681,920
Ft. Peck, MT	–	850,210	850,210
Gila River, AZ	371,422	–	371,422
Hopi, AZ	2,472,320	–	2,472,320
Laguna, NM	101,511	–	101,511
Menominee, WI	231,680	–	231,680
Navajo, AZ,UT,NM	11,355,034	328,963	11,683,997
Northern Cheyenne, MT	489,500	–	489,500
Papago, AZ	2,129,114	–	2,129,114
Pine Ridge, SD	161,565	2,363,813	2,525,378
Red Lake, MN	543,528	–	543,528
Rosebud, SD	–	1,867,716	1,867,716
San Carlos, AZ	1,834,240	–	1,834,240
Standing Rock, SD–ND	–	1,388,411	1,388,411
Turtle Mtn., ND	–	43,820	43,820
Wind River, WY	1,857,228	245,058	2,102,286
Yakima, WA	412,404	451,922	864,326
Zuni, NM	288,040	–	288,040

Source: Annual Report of the Commissioner of Indian Affairs, 1920
        (Washington: Government Printing Office, 1920), pp. 82–85.

Table 2.18
Area and Land Status, Selected Reservations, 1974 (Acres)

Reservation	Tribal	Allotted	Government Owned	Total
Blackfeet, MT	119,806	775,413	11,223	906,442
Cherokee, NC	56,573	–	–	56,573
Cheyenne River, SD	911,467	503,483	4,554	1,419,504
Crow, MT	344,304	1,209,949	–	1,554,253
Flathead, MT	562,277	50,752	1,017	614,046
Ft. Apache, AZ	1,664,872	–	–	1,664,872
Ft. Peck, MT	233,153	645,114	86,597	964,864
Gila River, AZ	274,462	97,467	–	371,929
Hopi, AZ	2,472,254	–	–	2,472,254
Laguna, NM	412,212	41,226	1,017	454,454
Menominee, WI	+	+	+	+
Navajo, AZ,UT,NM	12,940,191	722,854	326,177	13,989,222
Northern Cheyenne, MT	262,296	171,298	*	433,594
Papago, AZ	2,814,871	41,003	–	285,587
Pine Ridge, SD	372,243	1,089,077	48,231	1,509,551
Red Lake, MN	564,426	–	–	564,426
Rosebud, SD	409,321	540,112	28,797	978,230
San Carlos, AZ	1,853,841	960	22,415	1,877,216
Standing Rock, SD–ND	294,840	542,701	10,258	847,799
Turtle Mtn., ND	35,579	34,144	517	70,240
Wind River, WY	1,776,136	109,344	1,076	1,886,556
Yakima, WA	842,978	274,988	23	1,117,989
Zuni, NM	405,034	2,213	–	407,247

Notes: + not given
        * less than 1 acre

Source: U.S. Department of Commerce, Federal and State Indian Reservations and Indian Trust Areas (Washington: Government Printing Office, 1974).

Table 2.19
Area and Land Status, Selected Reservations, 1983 (Acres)

Reservation	Tribal	Allotted	Government	Total
Blackfeet, MT	251,907	692,314	136	944,357
Cherokee, NC	56,461	–	112	56,573
Cheyenne River, SD	952,785	442,944	176	1,395,905
Crow, MT	406,935	1,116,239	1,401	1,524,575
Flathead, MT	570,747	47,511	1,017	619,275
Ft. Apache, AZ	1,664,972	–	–	1,664,972
Ft. Peck, MT	391,769	521,521	–	913,290
Gila River, AZ	274,538	97,392	3	371,933
Hopi, AZ	1,560,993	220	–	1,561,213
Laguna, NM	458,933	2,165	–	461,098
Menominee, WI	222,552	–	–	222,552
Navajo, AZ,UT,NM	14,616,998	711,540	253,801	15,582,339
Northern Cheyenne, MT	313,255	123,675	1	436,931
Papago, AZ	2,773,850	320	380	2,774,550
Pine Ridge, SD	695,613	1,089,344	1,231	1,786,188
Red Lake, MN	564,452	–	–	564,452
Rosebud, SD	527,640	429,170	42	956,852
San Carlos, AZ	1,826,541	–	–	1,826,541
Standing Rock, SD–ND	351,409	497,133	2	848,544
Turtle Mtn., ND	8,613	24,489	140	33,242
Wind River, WY	1,792,891	94,325	1,296	1,888,462
Yakima, WA	899,869	229,593	23	1,129,485
Zuni, NM	406,351	2,213	–	408,564

Source: Bureau of Indian Affairs, Annual Report of Indian Lands, 1983
          (Washington: Department of the Interior, 1983).

Table 2.20
Average Temperature, Selected Reservations, by Month (°F)

	Jan	Feb	Mar	April	May	June	July	Aug	Sept	Oct	Nov	Dec	Annual Average
Blackfeet, MT	18.0	19.8	26.9	38.6	47.9	54.3	60.8	59.4	49.8	41.0	28.6	21.4	38.8
Cherokee, NC	39.5	41.5	47.6	55.5	62.7	70.2	73.1	72.4	68.4	57.7	46.0	39.8	56.2
Cheyenne River, SD	15.7	20.1	32.4	46.0	56.0	66.9	73.7	71.5	62.0	49.5	34.1	20.0	45.7
Crow, MT	18.9	21.8	33.6	46.4	54.7	65.1	72.4	69.0	58.7	47.4	33.6	23.6	45.4
Flathead, MT	23.0	27.6	35.8	45.0	52.4	59.0	66.5	64.8	50.0	45.0	34.0	26.0	44.5
Ft. Apache, AZ	35.8	39.9	45.3	51.8	59.9	69.0	73.3	71.3	65.8	55.4	46.1	37.2	54.2
Ft. Peck, MT	7.0	9.5	24.7	43.9	54.9	64.4	70.7	68.0	56.9	44.6	28.1	13.7	40.5
Gila River, AZ	50.0	54.3	59.2	65.8	73.5	83.1	87.9	86.5	81.2	69.1	58.1	50.1	68.2
Hopi, AZ	30.4	34.2	41.7	48.6	55.3	65.1	71.0	69.1	62.2	51.2	41.1	30.3	50.0
Laguna, NM	33.4	37.6	44.0	52.6	60.2	70.0	74.1	72.2	65.4	53.1	41.7	31.6	53.0
Menominee, WI	14.7	16.6	28.1	42.6	53.8	64.8	69.4	66.5	59.1	47.7	33.0	20.7	43.1
Navajo, AZ	32.0	39.2	45.9	53.8	61.7	71.1	76.8	77.8	67.6	55.7	43.4	32.3	54.8
Navajo, NM	30.0	37.0	44.5	53.2	60.9	69.0	75.8	73.6	66.2	54.0	40.3	28.7	52.8
Northern Cheyenne, MT	17.0	20.6	31.5	44.1	52.2	62.0	69.2	67.4	57.2	45.1	32.8	20.6	43.3
Papago, AZ	49.0	52.5	56.2	62.8	70.7	80.0	81.4	79.1	76.5	66.5	55.7	48.9	64.9
Pine Ridge, SD	22.4	23.5	34.2	45.4	54.3	64.4	73.0	70.0	60.7	47.4	36.7	23.9	46.3
Red Lake, MN	1.8	7.9	22.5	40.1	52.7	63.0	68.1	65.3	57.3	43.9	27.2	11.9	38.5
Rosebud, SD	22.8	22.5	32.8	47.0	56.7	66.7	73.4	70.9	61.0	49.0	36.2	23.7	46.9
San Carlos, AZ	44.4	49.6	55.2	61.8	70.0	79.8	85.9	83.7	77.3	64.5	52.3	45.2	64.1
Standing Rock, ND, SD	9.2	11.8	26.3	44.9	56.1	66.2	71.7	69.3	59.8	46.4	29.8	18.4	42.5
Turtle Mountain, ND	.6	4.2	20.1	39.1	51.3	61.3	66.6	64.1	54.9	41.0	23.6	7.4	36.2
Wind River, WY	14.5	23.4	32.8	44.0	53.1	62.0	69.4	66.6	56.5	43.4	27.1	15.1	42.3
Yakima, WA	24.8	34.6	45.2	51.7	58.2	65.3	70.3	68.5	58.8	49.3	38.0	29.6	49.5
Zuni, NM	29.0	34.4	40.0	46.6	55.8	65.9	70.8	68.6	62.6	51.6	39.7	30.2	49.6

Source: U.S. Weather Bureau, Climatic Survey of the United States (1930-31)

Table 2.20–A
Average Temperature—Reporting Stations

	Station	Number of Years
Blackfeet, MT	Browning, MT	29
Cherokee, NC	Cullowhee, NC	21
Cheyenne River, SD	Hopewell, SD	21
Crow, MT	Crow Agency, MT	47
Flathead, MT	St. Ignatius, MT	24
Ft. Apache, AZ	Ft. Apache, AZ	58
Ft. Peck, MT	Poplar, MT	44
Gila River, AZ	Sacaton, AZ	23
Hopi, AZ	Keams Canyon, AZ	16
Laguna, NM	Laguna, NM	16
Menominee, WI	Shawano, WI	35
Navajo, AZ	Tuba City, AZ	29
Navajo, NM	Shiprock, NM	5
Northern Cheyenne, MT	Busby, MT	27
Papago, AZ	Fresnell School Ranch, AZ	9
Pine Ridge, SD	Pine Ridge, SD	14
Red Lake, MN	Redby, MN	25
Rosebud, SD	Rosebud, SD	21
San Carlos, AZ	San Carlos Reservior, AZ	36
Standing Rock, ND	Ft. Yates, ND	27
Turtle Mountain, ND	Bottineau, ND	36
Wind River, WY	Riverton, WY	16
Yakima, WA	Toppenish, WA	7
Zuni, NM	Blackrock, NM	21

Table 2.21

Average Maximum Temperature, Selected Reservations, by Month (°F)

	Jan	Feb	Mar	April	May	June	July	Aug	Sept	Oct	Nov	Dec	Annual Average
Blackfeet, MT	28.7	30.7	38.3	51.2	61.3	68.3	77.4	76.9	64.1	53.4	39.1	31.3	51.6
Cherokee, NC	51.1	54.4	61.3	69.8	76.7	82.9	85.1	84.3	80.9	71.9	60.5	52.5	69.3
Cheyenne River, SD	26.8	31.3	44.9	59.6	69.4	80.1	87.9	86.4	76.0	63.0	45.6	30.5	58.5
Crow, MT	31.6	34.6	46.4	60.5	68.2	80.4	89.7	86.4	75.4	62.5	47.1	35.5	59.9
Flathead, MT	32.0	37.0	47.1	58.2	66.8	74.5	84.4	82.8	70.4	57.8	43.0	33.8	57.3
Ft. Apache, AZ	53.7	56.8	62.8	70.2	78.3	88.5	89.6	87.4	83.1	74.6	69.2	53.6	71.8
Ft. Peck, MT	20.2	22.4	37.1	56.7	68.8	77.6	86.0	84.6	72.5	59.3	40.3	25.6	54.3
Gila River, AZ	65.8	70.5	75.8	83.6	92.4	102.1	102.5	100.9	97.7	87.1	76.0	65.6	85.0
Hopi, AZ	43.2	47.4	56.3	64.8	71.7	83.6	87.5	84.3	78.7	66.7	56.5	43.2	65.3
Laguna, NM	47.0	51.6	59.2	68.8	78.0	88.1	89.5	87.0	81.3	69.9	56.1	45.1	68.5
Menominee, WI	22.2	25.2	37.8	54.0	66.1	76.1	80.3	77.2	69.4	59.6	39.9	26.5	52.9
Navajo, AZ	44.4	52.3	60.4	69.4	79.1	89.5	91.9	91.0	84.7	71.9	58.3	44.8	69.8
Navajo, NM	44.8	52.8	61.6	71.6	80.2	89.4	93.1	90.7	84.9	73.6	56.6	44.0	70.3
Northern Cheyenne, MT	31.2	35.3	45.6	58.9	66.7	77.6	86.8	85.6	74.4	60.8	47.0	34.5	58.7
Papago, AZ	63.6	66.8	70.9	78.7	87.3	96.2	94.2	92.4	89.0	82.0	70.2	61.9	79.4
Pine Ridge, SD	35.7	36.8	47.6	59.1	68.1	77.8	88.3	85.8	77.7	63.8	52.0	37.1	60.8
Red Lake, MN	13.9	19.2	34.0	51.3	63.8	73.8	79.5	76.9	68.4	54.0	34.3	20.5	49.1
Rosebud, SD	34.6	34.6	45.8	61.3	71.3	81.3	88.6	85.8	76.7	64.4	49.5	35.2	60.8
San Carlos, AZ	62.1	67.7	73.7	80.5	89.9	100.6	101.5	98.6	95.0	84.5	71.2	60.2	82.1
Standing Rock, ND, SD	25.3	27.5	40.9	55.1	66.6	76.2	85.5	83.3	72.2	58.3	40.8	25.0	54.7
Turtle Mountain, ND	12.6	16.3	31.6	52.6	66.0	74.4	80.3	79.0	69.2	55.3	34.4	20.0	49.3
Wind River, WY	29.3	38.0	47.9	59.5	68.6	78.5	87.0	84.3	73.8	59.1	40.7	29.1	58.0
Yakima, WA	32.5	45.1	58.8	67.2	74.0	81.9	89.2	87.6	76.3	64.7	48.8	37.7	63.6
Zuni, NM	44.6	49.1	55.1	62.6	73.5	84.9	86.1	83.7	78.7	68.3	55.7	44.8	65.6

Source: U.S. Weather Bureau, Climatic Survey of the United States (1930-31)

Table 2.21-A
Average Maximum Temperature—Reporting Stations

	Station	Number of Years
Blackfeet, MT	Browning, MT	29
Cherokee, NC	Cullowhee, NC	21
Cheyenne River, SD	Hopewell, SD	21
Crow, MT	Crow Agency, MT	47
Flathead, MT	St. Ignatius, MT	24
Ft. Apache, AZ	Ft. Apache, AZ	30
Ft. Peck, MT	Poplar, MT	36
Gila River, AZ	Sacaton, AZ	24
Hopi, AZ	Keams Canyon, AZ	16
Laguna, NM	Laguna, NM	16
Menominee, WI	Shawano, WI	37
Navajo, AZ	Tuba City, AZ	29
Navajo, NM	Shiprock, NM	5
Northern Cheyenne, MT	Busby, MT	27
Papago, AZ	Fresnell School Ranch, AZ	9
Pine Ridge, SD	Pine Ridge, SD	14
Red Lake, MN	Redby, MN	25
Rosebud, SD	Rosebud, SD	21
San Carlos, AZ	San Carlos Reservior, AZ	24
Standing Rock, ND	Ft. Yates, ND	18
Turtle Mountain, ND	Bottineau, ND	30
Wind River, WY	Riverton, WY	16
Yakima, WA	Toppenish, WA	7
Zuni, NM	Blackrock, NM	21

Table 2.22
Average Minimum Temperature, Selected Reservations, by Month (°F)

	Jan	Feb	Mar	April	May	June	July	Aug	Sept	Oct	Nov	Dec	Annual Average
Blackfeet, MT	7.2	8.9	15.5	26.1	34.5	40.3	44.1	42.8	35.5	28.5	18.1	11.4	26.1
Cherokee, NC	27.3	28.7	33.8	41.2	48.7	57.4	61.1	60.4	55.8	43.5	31.4	27.1	43.0
Cheyenne River, SD	4.6	8.8	19.8	32.5	42.7	53.7	59.4	56.6	48.0	35.9	22.6	9.6	32.8
Crow, MT	6.2	9.0	20.9	32.2	41.2	49.8	55.1	51.5	42.0	32.3	20.1	11.7	31.0
Flathead, MT	13.9	18.1	24.6	31.7	38.0	43.6	48.6	46.7	39.7	32.1	25.1	18.2	31.7
Ft. Apache, AZ	20.2	24.3	28.6	33.7	40.2	48.0	55.7	54.7	48.4	36.3	27.0	20.4	36.5
Ft. Peck, MT	-1.4	-1.2	12.5	30.9	41.5	51.1	56.1	52.4	41.7	30.3	16.4	3.2	27.8
Gila River, AZ	33.6	38.4	42.3	48.1	54.9	64.4	73.6	72.1	65.1	51.1	40.1	34.1	51.6
Hopi, AZ	17.6	21.0	27.1	32.3	38.7	46.9	55.1	53.9	45.7	35.8	25.6	17.4	34.8
Laguna, NM	19.8	23.6	28.8	36.5	42.5	52.0	58.7	57.3	49.6	36.3	27.3	18.2	37.6
Menominee, WI	3.5	5.0	17.4	31.2	41.4	51.2	55.6	52.9	46.5	35.7	24.1	11.1	31.3
Navajo, AZ	20.0	25.8	31.4	38.2	45.1	53.9	61.6	61.9	51.2	39.4	28.7	20.2	39.8
Navajo, NM	15.3	21.3	27.4	34.7	41.6	48.5	58.6	56.6	47.4	34.5	24.0	13.4	35.3
Northern Cheyenne, MT	2.9	6.0	17.4	29.3	37.8	46.3	51.5	49.3	39.9	29.4	18.7	6.7	27.9
Papago, AZ	34.4	38.2	41.4	46.9	54.6	63.9	68.6	65.9	62.1	52.4	41.3	35.8	50.5
Pine Ridge, SD	9.1	10.2	20.8	31.6	40.4	51.1	57.6	54.2	43.7	31.0	21.3	2.2	31.1
Red Lake, MN	-8.6	-3.2	10.9	27.6	40.8	52.1	57.6	53.8	46.2	33.7	19.3	1.9	27.7
Rosebud, SD	10.9	10.5	19.9	32.6	42.1	52.2	58.2	56.0	45.3	33.7	22.6	11.6	33.0
San Carlos, AZ	29.2	33.8	37.8	42.1	49.7	58.8	69.5	68.3	60.8	45.9	35.9	30.8	46.9
Standing Rock, ND, SD	2.7	5.6	18.2	29.4	40.2	50.5	56.9	54.2	43.9	31.9	19.1	5.3	29.8
Turtle Mountain, ND	-10.8	-6.5	7.8	26.6	37.0	47.6	51.1	48.2	39.2	27.5	10.8	-2.6	23.0
Wind River, WY	-.3	8.7	17.6	28.4	36.6	45.4	51.7	48.9	39.2	27.7	13.5	1.1	26.6
Yakima, WA	17.2	24.2	31.5	36.2	42.3	48.7	51.4	49.4	41.2	33.9	27.2	21.6	35.4
Zuni, NM	13.4	19.8	24.8	30.5	38.0	46.9	55.5	53.6	46.6	34.9	23.7	15.7	33.6

Source: U.S. Weather Bureau, Climatic Survey of the United States (1930-31)

Table 2.22-A
Average Minimum Temperature—Reporting Stations

	Station	Number of Years
Blackfeet, MT	Browning, MT	29
Cherokee, NC	Cullowhee, NC	21
Cheyenne River, SD	Hopewell, SD	21
Crow, MT	Crow Agency, MT	47
Flathead, MT	St. Ignatius, MT	24
Ft. Apache, AZ	Ft. Apache, AZ	30
Ft. Peck, MT	Poplar, MT	36
Gila River, AZ	Sacaton, AZ	24
Hopi, AZ	Keams Canyon, AZ	16
Laguna, NM	Laguna, NM	16
Menominee, WI	Shawano, WI	37
Navajo, AZ	Tuba City, AZ	29
Navajo, NM	Shiprock, NM	5
Northern Cheyenne, MT	Busby, MT	27
Papago, AZ	Fresnell School Ranch, AZ	9
Pine Ridge, SD	Pine Ridge, SD	14
Red Lake, MN	Redby, MN	25
Rosebud, SD	Rosebud, SD	21
San Carlos, AZ	San Carlos Reservior, AZ	24
Standing Rock, ND	Ft. Yates, ND	18
Turtle Mountain, ND	Bottineau, ND	30
Wind River, WY	Riverton, WY	16
Yakima, WA	Toppenish, WA	7
Zuni, NM	Blackrock, NM	21

Table 2.23

Average Monthly Precipitation, Selected Reservations (Inches)

	Jan	Feb	Mar	April	May	June	July	Aug	Sept	Oct	Nov	Dec	Annual Average
Blackfeet, MT	.66	.59	.84	.99	2.05	2.66	1.54	1.46	1.87	.86	.86	.67	15.02
Cherokee, NC	4.86	5.14	5.98	4.28	4.35	4.79	5.27	4.82	3.44	2.85	3.25	4.83	53.86
Cheyenne River, SD	.42	.36	1.32	1.87	3.43	1.73	2.85	1.98	.93	.44	.24	.35	15.92
Crow, MT	.83	.66	.95	1.36	2.47	2.50	1.38	.86	1.17	1.30	.87	.74	15.09
Flathead, MT	.96	.75	.98	1.45	2.13	2.28	1.18	1.07	1.74	1.27	1.24	.92	15.97
Ft. Apache, AZ	1.48	1.56	1.59	.85	.57	.51	3.07	3.31	1.59	1.13	1.14	1.43	18.23
Ft. Peck, MT	.52	.40	.69	.86	1.85	3.03	1.72	1.10	1.08	.69	.62	.40	12.96
Gila River, AZ	.87	.66	.97	.37	.21	.11	1.78	1.54	.92	.43	.74	1.24	9.84
Hopi, AZ	1.31	.95	.90	.66	.39	.27	2.41	1.81	.70	1.25	.70	1.08	12.43
Laguna, NM	.36	.64	.63	.96	.54	.56	2.47	1.73	1.47	.71	.55	.81	11.43
Menominee, WI	1.22	1.14	1.63	2.62	3.16	3.63	3.71	2.93	3.18	2.53	1.79	1.28	28.82
Navajo, AZ	.55	.54	.43	.53	.19	.34	.93	.84	.68	.78	.53	.58	6.92
Navajo, NM	.38	.60	.57	1.00	.83	.52	1.58	1.19	1.60	.40	.49	.41	9.57
Northern Cheyenne, MT	.75	.46	.69	1.17	2.22	2.34	1.52	.99	1.43	1.11	.59	.60	13.87
Papago, AZ	.84	1.07	1.74	.56	.37	.57	3.35	4.17	1.75	.53	1.45	1.60	18.00
Pine Ridge, SD	.34	.40	.76	1.86	2.63	2.80	2.56	2.13	1.38	1.47	.29	.54	17.16
Red Lake, MN	.67	.60	.82	1.36	2.42	4.29	3.09	2.81	2.74	1.57	.95	.69	22.01
Rosebud, SD	.87	.71	1.32	2.07	2.66	2.63	2.78	2.05	1.15	1.01	.60	.97	18.82
San Carlos, AZ	1.29	1.37	1.12	.42	.27	.19	1.87	2.14	.92	.81	.87	1.36	12.63
Standing Rock, ND, SD	.52	.62	.94	1.59	1.97	3.50	2.42	2.00	1.15	.91	.55	.48	16.65
Turtle Mountain, ND	.69	.82	.97	1.74	1.94	4.01	2.55	1.75	1.76	1.41	1.14	.72	19.50
Wind River, WY	.11	.25	.43	1.07	2.16	1.23	1.10	.70	1.13	1.39	.38	.24	10.19
Yakima, WA	1.21	.64	.27	.28	.32	.25	.01	.12	.52	.35	1.08	.83	5.88
Zuni, NM	.79	.73	.92	.73	.61	.40	2.59	1.99	1.33	.89	.55	.80	12.33

Source: U.S. Weather Bureau, Climatic Survey of the United States (1930-31)

Table 2.23–A
Average Monthly Precipitation—Reporting Stations

	Station	Period
Blackfeet, MT	Browning, MT	1894–1930
Cherokee, NC	Bryson City, NC	1888–1930
Cheyenne River, SD	Eagle Butte, SD	1911–1919
Crow, MT	Crow Agency, MT	1879–1930
Flathead, MT	St. Ignatius, MT	1896–1930
Ft. Apache, AZ	Ft. Apache, AZ	1872–1930
Ft. Peck, MT	Poplar, MT	1882–1930
Gila River, AZ	Sacaton, AZ	1908–1930
Hopi, AZ	Keams Canyon, AZ	1894–1895
		1906–1921
		1928–1930
Laguna, NM	Laguna, NM	1850–1851
		1905–1921
		1927–1930
Menominee, WI	Shawano, WI	1891–1930
Navajo, AZ	Tuba City, AZ	1897–1930
Navajo, NM	Shiprock, NM	1926–1930
Northern Cheyenne, MT	Busby, MT	1903–1930
Papago, AZ	Fresnell School Ranch, AZ	1922–1930
Pine Ridge, SD	Pine Ridge, SD	1901–1924
Red Lake, MN	Redby, MN	1893–1895
		1908–1930
Rosebud, SD	Rosebud, SD	1892–1922
	St. Francis, SD	1922–1930
San Carlos, AZ	San Carlos Reservior, AZ	1881–1930
Standing Rock, ND	Ft. Yates, ND	1882–1930
Turtle Mountain, ND	Bottineau, ND	1891–1900
Wind River, WY	Riverton, WY	1907–1930
Yakima, WA	Toppenish, WA	1925–1930
Zuni, NM	Blackrock, NM	1908–1930

Table 2.24
Average Annual Snowfall, Selected Reservations

	Annual Snowfall (Inches)	Station	# of Years
Blackfeet, MT	63.3	Browning, MT	29
Cherokee, NC	11.9	Brywon City, NC	35
Cheyenne River, SD	37.7	Hopewell, SD	21
Crow, MT	44.0	Crow Agency, MT	38
Flathead, MT	45.2	St. Ignatius, MT	24
Ft. Apache, AZ	18.0	Fort Apache, AZ	30
Ft. Peck, MT	32.9	Poplar, MT	35
Gila River, AZ	T	Phoenix, AZ	35
Hopi, AZ	32.3	Keams Canyon, AZ	15
Laguna, NM	20.6	Laguna, NM	17
Menominee, WI	50.1	Shawano, WI	34
Navajo, AZ	12.2	Tuba City, AZ	29
Navajo, NM	6.1	Shiprock, NM	5
Northern Cheyenne, MT	51.5	Busby, MT	26
Papago, AZ	1.0	Tucson, AZ	14
Pine Ridge, SD	36.3	Pine Ridge, SD	14
Red Lake, MN	37.6	Redby, MN	24
Rosebud, SD	44.5	Rosebud, SD	22
San Carlos, AZ	5.0	Globe, AZ*	29
Standing Rock, ND, SD	25.9	Ft. Yates, ND	16
Turtle Mountain, ND	37.3	Pembina, ND	20
Wind River, WY	35.3	Riverton, WY	15
Yakima, WA	11.1	Toppenish, WA	5
Zuni, NM	27.7	Blackrock, NM	21

Notes: * - Elevation 3440 feet
        T - Trace

Source: Weather Bureau, Climatic Survey of the United States (1930-31)

Table 2.25
Weather Stations and Elevations, Selected Reservations

	Station	Elevation (feet)
Blackfeet, MT	Browning, Glacer Co., MT	4,440
Cherokee, NC	Bryson City, Swain Co., NC	2,000
Cheyenne River, SD	Eagle Butte, Dewey Co., SD	2,415
Crown, MT	Crow Agency, Big Horn Co., MT	3,036
Flathead, MT	St. Ignatius, Lake Co., MT	2,900
Ft. Apache, AZ	Ft. Apache, Navajo Co., AZ	5,300
Ft. Peck, MT	Popular, Roosevelt Co., MT	1,994
Gila River, AZ	Sacaton, Pinal Co., AZ	1,280
Hopi, AZ	Keams Canyon, Navajo Co., AZ	6,600
Laguna, NM	Laguna, Valencia Co., NM	5,840
Menominee, WI	Shawano, Shawano Co., WI	796
Navajo, AZ	Tuba City, Coconino Co., AZ	4,500
Navajo, NM	Shiprock, San Juan Co., NM	4,950
Northern Cheyenne, MT	Busby, Big Horn Co., MT	3,500
Papago, AZ	Fresnal School Ranch, Pima Co., AZ	4,000
Pine Ridge, SD	Pine Ridge, Shannon Co., SD	3,232
Red Lake, MN	Redby, Beltrami Co., MN	1,158
Rosebud, SD	Rosebud, Todd Co., SD	2,600
San Carlos, AZ	San Carlos Reservoir, Gila Co., AZ	2,532
Standing Rock, ND-SD	Fort Yates, Sioux Co., ND	1,670
Turtle Mountain, ND	St. John, Rolette Co., ND	1,945
Wind River, WY	Riverton, Fremont Co., WY	4,954
Yakima, WA	Toppenish, Yakima Co., WA	765
Zuni, NM	Blackrock, McKinley Co., NM	6,455

Source: Weather Bureau, Climatic Survey of the United States (1930-31)

3

Population

American Indian population began increasing in the early twentieth century after a decline that began at first contact with Europeans. While authorities differ regarding the exact figures, a broad concensus exists that Indian populations declined precipitously after contact with Europeans as a result of infectious disease, disruption of food supplies, warfare, forced labor, and enslavement. In addition, during the historic period, some American Indian groups had high rates of alcoholism, homicide, and suicide, which has resulted in population losses as a result of high death rates (see Chapter 5). Since, at the time of contact, American Indians had not been exposed to European diseases, small pox, measles, and other infectious diseases were devastating to American Indian populations. American Indians had not acquired the immunities built up by Europeans. Disruptions in the food supply, particularly as a result of the extermination of wild animals and the forced removal of Indians from sources of animal and vegetable nourishment, led to starvation and death. Indians also have had high rates of infectious diseases, particularly of such water-borne diseases as diarrhea, as a result of crowding and poor sanitation in the historical period. Indian population reached its nadir in the early twentieth century; since then, as a result of a high birth rate, improvements in the food supply, and the provision of medical resources, Indian population has grown.

However, a part of the increase shown in census returns, particularly in the last quarter-century, results from changes in methods of gathering census information and, as a result of increased ethnic pride, from an increased willingness on the part of persons to identify themselves as Indian or to seek official recognition for that designation. Since 1960, the

Census Bureau has relied increasingly on self-reporting to enumerate ethnic groups. As a result, an unknown but substantial number of persons who were classified as white or identified as members of other groups prior to 1960, were enumerated as American Indians at that and subsequent censuses.[1]

Data from three major sources are included in the tables accompanying this chapter. Included are estimates of the American Indian population in 1492 by anthropologists and historians, estimates of Indian population before the 1890 census, and returns from the United States decennial census as of 1890 and after and Bureau of Indian Affairs (BIA) censuses of the nineteenth and twentieth centuries. Even when the census and BIA figures are for the same years, they often differ from each other. In part, this is a result of the vicissitudes of enumerating poor, culturally different populations; in part, it is a result of the migratory habits of many American Indian people; and, in part, it is a result of unstable economic conditions leading to rapid changes in the populations of reservation areas.

Scholars of pre-Columbian Indian population have differed radically from one another in their estimates of the Indian population at first contact with Europeans. Table 3.1 shows the estimates of a number of scholars, arranged in order of the date of the estimate, of Indian population in 1492, the date of the European discovery of the Western Hemisphere. Both hemispheric and North American estimates are given. While there are exceptions to the trend, in general scholars tended to estimate higher populations for American Indians in 1492 as time went on during the twentieth century. These higher population estimates are the result of the progress of archaeological investigations, of detailed investigations of the food sources available to American Indians in 1492, and of a reassessment of some of the sources, particularly the population estimates of the early Spanish explorers. Henry Dobyns, who has been a leader in this reappraisal, has consistently estimated the highest numbers.[2] While some have questioned the size of his estimates, the general point that Indian population was much higher than previously supposed has been generally accepted. In several regions, population densities in the Western Hemisphere rivaled those found in Europe in the fifteenth century.

Prior to the 1890 census, the first census in which a concerted attempt was made to enumerate the American Indian population, only scattered estimates of Indian population are available. Some of these are shown in Table 3.2. Many are of doubtful accuracy, although the later estimates are probably more accurate than the earlier ones, because of increased white-Indian contact. Despite the problems, the general decline in enumerated Indian populations through the nineteenth century reflects the destructive impact of early contact with whites on American Indian population.

The Bureau of Indian Affairs estimates of Indian reservation population in the late nineteenth century (Table 3.3) reveal a roughly comparable trend. These figures show American Indian population reaching a nadir in 1890, and gradually increasing during the last decade of the nineteenth century and into the twentieth century. The rate of increase was quite low until the 1960s, however. The decennial censuses of 1890 through 1980 (Tables 3.4 and 3.5) show uneven growth in the American Indian population during the first half of the twentieth century and much more rapid growth in Indian population after 1950. Indian population was probably consistently underestimated by both the Bureau of Indian Affairs and the Census Bureau, particularly during the first half of the twentieth century. However, the trend toward increasing Indian population is clear.

Tables 3.3 and 3.4 show the Alaska Native population separately, since data were not gathered on the population of Alaska Natives consistently during this period. The aboriginal population of Alaska includes Aleuts and Eskimos in addition to American Indians. Table 3.6 shows the numbers of Aleuts, Eskimos, and American Indians for most census years between 1920 and 1980. The aboriginal population of Alaska, like that of the United States as a whole, increased gradually prior to the 1950s. Since then it has increased at a more rapid rate. Table 3.7 presents the American Indian population by state for selected census years between 1890 and 1980.

Tribal population is probably a more meaningful statistic than the population of Indians in a particular state, since most American Indians identified themselves primarily as tribal members, not as American Indians or state residents. Table 3.8 shows the population of selected tribes at the decennial censuses of 1910, 1930, and 1970. These were years in which the Bureau of the Census made a special attempt to enumerate the Indian population completely and to present special data on American Indian populations, including tribal population counts. While making comparisons is complicated by the sometimes shifting tribal groups for which the data are reported, it is possible to trace changes in the population size of many tribal groups and in the proportion of all American Indians accounted for by the tribe using the data reported for these three years.

Table 3.9 shows, by state, the Indian reservation population under BIA jurisdiction for the years 1953, 1962, and 1983. Table 3.10 shows the population of selected reservations using both BIA and census enumerations for selected years between 1875 and 1983. Considerable fluctuation in population size occurred. This resulted in part from rapid changes in reservation conditions including, in the early years, removal and transfer of Indian populations to other reservations, and, in later years, rapidly changing economic opportunities both on reservations and in off-reservation areas.

Tables 3.11 through 3.17 provide data on the age and sex distribution of the Indian population in the twentieth century. Table 3.11 provides data on the sex distribution of the Indian population at selected censuses between 1890 and 1980. The ratio of females to males gradually increased during this period, as improvements in maternal health were achieved and as female life expectancy exceeded male life expectancy. Tables 3.12 through 3.17 provide detail on the age and sex distribution of the Indian population for the census years of 1910, 1930, 1950, 1960, 1970, and 1980. The gradual trend toward an increasing median age and decreasing proportions of very young Indian people is revealed in these tables, taken from the reports of the decennial censuses.

Despite the relative aging of the Indian population, the American Indian population remains a young one when compared to non-Indians. American Indian population today is rapidly growing as a result of improvements in health status, a high birth rate, and a relatively young population. (Developments in the Indian birth rate and health status are discussed in Chapter 5. The changing geographical distribution of the American Indian population is discussed in Chapter 4.)

The earliest nineteenth-century sources of statistical data on Indian population are Jedidiah Morse's *Report on Indian Affairs* (1822) and Henry Schoolcraft's *Indian Tribes of the United States* (1851-1857). Both of these surveys were undertaken for the federal government and, while they are necessarily inexact and vague, they do provide the population estimates for most of the known tribes in the United States at the time. Other nineteenth-century estimates and their sources are listed in the report of the 1890 census on American Indians, U.S. Bureau of the Census, *Report on Indians Taxed and Indians Not Taxed in the United States (Excluding Alaska) at the Eleventh Census: 1890* (1894), the first in a series of special census reports on American Indians. The 1890 census represented the first sustained attempt to gather statistical data on all American Indians in the United States and remains a useful source. Indian population for the nation, for states, for reservations, and, for Indians living off reservation, by county, is provided. Other nineteenth- and early twentieth-century population data are provided in the *Annual Reports* of the Commissioner of Indian Affairs, published prior to 1906. In addition to American Indian population statistics, Indian agents reported such things as crops raised, the number of births and deaths, participation in educational activities, and "statistics of civilization," including the number of Indians able to speak English, the number wearing "citizen's dress," and the number engaged in farming and agriculture.

The censuses of 1910, 1930, 1950, 1960, 1970, and 1980 made special efforts to cover the Indian population. These were reported on in a series of special publications of the Bureau of the Census including *Indian*

Population in the United States and Alaska: 1910 (1915) on the 1910 census; *The Indian Population of the United States and Alaska: 1930* (1937) on the 1930 census; *Census of Population, 1950, Special Reports: Nonwhite Population by Race* (1953) on the 1950 census; *Census of Population, 1960, Subject Reports: Nonwhite Population by Race* (1963) on the 1960 census; and *Census of Population, 1970, Subject Reports: American Indians* (1973) on the 1970 census. For the 1980 census, data on American Indians are included for the first time in the summary volumes, including *General Social and Economic Characteristics* (1983) and *Detailed Characteristics of the Population* (1984). The estimates of population completed by the Bureau of Indian Affairs may be found in a variety of Bureau publications. Summary population figures were included in many *Annual Reports* published after 1906. The Statistical Supplements to the *Annual Reports of the Commissioner of Indian Affairs* for the fiscal years 1938-1946 provide more detailed population statistics. These were mimeographed and may be found in some government documents depositories. More recently, the Bureau of Indian Affairs has published periodically *Local Estimates of Resident Indian Population and Labor Force Data.* Bureau publications enumerate only American Indians living on or near reservation lands. Most BIA population estimates provide information on reservation Indian population broken down by reservation and, after the 1940s, by BIA area.

The Columbian Exchange: Biological and Cultural Consequences of 1492, by Alfred W. Crosby, Jr., (1972) provides a good introduction to the demographic and social results of European contact on American Indian populations. Henry F. Dobyns' *Their Number Become Thinned: Native American Population Dynamics in Eastern North America* (1983) is the most recent statement by the leading proponent of increasing precontact population estimates. Dobyns is also the author of *Native American Historical Demography: A Critical Bibliography* (1976), which provides an excellent introduction to the literature in this field.

The report of the U.S. National Resource Board, *Indian Land Tenure, Economic Status, and Population Trends* (1935), prepared by the Bureau of Indian Affairs, includes an excellent discussion of the problems of estimating Indian population. J. Nixon Hadley, "The Demography of American Indians," in *The Annals of the American Academy of Political and Social Science* 311 (May 1957): 23-30, and Sam Stanley and Robert K. Thomas, "Current Demographic and Social Trends among North American Indians," *The Annals of the American Academy of Political and Social Science* 436 (March 1978): 111-120, provide overviews of recent demographic trends affecting American Indians. The report of the U.S. Congress, Office of Technology Assessment, *Indian Health Care,* OTA-H-290 (1986), pp. 59-82, includes a discussion of the contemporary

Indian population. Ira S. Lowry, "The Science and Politics of Ethnic Enumeration," in *Ethnicity and Public Policy* (1982), edited by Winston A. Van Horne, pp. 42-61, discusses issues in the enumeration of ethnic groups, including the Census Bureau's use of respondents' ethnic self-identification.

NOTES

1. See Ira S. Lowry, "The Science and Politics of Ethnic Enumeration," in Winston A. Van Horne, ed., *Ethnicity and Public Policy* (Milwaukee: University of Wisconsin System American Ethnic Studies Coordinating Committee, 1982), pp. 41-61.

2. For an early example, see Henry F. Dobyns, "Estimating Aboriginal American Population: An Appraisal of Techniques with a New Hemispheric Estimate," *Current Anthropology* 7 (1966): 395-416.

TABLES

Table 3.1
Estimates of Indian Population at Contact

Date of Estimate	Author	Western Hemisphere	North America
1910	Mooney	–	1,150,000
1924	Rivet	40–50,000,000	1,148,000
1924	Supper	40–50,000,000	2–3,500,000
1928	Spinden	50–75,000,000	–
1928	Mooney	–	1,153,000
1931	Wilcox	13,101,000	1,002,000
1939	Kroeber	8,400,000	900,000
1945	Rosenblat	13,385,000	1,000,000
1945	Steward	13,170,000	1,000,000
1949	Steward	15,490,800	1,000,000
1964	Borah	100,000,000	–
1966	Dobyns	90,043,000	9,800,000
1976	Ubelaker	–	2,171,125
1981	Thornton and Marsh-Thornton	–	7,705,000
1983	Dobyns	–	18,000,000

Sources: Henry Dobyns, Their Number Became Thinned: Native American Population Dynamics in Eastern North America (Knoxville: University of Tennessee Press, 1983), pp. 33–45; Russell Thornton and Jeanne Marsh-Thornton, "Estimating Prehistoric American Indian Population Size for United States: Implications of the Nineteenth Century Population Decline and Nadir," American Journal of Physical Anthropology, 55 (1981): 47–53; and Douglas H. Ubelaker, "Prehistoric New World Population Size: Historical Review and Current Appraisal of New World Estimates," American Journal of Physical Anthropology 45 (1976): 661–666.

Table 3.2
Estimates of Indian Population before the 1890 Census

Year	Population	Source
1800	600,000	Office of Indian Affairs (1943)
1822	471,417	Jedediah Morse
1829	312,930	Secretary of War
1834	312,610	Secretary of War
1850	388,229	H.R. Schoolcraft
1850	400,764	U.S. Census
1860	339,421	U.S. Census
1867	306,925*	Commissioner of Indian Affairs
1870	313,712	U.S. Census
1880	306,543	U.S. Census and Indian Office
1890	248,253	U.S. Census

Note:

*excludes Citizen Indians

Source: U.S. Bureau of the Census, Report of Indians Taxed and Indians No
Taxed in the United States (excluding Alaska) at the Eleventh Cen
1890 (Washington: Government Printing Office, 1894); U.S. Office
Indian Affairs, "In Fifty Years There May Be As Many Indians As
Before the White Man's Arrival," Indians at Work 11, no. 2 (July-
August, 1943): 24-28.

Table 3.3
BIA Estimates of Indian Reservation Population,
Selected Years, 1865-1983

Year	U.S., except Alaska	Alaska[1]	Combined
1865	294,574	–	–
1870	288,646	–	–
1875	279,337	25,831[2]	305,168
1880	256,127	–	–
1885	259,244	–	–
1890	243,534	–	–
1895	248,340	–	–
1900	270,544	–	–
1905	284,079	–	–
1910	304,950	–	–
1915	330,010	–	–
1920	336,337	–	–
1925	349,595	–	–
1930	340,541[3]	–	–
1939	351,878	29,983	381,861
1945	393,622	32,750	426,372
1953	368,401[4]	34,670[4]	403,071[4]
1962	328,857	38,332	367,179
1983	690,231	64,970	755,201

Notes:

1. Includes Eskimos, Aleuts, and Indians.
2. Excludes 1,500 "half-breeds or creoles."
3. Includes an estimated 118,733 Indians not enumerated.
4. Includes persons on tribal rolls only.

Sources: Commissioner of Indian Affairs, Annual Reports, 1865, 1870, 1875,
1880, 1885, 1890, 1895, 1900, 1905, 1910, 1915, 1920, 1925, 1930;
Statistical Supplements to the Annual Reports of the Commissioner of
Indian Affairs, 1939, 1945; U.S. House, Committee on Interior and
Insular Affairs, Investigation of Indian Affairs (Washington:
Government Printing Office, 1953); U.S. Bureau of Indian Affairs,
U.S. Indian Population and Land, 1962 (Washington: Bureau of Indian
Affairs, 1963); U.S. Bureau of Indian Affairs, Indian Service
Population and Labor Force Estimates, January 1983 (Washington:
Bureau of Indian Affairs, 1983).

Table 3.4
Indian Population of the United States and Alaska
at the Decennial Census, 1890–1980

	United States (except Alaska)	Alaska Natives[1]	Total
1890	248,253	25,354	273,607
1900	237,196	29,536	266,732
1910	265,683	25,331	291,014
1920	244,437	26,558	270,995
1930	332,397	29,983[2]	362,380
1940	333,969	32,458[3]	366,427
1950	343,410	33,863	377,273
1960	509,147	42,489	551,636
1970	776,454	50,819	827,273
1980	1,356,297[4]	64,103	1,420,400

Notes:

1. Includes Eskimos, Aleuts, and Indians living in Alaska.
2. Census of 1929.
3. Census of 1939.
4. Includes Alaska Natives residing in states other than Alaska.

Source: U.S. Bureau of the Census, 15th Census of the United States: 1930.
         The Indian Population of the United States and Alaska (Washington:
         Government Printing Office, 1937), p. 2; 16th Census of Population:
         1940, Characteristics of the Population: U.S. Summary (Washington:
         Government Printing Office, 1943), p. 46; Census of Population: 1950.
         Characteristics of the Population, Part 1: U.S. Summary (Washington:
         Government Printing Office, 1953), pp. 1–106; Census of Population:
         1950: Characteristics of the Population, Parts 51–54, Territories and
         Possessions (Washington: Government Printing Office, 1953), pp. 51–54;
         U.S. Census of Population: 1960. Characteristics of the Population:
         U.S. Summary (Washington: Government Printing Office, 1964), pp. 1–
         164; Census of Population: 1970. Characteristics of the Population,
         U.S. Summary (Washington: Government Printing Office, 1973), pp. 1–
         293; Census of Population: 1980. Characteristics of the Population,
         U.S. Summary (Washington: Government Printing Office, 1983), pp. 1–
         125.

Table 3.5
Indian Population of the United States, Including Alaska Natives,
at the Decennial Census, 1890–1980

CENSUS YEAR	INDIAN POPULATION*	% CHANGE
1980	1,420,400	+71.1
1970	827,273	+50.0
1960	551,636	+46.2
1950	377,273	+ 3.0
1940	366,427	+ 1.1
1930	362,380	+33.7
1920	270,995	− 6.9
1910	291,014	+ 9.1
1900	266,732	− 2.5
1890	273,607	—

Notes:

    * Including Alaska Natives in Alaska, 1890–1970, and Alaska Natives
    in all states, 1980.

Source: Table 3.4

Table 3.6
Composition of the Aboriginal Population of Alaska, 1920–1980

Year	Aleut	Eskimo	Indian	Total
1920	2,942	13,698	9,918	26,558
1929	N.A.	N.A.	N.A.	29,983
1939	5,599	15,576	11,283	32,458
1950	3,892	15,882	14,089	33,863
1960	5,722	22,323	14,444	42,489
1970	6,352	28,186	16,281	50,819
1980	8,090	34,144	21,869	64,103

Source: U.S. Bureau of the Census. Census of Population: 1950. Characteristics of the Population, Parts 51-54, Territories and Possessions (Washington: Government Printing Office, 1953); Census of Population: 1960. Characteristics of the Population, Part 2, Alaska (Washington: Government Printing Office, 1964); Census of Population: 1970. Characteristics of the Population, Part 2, Alaska (Washington: Government Printing Office, 1973); Census of Population: 1980. Characteristics of the Population, U.S. Summary (Washington: Government Printing Office, 1983).

Table 3.7
Indian Population by State, Selected Years, 1890–1980

	1890	1910	1930	1950	1970	1980[2]
Alaska[1]	25,354[3]	25,331	29,983	33,863	50,819	64,103
Alabama	1,143[3]	909	465	928	2,443	7,583
Arizona	29,981	29,201	45,726	65,781	95,812	152,745
Arkansas	250	460	408	533	2,014	9,428
California	16,624	16,371	19,212	19,947	91,018	201,369
Colorado	1,092	1,482	1,395	1,567	8,836	18,068
Connecticut	228	152	162	333	2,222	4,533
Delaware	4	5	5	-	656	1,328
District of Columbia	25	68	40	330	956	1,031
Florida	171	74	587	1,011	6,677	19,257
Georgia	68	95	43	333	2,347	7,616
Hawaii	-	-	-	-	1,126	2,768
Idaho	4,223	3,488	3,638	3,800	6,687	10,521
Illinois	98	188	469	1,443	11,413	16,283
Indiana	343	279	285	438	3,887	7,836
Iowa	457	471	660	1,084	2,992	5,455
Kansas	1,682	2,444	2,454	2,381	8,672	15,373
Kentucky	71	234	22	234	1,531	3,610
Louisiana	628	780	1,536	409	5,294	12,065
Maine	559	892	1,012	1,522	2,195	4,087
Maryland	44	55	50	314	4,239	8,021
Massachusetts	428	688	674	1,201	4,475	7,743
Michigan	5,625	7,519	7,080	7,000	16,854	40,050
Minnesota	10,096	9,053	11,077	12,533	23,128	35,016
Mississippi	2,036	1,253	1,458	2,502	4,113	6,180
Missouri	128	313	578	547	5,405	12,321
Montana	11,206	10,745	14,798	16,606	27,130	37,270
Nebraska	6,431	3,502	3,256	3,954	6,624	9,195
Nevada	5,156	5,240	4,871	5,025	7,933	13,308
New Hampshire	16	34	64	74	361	1,352
New Jersey	84	168	213	621	4,706	8,394
New Mexico	15,044	20,573	28,941	41,901	72,788	106,119
New York	6,044	6,046	6,973	10,640	28,355	39,582
North Carolina	1,516	7,851	16,579	3,742	44,406	64,652
North Dakota	8,174	6,486	8,387	10,766	14,369	20,158
Ohio	206	127	435	1,146	6,654	12,239
Oklahoma	64,456	74,825	92,725	53,769	98,468	169,459
Oregon	4,971	5,090	4,776	5,820	13,510	27,314
Pennsylvania	1,081	1,503	523	1,141	5,533	9,465
Rhode Island	180	284	318	385	1,390	2,898
South Carolina	173	331	959	554	2,241	5,757
South Dakota	19,854	19,137	21,833	23,344	32,365	44,968
Tennessee	146	216	171	339	2,276	5,104
Texas	708	702	1,001	2,736	17,957	40,075
Utah	3,456	3,123	2,869	4,201	11,273	19,256
Vermont	34	26	36	30	229	984
Virginia	349	539	799	1,056	4,853	9,454
Washington	11,181	10,997	11,253	13,816	33,386	60,804
West Virginia	9	36	18	160	751	1,610
Wisconsin	9,930	10,142	11,548	12,196	18,924	29,499
Wyoming	1,844	1,486	1,845	3,237	4,980	7,094
TOTAL	273,607	291,014	362,380	377,273	827,237	1,420,400

Notes:

1. Includes Eskimos and Aleuts for all years.
2. Includes Eskimos and Aleuts in all states.
3. Includes 384 Apache captives.

Source: See Table 3.4

Table 3.8
Population of Selected Tribes at the Censuses of 1910, 1930, and 1970

	1910	% [*]	1930	% [*]	1970	% [*]
Apache	4,973	1.7	6,537	1.8	22,993	3.0
Arapaho	1,419	0.5	1,241	0.3	2,993	0.4
Blackfeet	2,367	0.8	3,145	0.9	9,921[1]	1.3
Chemhuevi	355	0.1	-	-	-	-
Cherokee	31,489	10.8	45,238	12.5	66,150	8.7
Cheyenne	3,055	1.0	2,695	0.7	6,872	0.9
Chickasaw	4,204	1.4	4,745	1.3	5,616	0.7
Chippewa	20,214	6.9	21,549	5.9	41,946[2]	5.5
Choctaw	15,917	5.5	17,757	4.9	23,562[2]	3.1
Colville	785	0.3	-	-	3,180[3]	0.4
Commanche	1,171[4]	0.4	1,423	0.4	4,250[4]	0.6
Creek	7,341[4]	2.5	9,083	2.5	17,004[4]	2.2
Crow	1,799	0.6	1,674	0.5	3,779[5]	0.5
Delaware	985	0.3	971	0.3	2,926[5]	0.4
Flathead[6]	486	0.2	-	-	3,702	0.5
Iroquois[6]	8,190	2.8	7,219	2.0	21,473[7]	2.8
Kaw	238	0.1	318	0.1	6,849[7]	0.9
Kiowa	1,126[8]	0.4	1,050[8]	0.3	4,337	0.6
Lumbee	6,195[8]	2.1	12,975[8]	3.6	27,520	3.6
Menominee	1,422	0.5	1,969	0.5	4,307	0.6
Navajo	22,455	7.7	39,064	10.8	96,743[9]	12.7
Omaha	1,105	0.4	1,103	0.3	-[9]	-
Osage	1,373[10]	0.5	2,344[10]	0.6	-[9]	-
Paiute	5,631[10]	1.9	5,060[10]	1.4	-[11]	-
Papago	3,798	1.3	5,205	1.4	16,690[11]	2.2
Pima	4,236	1.5	4,382	1.2	-[12]	-
Ponca	875	0.3	939	0.3	-[9]	-
Potawatomie	2,440	0.8	1,854	0.5	4,626	0.6
Pueblo	10,843	3.7	12,047	3.3	30,971[9]	4.1
Quapaw	231	0.1	222	0.1	-	-
Seminole	1,729	0.6	2,048	0.6	5,055[13]	0.7
Shoshone	3,840	1.3	3,994	1.1	14,248[13]	1.9
Sioux (Dakota)	22,778	7.8	25,934	7.2	47,875[14]	6.3
Stockbridge	533	0.2	-	-	-	-
Tlingit-Haida	-	-	5,050	1.4	7,543	1.0
Ute	2,244	0.8	1,980	0.5	3,815	0.5
Winnebago	1,820	0.6	1,446	0.4	2,832	0.4
Yakima	1,362	0.5	-	-	3,856	0.5
Yuman	4,267	1.5	4,537	1.3	7,635	1.0

Notes:

[*] Percent of total Indian population for year. See Table 3.5
1. Combined with Shoshone
2. Includes Houma
3. Includes Lakes
4. Includes Alabama and Coushatta
5. Includes Stockbridge
6. Includes Cayuga, Mohawk, Oneida, Onondaga, Seneca, Tuscarora, and Wyandotte
7. Includes Omaha, Osage, Ponca and Quapaw
8. Croatan, Virginia-Carolina Algonquian Indians
9. Combined with Kaw
10. Combined with Mono and Paivotso
11. Includes Pima
12. Combined with Papago
13. Includes Paiute and Chemhuevi
14. Combined with Delaware

Source: U.S. Bureau of the Census, Indian Population in the United States and Alaska, 1910 (Washington: Government Printing Office, 1913), pp. 17-21; U.S. Bureau of the Census, Fifteenth Census of the United States: 1930. The Indian Population of the United States and Alaska (Washington: Government Printing Office, 1937), pp. 56-69; U.S. Bureau of the Census, 1970 Census of Population: Subject Report: American Indians (Washington: Government Printing Office, 1973), pp. 188-189.

Table 3.9
Indian Population under BIA Jurisdiction, by State, 1953–1983

State	1953	1962	1983
Alaska	34,670	38,332	64,970
Arizona	93,374	81,924	154,818
California	38,650	8,861	23,625
Colorado	1,119	1,411	2,661
Florida	846	1,003	1,921
Idaho	4,557	4,134	7,108
Iowa	579	531	662
Kansas	2,471	1,289	2,243
Louisiana	392	268	717
Maine	–	–	2,261
Michigan	2,202	1,216	5,829
Minnesota	19,430	11,580	18,260
Mississippi	2,838	3,594	4,487
Montana	22,221	20,566	27,529
Nebraska	4,933	2,196	4,404
Nevada	4,318	4,168	8,259
New Mexico	19,403	52,188	105,973
New York	–	–	11,167
North Carolina	2,540	5,500	5,971
North Dakota	17,422	11,490	21,552
Oklahoma	57,923	61,769	159,852
Oregon	4,338	2,305	4,301
South Carolina	509	–	–
South Dakota	31,588	27,669	46,101
Texas	415	–	–
Utah	2,082	4,885	7,140
Washington	15,857	11,220	39,726
Wisconsin	15,058	5,322	18,279
Wyoming	3,337	3,758	5,385
TOTAL	403,071	367,179	755,201

Source: U.S. House, Committee on Interior and Insular Affairs, Investigation
of Indian Affairs (Washington: Government Printing Office, 1953),
p. 54; Report on Indian Population and Land (Washington: Bureau of
Indian Affairs, 1962); Indian Service Population and Labor Force
Estimates (Washington: Bureau of Indian Affairs, 1983).

Table 3.10
Population of Selected Reservations, BIA and Census Enumerations, Selected Years, 1875–1983

	1875 (BIA)	1885 (BIA)	1895 (BIA)	1905 (BIA)	1915 (BIA)	1925 (BIA)	1932 (BIA)	1943 (BIA)	1970 (Census)	1980 (Census)	1983 (BIA)
Blackfeet, MT	7,200	2,000	1,837	2,063	2,724	3,244	3,812	4,904	4,757	5,080	6,555
Cherokee, NC	1,700	3,000	1,479	1,455	2,211	2,611	3,230	3,665	3,455	4,844	5,971
Cheyenne River, SD	7,586	2,907	2,539	2,526	2,708	2,964	3,168	3,751	3,440	1,529	4,649
Crow, MT	4,200	3,870	2,133	1,794	1,699	1,781	1,987	2,424	3,049	3,953	5,288
Flathead, MT	1,566	1,816	2,101	2,131	2,302	2,719	2,929	3,349	2,537	3,771	3,225
Ft. Apache, AZ	-[1]	3,600	1,739	2,090	2,388	2,602	2,705	3,103	5,903	6,880	8,140
Ft. Peck, MT	6,124	3,404	1,992	1,689	1,943	2,273	2,552	3,079	3,182	4,273	5,022
Gila River, AZ	-[1]	-[1]	3,926	-[1]	-[1]	5,691	4,588	5,095	4,573	7,076	9,784
Hopi, AZ	1,600	2,139	2,029	2,150	2,455	2,719	6,038	3,558	4,404[2]	6,601	8,755
Laguna, NM	-[1]	-[1]	-[1]	1,384	-[1]	1,927	2,191	2,686	2,579	3,564	6,525
Menominee, WI	1,522	1,308	1,286	1,370	1,730	1,890	1,988	2,454	2,445	2,377	3,373
Navajo, AZ-NM-UT	11,768	21,003	20,500	28,390	29,421	31,985	38,605	49,373	56,949[2]	104,968	158,917
Northern Cheyenne, MT	-[1]	-[1]	1,333	1,412	1,456	1,408	1,508	1,694	2,357	3,101	3,197
Papago, AZ	6,000	7,000	2,647	4,823	6,990	-[1]	4,914	5,684	4,879	6,959	10,610
Pine Ridge, SD	12,873	7,649	6,381	6,703	7,240	7,628	8,220	9,774	8,280	11,882	18,397
Red Lake, MN	1,141	1,069	1,341	1,353	1,486	1,698	1,881	2,406	2,741	2,823	4,782
Rosebud, SD	9,610	8,292	4,316	4,989	5,519	5,700	6,215	7,150	5,656	5,688	9,674
San Carlos, AZ	4,233	5,000	1,235	1,053	2,608	2,533	2,715	3,290	4,525	5,872	6,695
Standing Rock, ND-SD	7,322	4,450	3,763	3,429	3,434	3,610	3,708	4,210	2,925	4,800	8,197
Turtle Mountain, ND	-[1]	914	2,184	2,207	3,123	4,043	5,527	7,330	3,386	4,021	9,583
Wind River, WY	1,800	1,841	1,748	1,694	1,705	1,808	2,097	2,579	3,319	4,150	5,385
Yakima, WA	3,650	1,272	2,000	2,300	3,146	3,001	2,908	3,001	2,509	4,983	8,395
Zuni, NM	-[1]	-[1]	-[1]	1,514	1,603	1,932	1,991	2,320	4,736	5,988	7,288

Notes: [1] Not given
[2] An Additional 7,726 Indians were enumerated in the Navajo-Hopi Joint Use in Arizona

Source: 1875–1932, Annual Reports of the Commissioner of Indian Affairs; 1943: Statistical Supplement to the Annual Report of the Commissioner of Indian Affairs; 1970: U.S. Bureau of the Census, Census of Population: 1970. Subject Report: American Indians, Table 17; 1980: U.S. Bureau of the Census, Census of Population: 1980, General Population Characteristics, U.S. Summary, Table 71; 1983, Bureau of Indian Affairs, Indian Service Population and Labor Force Estimates, January, 1983.

Table 3.11
Sex of the Indian Population, 1890–1980

YEAR	INDIAN POPULATION	MALES	FEMALES	RATIO OF FEMALES TO MALES
1890	248,253	125,719	122,534	0.97
1910	265,683	135,133	130,550	0.97
1930	332,397	170,350	162,047	0.96
1950	342,226	178,172	164,054	0.92
1960	546,228	273,526	272,702	0.99
1970	763,594	375,384	388,210	1.03
1980*	1,420,400	702,228	718,172	1.02

Note:
  * Includes Alaska natives.

Source: Same as Table 3.4

Table 3.12
Age and Sex of the Indian Population, 1910

AGE	TOTAL		MALE		FEMALE	
	NUMBER	PERCENT	NUMBER	PERCENT	NUMBER	PERCENT
Total	265,683	100.0	135,133	100.0	130,550	100.0
Under 5	40,384	15.2	20,202	14.9	20,182	15.5
5 to 9	36,541	13.8	18,349	13.6	18,192	13.9
10 to 14	31,393	11.8	16,199	12.0	15,194	11.6
15 to 19	28,486	10.7	14,612	10.8	13,874	10.6
20 to 24	21,844	8.2	11,265	8.3	10,579	8.1
25 to 29	18,137	6.8	9,237	6.8	8,900	6.8
30 to 34	15,243	5.7	7,756	5.7	7,487	5.7
35 to 39	14,834	5.6	7,721	5.7	7,113	5.4
40 to 44	11,961	4.5	6,126	4.5	5,835	4.5
45 to 49	9,887	3.7	5,103	3.8	4,784	3.7
50 to 54	9,343	3.5	4,914	3.6	4,429	3.4
55 to 59	7,171	2.7	3,706	2.7	3,465	2.7
60 to 64	6,524	2.5	3,332	2.5	3,192	2.4
65 to 69	4,482	1.7	2,259	1.7	2,223	1.7
70 to 74	3,382	1.3	1,561	1.2	1,821	1.4
75 and over	5,122	1.9	2,310	1.7	2,812	2.2
Age unknown	949	0.4	481	0.4	468	0.4

Source: U.S. Bureau of the Census, The Indian Population of the United
States and Alaska, 1930 (Washington, D.C.: U.S. Government
Printing Office, 1937), p. 87

Table 3.13
Age and Sex of the Indian Population, 1930

AGE	TOTAL		MALE		FEMALE	
	NUMBER	PERCENT	NUMBER	PERCENT	NUMBER	PERCENT
Total	332,397	100.00	170,350	100.00	162,047	100.00
Under 5	46,680	14.0	23,447	13.8	23.233	14.3
5 to 9	46,736	14.1	23,434	13.8	23,302	14.4
10 to 14	39,456	11.9	20,028	11.8	19,428	12.0
15 to 19	36,219	10.9	18,154	10.7	18,065	11.1
20 to 24	28,843	8.7	14,697	8.6	14,146	8.7
25 to 29	23,491	7.1	12,127	7.1	11,364	7.0
30 to 34	19,309	5.8	10,032	5.9	9,277	5.7
35 to 39	17,941	5.4	9,404	5.5	8,537	5.3
40 to 44	15,090	4.5	7,881	4.6	7,209	4.4
45 to 49	13,416	4.0	7,131	4.2	6,285	3.9
50 to 54	11,623	3.5	6,272	3.7	5,351	3.3
55 to 59	9,236	2.8	5,118	3.0	4,118	2.5
60 to 64	7,551	2.3	4,060	2.4	3,491	2.2
65 to 69	5,840	1.8	3,104	1.8	2,736	1.7
70 to 74	4,190	1.3	2,153	1.3	2,037	1.3
75 and over	6,327	1.9	3,079	1.8	3,248	2.0
Age unknown	449	0.1	229	0.1	220	0.1

Source: U.S. Bureau of the Census, The Indian Population of the United States and Alaska, 1930 (Washington, D.C.: U.S. Government Printing Office, 1937), p. 87.

Table 3.14
Age and Sex of the Indian Population, 1950

AGE	TOTAL		MALE		FEMALE	
	NUMBER	PERCENT	NUMBER	PERCENT	NUMBER	PERCENT
Total	342,226	100.0	178,172	100.0	164,054	100.0
Under 5	51,988	15.2	26,386	14.8	25.602	15.6
5 to 9	44,301	12.9	22,295	12.5	22,006	13.4
10 to 14	43,575	12.7	23,321	13.1	20,254	12.3
15 to 19	33,829	9.9	16,912	9.5	16,917	10.3
20 to 24	30,122	8.8	16,257	9.1	13,865	8.5
25 to 29	23,510	6.9	12,080	6.8	11,430	7.0
30 to 34	19,574	5.7	9,929	5.6	9,645	5.9
35 to 39	18,917	5.5	9,709	5.4	9,208	5.6
40 to 44	15,489	4.5	8,044	4.5	7,445	4.5
45 to 49	14,340	4.2	7,799	4.4	6,541	4.0
50 to 54	11,551	3.4	6,360	3.6	5,191	3.2
55 to 59	9,292	2.7	5,216	2.9	4,076	2.5
60 to 64	7,694	2.2	4,263	2.4	3,431	2.1
65 to 69	7,185	2.1	3,846	2.2	3,339	2.0
70 to 74	4,517	1.3	2,431	1.4	2,086	1.3
75 and over	6,342	1.9	3,324	1.9	3,018	1.8

Source: U.S. Bureau of the Census, Census of Population: 1950. Special
Reports: Nonwhite Population by Race (Washington, D.C.: U.S.
Government Printing Office, 1953), p. 17.

Table 3.15
Age and Sex of the Indian Population, 1960

	TOTAL		MALE		FEMALE	
	NUMBER	PERCENT	NUMBER	PERCENT	NUMBER	PERCENT
TOTAL	546,228	100.0	273,526	100.0	272,702	100.0
Under 5	91,287	16.7	45,926	16.8	45,361	16.6
5-9	75,947	13.9	37,784	13.8	38,163	14.0
10-14	63,499	11.6	32,132	11.7	31,367	11.5
15-19	49,897	9.1	25,615	9.4	24,282	8.9
20-24	39,667	7.3	20,032	7.3	19,635	7.2
25-29	33,026	6.0	16,312	6.0	16,714	6.1
30-34	30,122	5.5	14,630	5.3	15,492	5.7
35-39	28,389	5.2	14,054	5.1	14,335	5.3
40-44	22,929	4.2	11,559	4.2	11,370	4.2
45-49	21,711	4.0	10,878	4.0	10,833	4.0
50-54	20,767	3.8	10,310	3.8	10,457	3.8
55-59	31,560	5.8	15,066	5.5	16,494	6.0
60-64	11,830	2.2	6,080	2.2	5,750	2.1
65-69	9,975	1.8	5,181	1.9	4,794	1.8
70-74	6,857	1.3	3,524	1.3	3,333	1.2
75 and over	8,765	1.6	4,443	1.6	4,322	1.6
Median Age	19.2 yrs		19.1 yrs		19.4 yrs	

Source: U.S. Bureau of the Census. U.S. Census of Population: 1960.
         Subject Reports. Nonwhite Population by Race. PC(2) - 1c.
         (Washington, D.C.: U.S. Government Printing Office, 1963),
         p. 2.

Table 3.16
Age and Sex of the Indian Population, 1970

	TOTAL		MALE		FEMALE	
	NUMBER	PERCENT	NUMBER	PERCENT	NUMBER	PERCENT
TOTAL	763,594	100.0	375,384	100.0	388,210	100.0
Under 5	91,456	12.0	46,017	12.3	45,439	11.7
5–9	102,105	13.4	51,043	13.6	51,062	13.2
10–14	98,129	12.9	49,088	13.1	49,041	12.6
15–19	84,105	11.0	41,963	11.2	42,142	10.9
20–24	65,147	8.5	31,934	8.5	33,213	8.6
25–29	51,878	6.8	25,693	6.8	26,185	6.7
30–34	46,591	6.1	22,665	6.0	23,926	6.2
35–39	39,486	5.2	18,883	5.0	20,653	5.3
40–44	36,144	4.7	17,624	4.7	18,520	4.8
45–49	31,822	4.2	15,337	4.1	16,485	4.2
50–54	27,922	3.7	13,300	3.5	14,622	3.8
55–59	24,986	3.3	11,627	3.1	13,359	3.4
60–64	20,021	2.6	9,558	2.5	10,463	2.7
65–69	17,239	2.3	8,242	2.2	8,997	2.3
70–74	11,121	1.5	5,260	1.4	5,861	1.5
75–79	7,468	1.0	3,507	0.9	3,901	1.0
80–84	4,234	0.6	2,037	0.5	2,197	0.6
85 and over	3,740	0.5	1,656	0.4	2,084	0.5
Median Age	20.4 yrs		19.9 yrs		20.9 yrs	

Source: U.S. Bureau of the Census, Census of Population: 1970. Subject
Reports: American Indians, PC(2)-1F (Washington, D.C.: U.S.
Government Printing Office, 1973), p.2.

Table 3.17
Age and Sex of the Indian, Eskimo, and Aleut Population, 1980

	TOTAL		MALE		FEMALE	
	NUMBER	PERCENT	NUMBER	PERCENT	NUMBER	PERCENT
TOTAL	1,420,400	100.0	702,228	100.0	718,172	100.0
Under 5	149,275	10.5	75,803	10.8	73,472	10.2
5-9	146,647	10.3	74,182	10.6	72,465	10.1
10-14	155,992	11.0	78,988	11.2	77,004	10.7
15-19	170,215	12.0	86,202	12.3	84,013	11.7
20-24	149,154	10.5	74,828	10.7	74,326	10.3
25-29	124,932	8.9	61,559	8.8	63,373	8.8
30-34	107,219	7.5	52,407	7.5	54,812	7.6
35-39	84,179	5.9	41,131	5.9	43,048	6.0
40-44	69,370	4.9	33,759	4.8	35,611	5.0
45-49	58,089	4.1	27,932	4.0	30,157	4.2
50-54	51,593	3.6	24,979	3.6	26,614	3.7
55-59	44,897	3.2	21,471	3.1	23,426	3.3
60-64	33,919	2.4	16,010	2.3	17,909	2.5
65-69	28,310	2.0	12,847	1.8	15,463	2.2
70-74	19,893	1.4	8,848	1.3	11,045	1.5
75-79	13,760	1.0	6,099	0.9	7,661	1.1
80-84	7,085	0.5	2,872	0.4	4,213	0.6
85 and over	5,871	0.4	2,311	0.3	3,560	0.5
Median Age	22.8 yrs		22.3 yrs		23.4 yrs	

Source: U.S. Bureau of the Census, Census of Population: 1980. U.S. Summary. PC 80-1-B1 (Washington, D.C.: U.S. Government Printing Office, 1983), pp. 32-33.

4

Removal, Relocation, and Urbanization

The United States made several attempts to change the geographical locations of Indian populations during the nineteenth century. At times, the federal government encouraged voluntary segregation of American Indians; at other times, coercive measures were used to force Indian removal from lands sought by whites. In the mid-twentieth century, an assisted migration program was devised to urbanize and integrate the American Indian population. Although each of the major federal efforts was controversial at the time, and while each continues to engender controversy among historians and others to this day, the three major efforts to relocate Indian populations which will be discussed in this chapter, the removal program of the 1820s and 1830s, the concentration program of the 1870s and 1880s, and the relocation program of the 1950s and 1960s, all had substantial and lasting effects on the geographic distribution of American Indian populations.

The removal program was intended to clear the lands east of the Mississippi River of Indians. This would permit the settlement of these lands by whites. Removal was significant in the development of the United States east of the Mississippi River. It resulted in the relocation of Indians from the Southeast, Northeast, and Great Lakes areas to regions west of the Mississippi River—the present states of Nebraska, Kansas, and Oklahoma. After the Civil War, the concentration program resulted from the westward movement of the white population and the use of travel routes through the present-day states of Kansas and Nebraska. The development of these areas as transportation routes and later as areas of permanent habitation for white agriculturists resulted in the removal of many of the tribes that had been removed to Kansas and Nebraska south to Indian Territory, the present-day state of Oklahoma. Tribes of the Northern Plains were concentrated in Dakota Territory and to the west; as the development of territories of Dakota, Montana, Idaho, and Wyoming proceeded, Indian groups were concentrated into smaller and smaller geographical areas in the Northwest. Isolated tribes in the states of California and in the Pacific Northwest, such as the Modocs and Nez Perces, were also relocated to Indian territory during the late nineteenth century.

The removal and concentration policies, while clearly motivated by a desire to encourage the development of Indian-held areas as white agricultural regions, were defended by some contemporaries as being in the best interest of the Indians. Removal, some thought, would give the Eastern tribes sufficient isolation from the worst elements of white society to allow acculturation to the realities of nineteenth-century American life. Concentration was defended by white "friends of the Indian" in the late nineteenth century as a way to save some land for the Indians in the face of seemingly insatiable white land hunger.[1] Historians have generally rejected the claims of the defenders of the concentration policy, although some, notably Francis Paul Prucha, have called for a reassessment of the motives of the removal policy. In particular, Prucha has argued that the motives of the removal policy, taken in the context of early nineteenth-century American political society, were benign and the charge that whites were sending Eastern Indians to what they believed to be a "Great American Desert," was false.[2] Similarly, one could question to what extent it would have been possible in the late nineteenth century to defend the retention by Indian groups of substantial portions of their domain in the face of white land hunger. However inevitable and however well intentioned removal and concentration may have been, both policies were executed in a coercive manner with much suffering for the Indians who were deprived of property and familiar geographic environments, compelled by force to comply with federal directives, and saw the funds held in trust for them manipulated by the federal government to achieve its objectives.[3]

The statistics on removal and concentration presented in this chapter must be used with caution. In part, this is because of the confusion and chaos that often accompanied coercive removal. Federal officials were not always able to observe accurately the results of the removal efforts. Some may have had an interest in exaggerating the numbers of Indians being removed. Even if the data were accurate, the goals of the removal policy were often frustrated by the Indians themselves. Individuals who were removed to a new territory frequently made unauthorized returns to their homeland, sometimes to be removed again. By the late nineteenth century, the Bureau of Indian Affairs had to make provisions for returned American Indians in a variety of geographical locations, including the Santee Sioux in Minnesota, Winnebagos and Pottawatomies

in Wisconsin, Cherokees in North Carolina, and Choctaws in Mississippi—and there were other groups for whom no provisions were made.[4]

A part of the removal effort involved the purchase of land from the
Indian tribes by the United States. After land was purchased, the federal
government could put the proceeds in a trust fund for the tribe or could
compensate the Indians for purchased lands with lands west of the
Mississippi River. Table 4.1 presents data on the acres of lands
purchased from American Indian tribes between 1795 and 1838 and the
compensation provided to the tribes, in trust funds or in lands. By 1838
nearly 420 million acres of land had been purchased from the Indians by
the federal government; these lands were sold to settlers and distributed
to territorial governments for the establishment of local governments,
schools, roads, and canals.

Table 4.2 presents data on the number of Indians removed from east of
the Mississippi River to west of the Mississippi by the United States
between 1828 and 1838. The table does not include voluntary removals
of Indian groups prior to 1828 and the figures must be used with caution.
These data are as accurate as possible. They were gathered by the Office
of Indian Affairs while Thomas Hartley Crawford was commissioner.
Crawford did much to regularize the operations of the Office of Indian
Affairs and was particularly interested in compiling accurate data.[5]

Table 4.3 presents data on the location of American Indian tribes in the
year 1834 and on lands reserved for the Indians west of the Mississippi.
This table is taken from the *Report* of the House of Representatives
Committee on Indian Affairs, "Regulating the Department of Indian
Affairs," a report that led to the creation of the Bureau of Indian Affairs.
While it was completed prior to Crawford's tenure, the data are broadly
comparable with later calculations made while Crawford was Commissioner of Indian Affairs. Table 4.3 also shows the acreage west of the
Mississippi River reserved for the area's indigenous and emigrant tribes.
The populations of the "emigrant" tribes includes tribal members who
had not yet actually moved west of the Mississippi, except in the case of
the Cherokees. The population of this tribe is divided into Eastern and
Western divisions. For the other tribes Indians who had "agreed to
emigrate" are listed as emigrants. The "agreement" had sometimes been
coerced and had sometimes been made by individuals who did not
represent the entire group. By 1834, in addition to 22.5 thousand
indigenous Indians living west of the state of Missouri and 5.5 thousand
north of Missouri, an additional sixty-seven thousand Indians were
members of tribes that had emigrated or had agreed to emigrate. An
addition 17.5 thousand members of tribes that had not agreed to
emigrate had lands reserved for them in the West. Nearly thirteen
thousand were members of Eastern tribes for which no plans for
emigration had been made.

By 1838, the removal of the emigrant tribes listed in Table 4.3 was well under way. Substantial numbers of Chickasaws, Creeks, Seminoles (listed as Florida Indians), and Cherokees were removed during 1838. Still awaiting removal were tribes in the Great Lakes region—Chippewas, Ottawas, Pottawatomies, Winnebagos, and the Indians of New York State (Table 4.4). Some of these groups were able to avoid removal, although many were removed during the next decade. Table 4.5 provides a count of Indians on the western frontier in the year 1842, after much of the removal program had been completed. Substantial numbers of Creeks and Choctaws were joined by members of Great Lakes and Mississippi River tribes and smaller numbers of Northeastern tribes in the West.

Tables 4.1 through 4.5 present data on the removal policy. Comparable data are not available on the concentration policy, in part because it was less well defined, covered a longer period of time, and was not centrally directed as the removal policy was. The results of removal and concentration on the geographic location of American Indian populations are clear, however. These are shown in Table 4.6. The table shows the 1910 population of Indian tribes identified as having a connection with Oklahoma by John R. Swanton.[6] Also shown is the proportion of the total tribal population residing in Oklahoma at the 1910 census. For tribes like the Cherokees, Choctaws, Chicksaws, Creeks, and Seminoles, which were removed from the Southeast, substantial proportions of the tribal population were found in Oklahoma in 1910. The historic Indian areas of Oklahoma had become traditional homelands for these tribes. Other tribes, such as the Delawares and Wyandots, which had been removed from the Northeast and Great Lakes areas, similarly had a high concentration of tribal population in Oklahoma in 1910. Some tribes from adjoining areas in the Great Plains also had high proportions of tribal population in Oklahoma. However, for other tribes, such as the Kickapoos, Ottawas, Pottawatomies, and the Sac and Fox, the proportions in Oklahoma were not as great, reflecting the tribes' partially successful attempts to avoid the concentration and removal policies.

A third major attempt to change the geographical location of American Indians was the relocation program of the 1950s and 1960s. Rather than attempting to provide a haven away from whites, as the defenders of removal claimed to be doing, the relocation program was intended to accelerate the pace of the integration of Indian people into the mainstream of American life. Rather than providing land for separate tribal development as the removal policy envisioned, the relocation program was not intended to create an Indian land base, but to integrate Indian people into an urban society. During the twentieth century, the United States became an urban and industrial society; the intention of the relocation program was to increase the urbanization of American

Indians and to help shift Indian occupations from agriculture to industrial and service occupations (see Chapter 8 for data on Indian occupations). This, it was believed, would further the integration of American Indians into American life and reduce the need for special services for Indians. The relocation program was initiated after World War II, a war that had seen the involvement of large numbers of Indian young men in military service and large numbers of Indian men and women in defense industries.

American Indian population in the early twentieth century was overwhelmingly rural. In 1890, more than three-quarters of American Indians lived in Indian areas, on reservations, in Indian territory, or on the lands of the six nations of New York and Pennsylvania. Less than one-quarter, classified as "citizen Indians," lived in off-reservation areas, many in rural areas (Table 4.7). At the census of 1910, more than 95 percent of the enumerated Indians lived in rural areas. This proportion declined very gradually during the early twentieth century; in 1930 more than 90 percent of all Indians still lived in rural areas, and by 1950 more than 80 percent were still in rural areas. As a result of the relocation program, as well as the mechanization of American agriculture, the proportion of Indians living in urban areas increased rapidly after 1950. By 1960, 30 percent of American Indians were living in urban areas. That proportion increased to 45 percent in 1970 and to more than one-half of the American Indian population in 1980 (Table 4.8).

This major change in the geographical location of the Indian population between 1950 and 1980 was in part the result of the relocation or employment assistance program of the Bureau of Indian Affairs. Beginning in 1952 with a direct employment program that assisted Indians willing to move to urban areas by finding them jobs and paying part of the cost of moving, the Bureau of Indian Affairs assisted the migration of an increasing number of American Indian people from reservations to cities. In 1958, an adult vocational training program was added. This program included both institutional training (in vocational schools) and on-the-job training in which the Bureau paid some of the employer's costs incurred as a result of the Indian's need for training. Initially much smaller than the direct employment program, the vocational training programs became larger by the mid-1960s. Table 4.9 shows the number of individuals assisted through direct employment and vocational training for the fiscal years between 1952 and 1967. The table is based on unpublished Bureau of Indian Affairs data made available to Elaine M. Neils for her research on relocation and Indian migration.[7]

Table 4.10 shows the growing importance of the relocation program within the Bureau of Indian Affairs. For the fiscal years between 1951 and 1972, the table shows the funds expended for the program (in thousands of dollars) and, for 1955 and subsequent years, the number of grants awarded. The data in this table are taken from the *Budget of the United States Government* for the fiscal years 1953-1974. These data do not match the figures provided to Elaine M. Neils, in part because they combine a number of programs and in part because they may include family members as well as the direct recipients of the grants. (For a continuation of data in this table, see Table 7.19.)

The relocation program was not the only influence affecting Indian migration to urban areas. During the 1950s and 1960s, a large number of rural people of all races moved to urban areas, particularly in states with high American Indian populations such as South Dakota, Arizona, and New Mexico. As occupational opportunities in such traditional agricultural occupations as farm labor became limited as a result of mechanization, pressure to migrate, with or without federal assistance, increased. However, the relocation program was significant beyond the mere numbers of persons who were assisted. When a group of individuals from a particular reservation was established with relocation assistance in an urban area they could provide assistance to family members, friends, and others from their home reservation who might migrate to urban areas without direct Bureau of Indian Affairs help. This was similar to the earlier patterns of European and black migration to urban areas. By 1970, only 28 percent of American Indians were living on reservations, in contrast to more than 75 percent eighty years earlier (see Table 4.11). By 1980, the proportion of American Indians on reservations had declined further to about one-fourth and the proportion of Alaska Natives in identified Alaska Native areas was only around 36 percent (Table 4.12). About two-thirds of American Indians were living outside of traditional American Indian areas, although about 60 percent of Eskimos were still living in identified Alaska Native villages.

The relocation program assisted the migration of American Indians to major urban areas. These were the areas that seemed to be growing rapidly and seemed to offer the best vocational opportunities in the 1950s and 1960s. Table 4.13 shows the American Indian population in 1970 for the fifteen cities with the largest American Indian population in that year. Also shown is the American Indian population in the same cities a decade later. New York, which was not the site of a BIA relocation field office, had the largest number of American Indians in 1970, but by 1980, New York had dropped to third place and Los Angeles had the largest number of American Indians. In general, Indian populations increased substantially in most cities between 1970 and 1980. However, in some cities, like Chicago, Dallas, Detroit, and San Francisco, the Indian population grew only gradually and in others, like Oakland, California, Indian population actually declined. This inconsistency was probably related to differing employment opportunities in the various cities as well as the attraction of other nearby urban areas. For example, San Jose, California, close to both San Francisco and Oakland, had the tenth largest urban Indian population in 1980, while it did not place in the top fifteen cities in 1970.

The fifteen cities with the largest American Indian population in 1980 are shown in Table 4.14. When the 1980 American Indian, Eskimo, and Aleut population is combined for urban areas (Table 4.15), the same fifteen cities are in the top fifteen in approximately the same order. The only major change is that Anchorage, with the fifteenth largest Indian population in 1980, had the seventh largest combined Indian, Eskimo, and Aleut population in 1980. Eskimos and Aleuts seem much less likely to live in large urban areas, except in Anchorage and to a lesser extent in such West Coast cities as Los Angeles and Seattle.

Table 4.16 and 4.17 present data on the American Indian population for the fifteen standard metropolitan statistical areas (SMSAs) with the largest American Indian population in 1980. Table 4.16 presents this data for the Indian population of these metropolitan areas in 1890, 1910, and 1930. Table 4.17 presents data on the Indian population of these SMSAs in 1960, 1970, and 1980. In addition to reflecting the influence of the relocation program, the data in these tables suggest that the proximity of some urban areas to reservations and other historic areas is significant in predicting American Indian population concentrations. Among the top fifteen standard metropolitan areas in 1980 are areas like Albuquerque, Oklahoma City, Phoenix, Seattle-Everett, Tucson, and Tulsa—all of which are located close to traditional Indian areas. Some of these areas, like Albuquerque, Phoenix, Tucson, and Tulsa, had significant numbers of Indian residents as early as 1910.

The coercive and voluntary efforts to assist migration had a significant impact on the geographical distribution of the American Indian population and the location of that population in rural and urban areas. However, government initiative does not tell the entire story of American Indian geographical mobility. Much mobility was the result of individual choices, although these were often the result of economic necessity, government inducements, and, at times, government pressure. One significant development of the twentieth century for American Indian people, as well as for many others, has been the decline of agriculture as a source of employment. That decline resulted in the urbanization of significant portions of the Indian population as well as of many others in American society.

Data on various aspects of Indian removal and concentration can be traced in a number of federal documents, including the *Annual Reports* of the Commissioner of Indian Affairs for the relevant years. Additional data may be found in special reports to Congress, which can be located in the serial set of congressional documents. Steven L. Johnson has compiled a useful *Guide to American Indian Documents in the*

Congressional Serial Set: 1817-1899 (1977). Special censuses of tribes have been exploited to provide information on the experience of particular groups; an example is the Cherokee census of the nineteenth century used by Russell Thornton in his estimate of "Cherokee Population Losses during the Trail of Tears: A New Perspective and a New Estimate," *Ethnohistory* 31 (November 1984): 289-300. A guide to some of these materials is provided by Michael F. Doran in "Population Statistics of Nineteenth Century Indian Territory," *Chronicles of Oklahoma* 53 (1975): 492-515.

The Bureau of Indian Affairs published very little statistical data on the relocation program; some data are included in Elaine M. Neils, *Reservation to City: Indian Migration and Federal Relocation* (1971). Data on Indian urbanization may be traced on the twentieth-century census reports discussed in Chapter 3.

The literature on Indian removal and concentration is voluminous. Useful starting points include Francis Paul Prucha, *American Indian Policy in the Formative Years: The Indian Trade Intercourse Acts, 1790-1834* (1962) and Ronald N. Satz, *American Indian Policy in the Jacksonian Era* (1975). The results of the removal process are described in Arrell Morgan Gibson, ed., *America's Exiles: Indian Colonization in Oklahoma* (1976), a collection of essays on tribes removed to Indian Territory during the nineteenth century. Gibson's essay, "The Great Plains as a Colonization Zone for Eastern Indians," appears in Frederick C. Luebke, ed., *Ethnicity on the Great Plains* (1980), pp. 19-37.

Historians are only beginning to examine the relocation program. Contemporary documents such as LaVerne Madigan, *The American Indian Relocation Program* (1956), remain valuable, as do such contemporary assessments as Neils' *Reservation to City*, mentioned above. American Indian urbanization has not been confined to the United States; for a study of Indian urbanization in Canada, see Mark Nagler, *Indians in the City: A Study of the Urbanization of Indians in Toronto* (1970). An interesting evaluation of the relocation program, based on census data, is James H. Gundlach, P. Nelson Reid, and Alden E. Roberts, "Migration, Labor Mobility, and Relocation Assistance: The Case of the American Indian," *Social Service Review* 51 (September 1977): 464-473. Historians' assessments of the program include Larry W. Burt, *Tribalism in Crisis: Federal Indian Policy, 1953-1960* (1982), pp. 56-58; and Kenneth R. Philp, "Stride Toward Freedom: The Relocation of Indians to Cities, 1952-1960," *Western Historical Quarterly* 16 (April 1985): 175-190.

NOTES

1. William T. Hagan, "The Reservation Policy: Too Little and Too Late," in Jane F. Smith and Robert M. Kvasnicka, eds., *Indian-White Relations: A Persistent Paradox* (Washington, D.C.: Howard University Press, 1976), pp. 157-169.

2. Francis Paul Prucha, "Andrew Jackson's Indian Policy: A Reassessment," *Journal of American History* 56 (December 1969): 527-539; Francis Paul Prucha, "Indian Removal and the Great American Desert," *Indiana Magazine of History* 59 (December 1963): 299-322. In the latter paper, Prucha erroneously asserts that the quality of Western land did not enter into the congressional debate on the removal policy at all. For evidence to the contrary, see Ronald N. Satz, *American Indian Policy in the Jacksonian Era* (Lincoln: University of Nebraska Press, 1975), pp. 26-27 and note 50, p. 37.

3. For a discussion of the use of trust funds to control Indian behavior during the removal period, see Satz, *American Indian Policy in the Jacksonian Era*, p. 154; and Ronald N. Satz, "Indian Policy in the Jacksonian Era: The Old Northwest as a Test Case," *Michigan History* 60 (Spring 1976): 76-93.

4. For example, many Santee Sioux returned to Minnesota within a decade after their removal following the Sioux uprising of 1863. See Tribal History Program, *History of the Flandreau Santee Sioux Tribe* (Flandreau, South Dakota: Flandreau Sioux Tribe, 1971), pp. 75-81.

5. On Thomas Hartley Crawford, see Ronald N. Satz, "Thomas Hartley Crawford, 1838-45," in Robert M. Kvasnicka and Herman J. Viola, eds., *The Commissioners of Indian Affairs, 1824-1977* (Lincoln: University of Nebraska Press, 1980), pp. 23-27.

6. See John R. Swanton, *The Indian Tribes of North America*, Smithsonian Institution, Bureau of American Ethnology, Bulletin 145 (Washington, D.C.: U.S. Government Printing Office, 1952).

7. Elaine M. Neils, *Reservation to City: Indian Migration and Federal Relocation*, Department of Geography, University of Chicago, Research Paper No. 131 (Chicago: University of Chicago, 1971).

TABLES

Table 4.1
Lands Purchased by the United States from the Indian Tribes, 1795–1838

YEAR	LANDS PURCHASED (ACRES)	CONSIDERATION IN MONEY OR IN LANDS (AT $1.25 PER ACRE)
1795	11,808,499	$ 210,000.00
1801	2,641,920	—*
1802	853,760	2,201.00
1803	10,950,250	16,000.00
1804	11,841,920	26,234.50
1805	9,167,300	155,600.00
1806	1,209,600	44,000.00
1807	7,862,400	100,400.00
1808	50,269,440	60,000.00
1809	3,395,840	20,700.00
1814	14,284,800	120,000.00
1816	2,814,080	77,000.00
1817	4,807,680	561,830.13
1818	51,925,120	482,600.00
1819	8,060,800	67,000.00
1820	4,510,240	5,000.00
1821	5,500,000	150,000.00
1823	amount unknown	106,000.00
1824	11,000,000	79,900.00
1825	85,699,680	2,451,400.00
1826	4,132,480	5,938,000.00
1827	1,337,780	533,718.18
1828	1,285,120	63,741.00
1829	990,720	189,795.00
1830	6,695,760	1,143,401.00
1831	24,092,000	23,409,661.00
1832	8,326,397	16,440,767.00
1833	19,122,280	6,958,187.00
1834	4,128,610	549,676.00
1835	5,113,920	7,631,619.00
1836	22,652,720	9,257,616.00
1837	4,698,240	1,082,083.00
1838	18,250,000	3,738,000.00
TOTAL	419,429,446	$81,672,824.81

Note:
* Included in figure for 1802.

Source: Secretary of War, "Indians Removed to West Mississippi From 1789," February 5, 1839, 25th Congress, 3rd session, House Documents, no. 147, serial 347, p. 9.

Table 4.2
Indians Removed West of the Mississippi River by
the United States, 1828–1838

YEAR	NUMBER
1828	7,422
1828–30	--
1831	5,407
1832	5,500
1833	5,462
1834	4,386
1835	2,330
1836	15,948
1837	9,688
1838	25,139
TOTAL 1828–1838	81,282

Source: Secretary of War, "Indians Removed to West Mississippi from 1789," February 5, 1839, 25th Congress, 3rd session, House Documents, no. 147, serial 347, p. 8.

Table 4.3
American Indian Tribes in the United States, Lands Reserved
for Indians West of the Mississippi, 1834

	POPULATION	ACRES
INDIGENOUS TRIBES WEST OF MISSOURI	22,496	31,500,800
Osages	5,200	7,564,820
Kanzas	1,496	6,400,000
Ottoes and Missourias	1,600	1,536,000
Pawnees	12,000	16,000,000
Omahas	1,400	—[1]
Poncas	800	—[1]
INDIGENOUS TRIBES NORTH OF MISSOURI	5,602	9,000,000
Sacs and Foxes	4,500	6,000,000
Ioways	1,102	3,000,000
EMIGRANT TRIBES[2]	67,300	51,202,000
Choctaws	18,000	15,000,000
Chicksaws	5,000	—
Creeks	20,000	13,140,000
Seminoles	5,000	—[4]
Cherokees, west	5,000	13,000,000[5]
Senecas and Shawnees	461	100,000
Quapaws	466	96,000
Piankashaws	185	160,000
Weas	220	—[6]
Peorias and Kaskaskias	128	96,000
Shawnees	1,250	1,600,000
Delawares	835	2,208,000
Kickapoos	555	768,000
Chippewas and Ottawatas	10,000	5,000,000
NON-EMIGRANT TRIBES WITH LAND IN WEST	17,591	2,304,000
Chippewas and Ottawas of Michigan Territory	3,000	—[7]
Winnegagoes	4,591	2,304,000
Cherokees, east	10,000	—[7]
NON-EMIGRANT TRIBES	12,817	—
Indians of New England	2,526	—
Indians of New York	5,774	—
Indians of Virginia	47	—
Indians of South Carolina	450	—
Wyandots of Ohio	527	—
Ottawas of Ohio	250	—
Miamies	1,100	—
Menomonies	2,143	—
UNAPPROPRIATED LANDS	—	34,846,380
West of Missouri	—	33,771,180
North of Missouri	—	1,075,200
TOTALS	125,806	128,853,180

Notes:
1. With Pawnees.
2. Includes tribes which had agreed to emigrate.
3. With Choctaws.
4. With Creeks.
5. Lands provided for whole Cherokee Nation, east as well as west
   of the Mississippi River.
6. With Piaknashaws.
7. With tribesmen west of the Mississippi River.

Source: "Regulating the Indian Department," May 20, 1834, in 23rd Congress, 1st session, House Reports, no. 474, serial 26, pp. 74-75, 87-89.

Table 4.4
Tribes Scheduled for Removal, Removed West of the Mississippi River, and Still to Be Removed, 1838

TRIBE	ORIGINALLY SCHEDULED FOR REMOVAL	NUMBER OF INDIANS					DAILY COST OF SUBSISTENCE
		REMOVED PRIOR TO 1837	REMOVED 1837-38	WEST OF THE MISSISSIPPI, 1838	STILL TO BE REMOVED 1838	UNDER SUBSISTENCE WEST OF MISSISSIPPI 1838	
Chippewas, Ottowas, and Pottawatomies	8,000	2,190	151	2,342	5,648	2,044	$153.00
Pottawatomies of Indiana	1,786	494	768[1]	1,262	150	768[1]	57.60
Choctaws	18,500	15,000	177	15,177	3,323	---	---
Quapaws	476	476	---	476	---	---	---
Creeks	22,000	20,437	4,106	24,543	750	4,106	574.84
Florida Indians	3,765	1,079	1,851[1]	2,730	835	1,651[1]	131.14
Cherokees	22,000	7,911	18,000[1]	25,911	---	18,000[1]	1,710.00
Kickapoos	588	588	---	588	---	---	---
Delawares	826	826	---	826	---	---	---
Shawnees	1,272	1,272	---	1,272	---	---	---
Ottowas	420	374	---	374	200	174	15.66
Weas	225	225	---	255	---	---	---
Piankeshaws	162	162	---	162	---	---	---
Peorias and Kaskaskias	132	132	---	132	---	132	---
Senecas from Sandusky	251	251	---	251	---	---	---
Senecas from Shawnees	211	211	---	211	---	---	---
Ottowas and Chippewas	6,500	---	---	---	6,500	---	---
Winnebagos	4,500	---	---	---	4,500	---	---
New York Indians	4,176	---	---	---	4,176	---	---
Chickasaws	5,000	---	4,600	4,600	400	4,600	544.00
TOTAL	100,790	51,628	29,653[1]	81,082	26,482	31,343[1]	$3,186.24

Note: 1. Includes Indians on route to the West in 1833.

Source: Annual Report of the Commissioner of Indian Affairs, 1838, p. 470.

Table 4.5
Indian Tribes on the Frontier, 1842

TRIBE	POPULATION	REMARKS
Choctaws	15,177	Removed west by Government.
Creeks	24,594	Removed west by Government.
Florida Indians	3,511	Removed west by Government.
Cherokee Indians	25,911	Removed west by Government.
Osages	5,120	Indigenous tribe.
Quapaws	476	Indigenous tribe.
Senecas & Shawnees	211	Removed west by Government.
Senecas	251	Removed west by Government.
Chippewas, Ottowas, and Pottawatomies	2,000	Removed west by Government.
Otoes & Missourias	1,000	Indigenous tribe.
Peorias and Kaskaskias	132	Removed west by Government.
Piankeshaws	162	Removed west by Government.
Weas	225	Removed west by Government.
Shawnees	1,272	Removed west by Government.
Kanzas	1,606	Indigenous Western tribe.
Delawares	826	Removed west by Government.
Kickapoos	588	Removed west by Government.
Swan Creek and Black River Chippewas	51	Removed west by Government.
Stockbridges, Munsees, and Delawares	180	Removed west by Government.
Iowas	1,500	Removed west by Government.
Sacs of Missouri	500	Removed west by Government.
Chicksaws	4,600	Removed west by Government.
Ottowas of Maumee	428	Removed west by Government.
TOTAL	90,320	

Source: "On Repealing the Act of 1819, for the Civilization of The Indians," June 10, 1842, in 27th Congress, 2nd session, House Reports, no. 854, serial 410, p. 14.

Table 4.6
Indian Tribes Removed to Indian Territory, 1828–1890,
with Population in Oklahoma in 1910

TRIBE	ORIGIN	POPULATION IN OKLAHOMA, 1910	PERCENT OF TOTAL TRIBAL POPULATION
Apache	Southwest	282	5%
Arapaho	Great Plains	685	48%
Caddo	Texas	436	96%
Cherokee	Southeast	29,610	94%
Cheyenne	Great Plains	1,522	50%
Chickasaw	Southeast	4,191	99%
Choctaw	Southeast	14,551	91%
Commanche*	Southern Plains	1,160	99%
Creek	Southeast	6,654	91%
Delaware	Northeast	895	91%
Iowa	Iowa	79	32%
Iroquois	Northeast	263	3%
Kansa	Kansas	232	97%
Kickapoo	Wisconsin	135	39%
Kiowa*	Southern Plains	1,107	98%
Kiowa Apache*	Southern Plains	139	100%
Miami and Illinois	Indiana and Illinois	241	67%
Osage	Missouri	1,345	98%
Oto and Missouri	Nebraska and Missouri	326	94%
Ottawa	Michigan	170	6%
Pawnee	Nebraska	573	91%
Ponca	Nebraska	619	71%
Potawatomie	Michigan	866	35%
Quapuw*	Arkansas and Oklahoma	221	96%
Saulk and Fox	Wisconsin	347	48%
Seminole	Florida	1,503	87%
Shawnee	Kansas	1,300	97%
Tonkawa	Texas	42	100%
Wichita and Kichai*	Southern Plains	295	88%
Wyandot	Ohio	320	91%
Yuchi	Southeast	74	98%

Note:
    * Indigenous tribe.

Source: John R. Swanton, The Indian Tribes of North America, Smithsonian
          Institution, Bureau of American Ethnology, Bulletin 145
          (Washington, D.C.: U.S. Government Printing Office, 1952); U.S.
          Bureau of the Census, The Indian Population of the United States
          and Alaska: 1910 (Washington, D.C.: U.S. Government Printing Office,
          1915).

Table 4.7
American Indians in 1890, by Place of Residence

	TOTAL	PERCENT
Off-Reservation (Citizen Indians)	58,806	23.7
In Indian Areas (Non-citizen Indians)	189,447	76.3
On Reservations	133,417	53.7
Five Civilized Tribes (in Indian Territory)	50,055	20.2
Six Nations (in New York and Pennsylvania)	5,407	2.2
Prisoners*	568	0.2
TOTAL	248,253	100.0

Note:
* Includes 384 Apache prisoners in Mount Vernon barracks, Alabama, and 184 Indians in prison for felonies.

Source: U.S. Census Office, Report on Indians Taxed and Indians Not Taxed In the United States (Except Alaska) at the Eleventh Census: 1890 (Washington, D.C.: Government Printing Office, 1894), p. 24.

Table 4.8
Indian Population, 1910–1980, by Urban and Rural Residence

YEAR	TOTAL INDIAN POPULATION	URBAN NUMBER	PERCENT	RURAL FARM NUMBER	PERCENT	RURAL NONFARM NUMBER	PERCENT
1910	265,683	11,925	4.5	—	—	253,758[1]	95.5
1930	332,397	32,816	9.9	188,946	56.8	110,635	33.3
1950	342,226	55,909	16.3	108,588	31.7	177,729	51.9
1960[2]	546,228	165,922	30.4	78,089	14.3	302,217	55.3
1970[3]	763,594	340,367	44.6	47,405	6.2	375,822	49.2
1980[4]	1,420,400	740,222	52.1	—	—	680,178[1]	47.9

Notes:

1. Rural farm and rural nonfarm combined.
2. Based on 25–percent sample.
3. Based on 20–percent sample. Includes Alaska natives.
4. Includes Alaska natives.

Source: U.S. Bureau of the Census, The Indian Population of the United States and Alaska, 1930 (Washington, D.C.: U.S. Government Printing Office, 1937), pp. 6, 7; U.S. Bureau of the Census, U.S. Census of Population 1950. Special Report: Nonwhite Population by Race, (Washington, D.C.: U.S. Government Printing Office, 1953), p. 17; U.S. Bureau of the Census, Census of Population: 1960. Subject Report PC(2)-1C: Nonwhite Population by Race (Washington, D.C.: U.S. Government Printing Office, 1963), p. 2; U.S. Bureau of the Census, Census of Population: 1970, Subject Report PC(2)-1F: American Indians (Washington, D.C.: U.S. Government Printing Office, 1973), p. 1; U.S. Bureau of the Census, Census of Population, 1980. Characteristics of the Population. U.S. Summary, PC 80-1-B1 (Washington, D.C.: U.S. Government Printing Office, 1983)

Table 4.9
Employment Assistance Activities, 1952–1967

FISCAL YEAR	PERSONS ENTERING DIRECT EMPLOYMENT	PERSONS ENTERING ADULT VOCATIONAL TRAINING		TOTAL
		INSTITUTIONAL	ON–THE–JOB	
1952	442	—	—	442
1953	697	—	—	697
1954	1,222	—	—	1,222
1955	1,500	—	—	1,500
1956	2,083	—	—	2,083
1957	2,882	—	—	2,882
1958	2,373	397	207	2,977
1959	1,655	1,141	168	2,964
1960	1,798	936	276	3,010
1961	1,822	1,226	506	3,554
1962	1,866	1,445	736	4,047
1963	1,696	1,747	476	3,919
1964	1,985	1,805	552	4,342
1965	2,015	2,719	656	5,390
1966	1,866	3,224	1,302	6,392
1967	2,649	3,441	1,344	7,434
TOTAL	28,551	18,081	6,223	52,855

Source: Bureau of Indian Affairs, reported in Elaine M. Neils, Reservation to City: Indian Migration and Federal Relocation, Research Paper No. 131 (Chicago: Department of Geography, University of Chicago, 1971), p. 71.

Table 4.10
Relocation Program, Bureau of Indian Affairs, 1951-1972

FISCAL YEAR	FUNDS EXPENDED (000's)	NUMBER OF GRANTS AWARDED
1951[1]	$263	N.R.
1952[1]	576	N.R.
1953	566	N.R.
1954	578	N.R.
1955	691	3,459
1956	973	5,300
1957	2,807	6,964
1958	3,069	5,728
1959	2,790	3,560
1960	2,618	3,674
1961	2,942	3,468
1962	6,933	5,282
1963	8,020	5,249
1964	9,120	5,871
1965	11,583	6,606
1966	12,143	8,590
1967	15,349	11,062
1968	21,454	11,517
1969	23,902	11,710
1970	33,899	12,374
1971	33,418	14,747
1972	38,386	13,760

Notes:

    N.R. - not reported
    1. Placement Program

Source: The Budget of the United States Government for the Fiscal Year
        Ending June 30, 1953-1974.

Table 4.11
American Indians in 1970, by Place of Residence

	NUMBER	PERCENT
On Identified Reservations	213,770	28.0
Not on Identified Reservations	549,824	72.0
TOTAL	763,594	100.0

Note:
Data based on 20-percent sample.

Source: U.S. Bureau of the Census, 1970 Census of Population. Subject Reports: American Indians, PC(2)-1F (Washington, D.C.: U.S. Government Printing Office, 1973), p. 190-191.

Table 4.12
American Indians and Alaska Natives in 1980, by Place of Residence

	TOTAL (Percent)	AMERICAN INDIAN (Percent)	ESKIMO (Percent)	ALEUT (Percent)
United States	1,423,043 (100.0%)	1,366,676 (100.0%)	42,162 (100.0%)	14,205 (100.0%)
In Identified Areas	525,988 (37.0%)	494,483 (36.2%)	26,718 (63.4%)	4,787 (33.7%)
Reservations	339,987 (23.9%)	339,836 (24.9%)	95 (0.2%)	56 (0.4%)
Tribal Trust Lands	30,274 (2.1%)	30,265 (2.2%)	4 (—)	5 (—)
Historic Areas of Oklahoma (excluding urbanized areas)	116,426 (8.2%)	116,359 (8.5%)	45 (0.1%)	22 (0.2%)
Alaska Native Villages	39,301 (2.8%)	8,023 (0.6%)	26,574 (63.0%)	4,704 (33.1%)
Outside Identified Areas	897,055 (63.0%)	872,193 (63.8%)	15,444 (36.6%)	9,418 (66.3%)

Note: Corrected count

Source: U.S. Bureau of the Census, 1980 Census of Population. Supplementary Report. American Indians and Alaska Native Villages, PC80-S1-13 (Washington, D.C.: U.S. Government Printing Office, 1984), p. 2.

Table 4.13
Fifteen Cities with Largest American Indian Population, 1970, with American Indian Population in 1980

		AMERICAN INDIAN POPULATION	
RANK	CITY	1970	1980
1	New York, NY	9,930	13,141
2	Los Angeles, CA*	9,172	18,371
3	Tulsa, OK	8,510	13,816
4	Oklahoma City, OK	7,361	11,186
5	Chicago, IL*	6,575	6,623
6	Phoenix, AZ	5,893	11,593
7	Minneapolis, MN	5,829	9,137
8	Seattle, WA	4,123	6,158
9	Dallas, TX*	3,437	3,848
10	Albuquerque, NM	3,351	7,093
11	Milwaukee, WI	3,300	5,304
12	Detroit, MI	2,914	3,837
13	San Francisco, CA*	2,900	3,374
14	Oakland, CA*	2,890	2,708
15	Denver, CO*	2,635	4,256

Note:
   * Location of Relocation Field Office.

Source: U.S. Bureau of the Census, Census of Population: 1970.
         Characteristics of the Population. U.S. Summary, vol. 1, pt. 1,
         sec. 1 (Washington, D.C.: U.S. Government Printing Office, 1973),
         pp. 329-333; U.S. Bureau of the Census, 1980 Census of Population.
         Characteristics of the Population, U.S. Summary, PC80-1-C1
         (Washington, D.C.: U.S. Government Printing Office, 1983),
         pp. 393-400.

Table 4.14
Fifteen Cities with Largest American Indian Population, 1980

RANK	CITY	AMERICAN INDIANS 1980	RANK IN 1970
1	Los Angeles, CA*	18,371	2
2	Tulsa, OK	13,816	3
3	New York, NY	13,141	1
4	Phoenix, AZ	11,593	6
5	Oklahoma, OK	11,186	4
6	Minneapolis, MN	9,137	7
7	Albuquerque, NM	7,093	10
8	Chicago, IL*	6,623	5
9	Seattle, WA	6,158	8
10	San Jose, CA*	5,694	---
11	San Diego, CA	5,670	—
12	Milwaukee, WI	5,304	11
13	Tucson, AZ	4,559	—
14	Denver, CO*	4,256	15
15	Anchorage, AK	4,186	—

Note:
    * Location of Relocation Field Office

Source: U.S. Bureau of the Census, 1980 Census of Population.
    Characteristics of the Population, U.S. Summary, PC80-1-C1
    (Washington, D.C.: U.S. Government Printing Office, 1983),
    pp. 393–400.

Table 4.15
Fifteen Cities with Largest American Indian, Eskimo, and Aleut Population, 1980

RANK	CITY	AMERICAN INDIANS, ESKIMOS, AND ALEUTS	ESKIMOS AND ALEUTS
1	Los Angeles, CA	19,296	925
2	Tulsa, OK	13,816	--
3	New York, NY	13,400	259
4	Phoenix, AZ	11,645	52
5	Oklahoma, OK	11,199	13
6	Minneapolis, MN	9,198	61
7	Anchorage, AK	9,022	4,836
8	Albuquerque, NM	7,163	70
9	Seattle, WA	6,821	663
10	Chicago, IL	6,804	181
11	San Diego, CA	5,833	163
12	San Jose, CA	5,801	107
13	Milwaukee, WI	5,348	44
14	Tucson, AZ	4,578	19
15	Denver, CO	4,318	62

Source: U.S. Bureau of the Census, 1980 Census of Population. Characteristics of the Population, U.S. Summary, PC 80-1-C1 (Washington, D.C.: U.S. Government Printing Office, 1983), pp. 393–400.

Table 4.16
American Indians in Counties Containing Central Cities of Fifteen SMSAs with Largest Indian Population in 1980, 1890–1930

	1890[1]	1910	1930
Albuquerque, NM *(Bernaillo County)	3,469	1,192	1,106
Anaheim – Santa Ana – Garden Grove, CA (Orange County)	5	21	125
Dallas – Fort Worth, TX (Dallas and Tarrant Counties)	14	16	53
Detroit, MI (Wayne County)	11	41	460
Los Angeles – Long Beach, CA (Los Angeles County)	144	97	997
Minneapolis – St. Paul, MN – WI (Hennepin and Ramsey Counties)	52	37	373
New York, NY (Bronx, New York, Richmond, Kings, and Queens Counties)	144	343	391
Oklahoma City, OK *(Oklahoma County)	2	112	698
Phoenix, AZ *(Maricopa County)	1	3,099	3,845
Riverside – San Bernardino – Ontario, CA *(Riverside and San Bernardino Counties)	399	2,163	1,795
San Diego, CA *(San Diego County)	478	1,516	1,722
San Francisco – Oakland, CA (San Francisco and Alameda Counties)	56	87	333
Seattle – Everett, WA *(King and Smohomish Counties)	675	1,157	1,173
Tucson, AZ *(Puma County)	904	3,495	5,305
Tulsa, OK *(Tulsa County)	—	1,381	3,674

Notes:
* County includes reservation or other historic Indian area.
1. Enumeration includes only Indians living out of reservation areas.

Source: U.S. Bureau of the Census, The Indian Population of the United States and Alaska, 1930 (Washington, D.C.: U.S. Government Printing Office, 1937), pp. 7–32.

Table 4.17
American Indians in Fifteen SMSAs with Largest American
Indian Population in 1980, 1960–1980

SMSA	1960	1970	1980
Albuquerque, NM	3,378	5,839	20,721
Anaheim – Santa Ana – Garden Grove, CA	730[1]	3,920	12,782
Dallas – Fort Worth, TX	2,120[2]	6,632	11,076
Detroit, MI	2,195	5,683	12,372
Los Angeles – Long Beach, CA	8,839	24,509	47,234
Minneapolis – St. Paul, MN – WI	3,285	9,852	15,831
New York, NY – NJ	4,366	12,160	13,440
Oklahoma City, OK	6,453	13,033	24,695
Phoenix, AZ	8,136	11,159	22,788
Riverside – San Bernardino – Ontario, CA	3,566	6,378	17,107
San Diego, CA	3,293	5,880	14,355
San Francisco – Oakland, CA	3,883	12,011	17,546
Seattle – Everett, WA	3,817	9,496	15,162
Tucson, AZ	7,307	8,837	14,880
Tulsa, OK	7,608	15,519	38,463

Note:

[1] Data for Orange County. Not a standard metropolitan statistical area in 1960.

[2] Data for Dallas SMSA and Fort Worth SMSA combined.

Sources: U.S. Bureau of the Census, 1960 Census of Population. General Population Characteristics (Washington, D.C.: U.S. Government Printing Office, 1962); U.S. Bureau of the Census, 1970 Census of Population. General Characteristics, U.S. Summary. (Washington, D.C.: U.S. Government Printing Office, 1973); U.S. Bureau of the Census, 1980 Census of Population. General Population Characteristics. U.S. Summary PC 80-1-B1 (Washington, D.C.: U.S. Government Printing Office, 1983). Table 4-3.

5

Vital Statistics and Health

Locating accurate data on Indian births, deaths, and other vital events has been a serious problem since statistics were first collected in the nineteenth century. Nineteenth-century data are highly questionable, and even many data collected in the twentieth century are suspect. The problem improved somewhat with the transfer of responsibility for Indian health care from the Bureau of Indian Affairs to the Public Health Service in 1955. However, in 1986, the Office of Technology Assessment identified deficits in data systems as a significant problem in Indian health.[1] (This echoed complaints about the quality of statistical reporting on Indians made as early as the Meriam Report of 1928.)[2] Today, most Indian Health Service (IHS) data are collected for "Indians in reservation states" rather than for Indians in IHS service units, that is, Indians living on reservations or in other traditional areas who are eligible for all IHS services. When the Office of Technology Assessment computed data based on IHS service areas rather than on reservation states, IHS data was found to significantly understate the incidence of disease and mortality. Very little is known about the health status and vital statistics of off-reservation Indians, either those living in rural areas or those in urban areas.

Despite serious and continuing problems with the quality of the data, the main lines of development in Indian health are known and generally accepted. The health status of American Indians has improved dramatically during the twentieth century, particularly after the transfer of Indian health to the Public Health Service in 1955. However, the health status of American Indians and Alaska Natives still lags behind that of the general population. The Indian death rate in 1981 was 1.4 times the death rate for the general population, with such causes as accidents and adverse effects (particularly automobile accidents), liver disease and cirrhosis, tuberculosis, and diabetes occurring with significantly greater frequency in Indian populations than in the general population.

Perhaps the greatest success of the Indian Health Service has been in the area of infant mortality. American Indian infant mortality rates were more than three times higher than the general population rates in the 1940s, but by the 1970s and 1980s they were approaching the national rates. Neonatal (zero to 27 day) Indian death rates were actually somewhat lower than the national rates in 1981, while postneonatal (twenty-eight days to one year) rates remain significantly higher than the national rates. These higher mortality rates reflect the continuing significance of such infectious diseases as influenza, pneumonia, and gastrointestinal diseases in accounting for American Indian deaths.

For much of the twentieth century, the Meriam Report's observation that the Indian population was characterized by "a high birth rate and a high death rate with excessively high infant mortality and a large proportion of deaths from tuberculosis" held true.[3] Birth rates significantly in excess of the general population rates were common, although Indian population size relative to that of the general population did not increase due to very high death rates.

Table 5.1 presents some nineteenth-century statistics on Indian births and deaths, taken from *Annual Reports* of the Commissioner of Indian Affairs. The table shows the number and rate per thousand of births and deaths on reservations (excluding the Five Civilized Tribes) for selected years between 1875 and 1900. The size of the population surveyed, the number of births and deaths, and the reported rates all fluctuate dramatically. Although in 1895 and 1900 the table includes the warning that births and deaths were "only partially reported," all of the figures are somewhat questionable. Probably the most accurate statistics are those for 1890, the year in which the Bureau of the Census and Bureau of Indian Affairs made a concerted effort to report accurately the Indian population and the occurrence of vital events. The birth rate of 27.8 per 1,000 and the death rate of 29.5 per 1,000, reported in 1890, were the highest rates reported in the late nineteenth century and those that are closest to those found in the early twentieth century.

The commissioner's reports for these years indicate births and deaths for each reservation. Some of these reports may be relatively accurate. However, even in cases where agency physicians made a concerted effort to identify all births and deaths and to report them, many vital events doubtless occurred distant from the agency and were not recorded. Many physicians were less than scrupulous. Charles Eastman, a Santee Sioux who served as agency physician at the Pine Ridge Reservation in 1890, commented as follows on the work of the late nineteenth-century Indian Service physician and his isolation from the Indian people:

The doctors who were in the Service in those days had an easy time of it. They scarcely ever went outside of the agency enclosure, and issued their pills in compounds after the most casual inquiry. As late as 1890, when the government sent me out as physician to ten-thousand Ogallalla Sioux and Northern Cheyennes at Pine Ridge agency, I found my predecessor still practicing his profession through a small hole in the wall between his office and the general assembly room of the Indians.[4]

Matters improved somewhat during the early twentieth century, when disease became recognized as a significant problem for American Indians. Trachoma and tuberculosis, two infectious diseases with significantly higher incidence rates in the Indian population than in the general population, were widely regarded as serious threats to Indian well-being by the 1910s. Although general statistical reporting of vital events for Indians was not yet being done on a nationwide basis, fairly accurate birth rates were available as well as data on the incidence of certain diseases. Table 5.2 reports Indian births and estimated Indian population for reservation areas that reported births in 1915, 1920, and 1925. For each of those years, the birth rate per 1,000 estimated Indian population was in excess of thirty-one, or about 50 percent higher than the national birth rate.

Indian and Alaska Native birth rates have continued to be significantly higher than the rate for the general population as well as higher than the rate for all nonwhites in the 1950s, 1960s, and 1970s, as shown by Table 5.3. The table shows American Indian and Alaska Native birth rates for reservation states for selected years between 1955 and 1982. For purposes of comparison, the birth rates for all races and nonwhites are shown as well. Despite a lower American Indian and Alaska Native birth rate in 1982 than in 1955, the ratio of the Indian birth rate to the birth rate of the general population increased from 1.5 in 1955 to 1.8 in 1982. Because of the relatively small number of events involved, compared to the general and nonwhite populations, the rates for American Indians and Alaska Natives presented in Table 5.3 and most subsequent tables in this chapter are three-year rates centered on the year specified.

Table 5.4 shows life expectancy at birth for American Indians and Alaska Natives born in 1940, 1950, 1960, 1970, and 1980. These data show gradual improvement in the life expectancy of American Indians and Alaska Natives, both in absolute terms and in relation to the white population. Life expectancy at birth for American Indians and Alaska Natives increased from 51.0 years in 1940 to 71.1 years in 1980. The 1940 life expectancy was 79 percent of white life expectancy in that year;

by 1980, Indian and Alaska Native life expectancy was 96 percent of white life expectancy. The data on American Indians and Alaska Natives presented in Table 5.4 are for the continental United States (1940 and 1950) and for states in which the Indian Health Service had responsibilities (1960, 1970, and 1980). Data focusing on reservation populations (that is, excluding urban and other off-reservation Indians in reservation states) would probably reveal a less positive picture.[5]

A second trend revealed by Table 5.4 is improvement in female life expectancy relative to male life expectancy for American Indians and Alaska Natives, as well as for whites. Female American Indian life expectancy was 101 percent of male life expectancy in 1940; by 1980, female life expectancy was 112 percent of male life expectancy among American Indians and Alaska Natives. This change was mirrored, less dramatically, in the white population.

Reduction in infant mortality is illustrated in Table 5.5. Rates are shown for selected years between 1944 and 1982; the combined Indian and Alaska Native infant mortality rate is based on three-year averages centered on the year specified. The ratios of American Indian and Alaska Native rates to the all races rate, and to the black rate are also shown. Between 1955, the first year for which comparable across-the-board data are presented, and 1970, the ratio of the Indian and Alaska Native infant mortality rate to that of the general population declined from 2.4 to 1.2. During the same period, the ratio of the Indian and Alaska Native infant mortality rate to the black infant mortality rate declined from 1.5 to 0.8. Infant mortality for all groups declined during the period, but the Indian and Alaska Native infant mortality rate declined more rapidly than that of the general popualtion or that of the black population. The infant mortality rate for Alaska Natives remained significantly higher than the rate for American Indians or any other group throughout the period.

Table 5.6 presents data on the composition of the Indian infant mortality rate. Again, the data presented are for reservation states. The table shows that the greatest progress in reducing infant mortality has been in reduction of neonatal (age zero to twenty-seven days) mortality. The postneonatal (age twenty-eight days to one year) infant mortality rate has also declined but remains significantly greater than the general population rate. Nonetheless, both rates in 1982 were about one-third of what they had been fifteen years before.

Maternal mortality is closely associated with infant mortality. Table 5.7 shows maternal deaths and death rates for American Indians and Alaska Natives living in reservation states for selected years between 1958 and 1982. For purposes of comparison, the U.S. all races and U.S. nonwhite rates are also shown. The American Indian and Alaska Native maternal death rate changed from double the all races rate in 1958 to near equality by the early 1980s. However, as with all of the vital data on

American Indians presented in this chapter, caution must be exercised in interpreting the changes in rates. Because of the relatively small number of persons and events involved, the rates, even three-year rates, may be relatively unstable.

Table 5.8 through 5.11 present data on the ten leading causes of American Indian death for the years 1952, 1973, 1976, and 1981. The significance of such causes of deaths as accidents, influenza, pneumonia, tuberculosis, diseases of early infancy, homicide, and suicide, is striking. Table 5.8 presents data on causes of death for American Indians in twenty-three reservation states in 1952. Tables 5.9 and 5.10 present data on causes of death for American Indians and Alaska Natives in reservation states in 1973 and 1976. Table 5.11 presents data on the ten leading causes of death in 1981 for Indian Health Service areas, rather than reservation states. For reference puposes, the ratio of American Indian deaths to the U.S. all races death rate is presented as well. Striking is the greater toll taken by such causes of death as accidents and adverse effects, liver disease and cirrhosis, pneumonia, diabetes mellitus, homicide, and suicide in accounting for American Indian deaths. The death rates for such causes as heart disease, cerebrovascular disease, and conditions arising in the perinatal period are quite close to the U.S. all races rates.

Table 5.12 presents incidence rates among American Indian and Alaska Natives of fifteen leading notifiable diseases for selected years between 1965 and 1978. These are annual rates per 100,000 population and are based upon hospitalizations in Indian Health Service hospitals, not reservation states. Significant declines in trachoma, mumps, and tuberculosis are somewhat offset by increases in acute otitis media, gastroenteritis, influenza, and infectious hepatitis. The persistence of infectious disease, in spite of reductions in death rates, suggests persistent and continuing problems in the health status of the American Indians and Alaska Natives.

Tables 5.13 through 5.19 present data on specific causes of death significant for American Indians and Alaska Natives, together with death rates for all races and nonwhites. Specific causes of death include diabetes mellitus (Table 5.13), gastrointestinal disease (Table 5.14), tuberculosis (Table 5.15), accidents (Table 5.16), alcoholism (Table 5.17), homicide (Table 5.18), and suicide (Table 5.19). While dramatic reductions in death rates for such causes of death as gastrointestinal disease and turberculosis have occurred, other causes of death, such as accidents, alcoholism, homicide, and suicide, remain significantly above the national all races rate. The diabetes death rate has increased as has the ratio of the Indian diabetes death rate to the all races diabetes death rate. Table 5.20 presents suicide mortality rates by age for American Indians and Alaska Natives, for all races, and for nonwhites for the year

1982. The pattern of age-specific suicide death rates for American Indians and Alaska Natives differs from the age-specific suicide death rates for all races. Suicide deaths peak in the fifteen- to twenty-four-year-old age group among the American Indians and Alaska Natives, while, among Americans of all races, the highest death rates are found in the seventy-five to eighty-four age cohort. Nonwhites have the highest suicide death rate in the twenty-five to thirty-four age cohort. For all three groups, suicide deaths for males are much higher than the rates for females in all age cohorts.

While significant declines in death rates in many areas have been recorded in the past twenty-five years, significant problems remain in Indian health. Particularly significant are causes of deaths having a behavioral component such as suicide, homicide, and alcohol-related deaths. Program statistics of the Indian Health Service are presented in Chapter 7.

Nineteenth-century Indian agents collected a wide variety of statistical data on births, health and disease, and deaths. Much of this data is presented in the *Annual Reports* of the Commissioner of Indian Affairs for years prior to 1906. These reports, while they contain some useful information and while they may be relatively accurate for certain reservations, need to be used with caution. At times, the amount of specificity and detail is impressive but the social situation of the Indian Service physician needs to be taken into account. Many nineteenth-century Indian Service physicians were isolated from their Indian patients. During the early twentieth century, available statistical data in published sources are sparse. Laurence F. Schmeckebier presents some health data in *The Office of Indian Affairs: Its History, Activities, and Organization* (1927) and Lewis Meriam and his associates present some vital data with a discussion of its shortcomings in *The Problem of Indian Administration* (1928).

The transfer of Indian health responsibilities from the Bureau of Indian Affairs to the Indian Health Service in 1955 placed the responsibility for reporting vital events in an organization of health care professionals with considerable expertise and commitment to generating accurate data. While this development did not solve all problems in data collection and handling, relatively good statistical data are available for the period from 1955 to the present. A variety of Indian Health Service publications, generated by the area offices and by headquarters, present valuable data on Indian health. The most useful current source of statistical data is the Indian Health Service *Chart Series Book* published periodically by IHS. An extremely valuable recent source, which includes an excellent bibliography and informed discussion of data problems, is the report of the U.S. Congress Office of Technology Assessment titled *Indian Health Care*, OTA-H-290 (1986).

A good deal of historical attention has been devoted to Indian deaths in the early Colonial period. Alfred W. Crosby Jr.'s *The Columbian Exchange* (1972) and Henry Dobyns' *Their Number Becomes Thinned* (1983), both mentioned in Chapter 3, are significant examples of this work. Many other examples exist; these are discussed in Dobyns' *Indian Historical Demography: A Critical Bibliography* (1976). However, historians have not examined the dramatic changes of the twentieth century in American Indian vital statistics in detail. An exception is an unpublished Ph.D. dissertation by Diane Putney, "Fighting the Scourge: American Indian Morbidity and Federal Policy, 1897-1928," Ph.D. dissertation, Marquette University, Milwaukee, 1980. This relative neglect is unfortunate since concern about high Indian death rates has been a significant factor in changing federal Indian policy and in program development. *The Problem of Indian Administration* (1928), the Report of the Commission on the Rights, Liberties, and Responsibilities of the American Indian, titled *The Indian: America's Unfinished Business* (1966), and the reports of the American Indian Policy Review Commission (1976) all contain material on the vital statistics of American Indians, particularly death rates. Probably the best recent source is the report of the Congressional Office of Technology Assessment, *Indian Health Care*, OTA-H-290 (1986).

NOTES

1. U.S. Congress, Office of Technology Assessment, *Indian Health Care*, OTA-H-290 (Washington, D.C.: U.S. Government Printing Office, 1986), pp. 251-255.

2. Lewis Meriam and others, *The Problem of Indian Administration*, Institute for Government Research, Studies in Administration (Baltimore: The Johns Hopkins Press, 1928), p. 196.

3. Ibid.

4. Charles A. Eastman, "The Indians' Health Problem," *The American Indian Magazine*, April/June 1916, quoted in Laurence F. Schmeckebier, *The Office of Indian Affairs: Its History, Activities, and Organization*, Institute for Government Research, Service Monographs of the United States Government, no. 48 (Baltimore: The Johns Hopkins Press, 1927), p. 228.

5. For a discussion of this and other problems in using "reservation states" rather than IHS service areas as the base for generating vital data, see U.S. Congress, *Indian Health Care*, pp. 85-89.

Table 5.1
Reported Births, Deaths, and Rates, Indians on Reservations, Excluding Five Civilized Tribes, 1875–1900 (Rates per 1,000 Population)

YEAR	INDIAN POPULATION	BIRTHS NUMBER	RATE	DEATHS NUMBER	RATE
1875	252,900	1,985	7.8	1,601	6.3
1880	196,940	3,430	17.4	2,020	10.3
1890	176,534	4,908	27.8	5,208	29.5
1895	182,370	3,502*	19.2	2,974*	16.3
1900	185,790	4,196*	22.6	3,698*	19.9

Note:
   * Only partially reported

Source: Commissioner of Indian Affairs, Annual Reports, 1875, 1880, 1890, 1895, 1900.

Table 5.2
Estimated Indian Population, Births, and Birth Rates in U.S. Birth Registration Area, 1915–1925 (Rates per 1,000 Population)

Year	Estimated Indian Population in Reporting Areas*	Reported Indian Births Number	Rate	Birth Rate in U.S. Birth Registration Area
1925	180,884	5,699	31.5	21.4
1920	206,868	6,510	31.5	23.7
1915	205,450	6,542	31.8	25.1

Note:
   * Estimated population of areas reporting births; estimate does not include all Indians, nor do the three estimates cover the same area.

Source: Lewis Meriam, et al., The Problem of Indian Administration (Baltimore: The Johns Hopkins Press, 1928), p. 198.

Table 5.3
Indian and Alaska Native Births and Birth Rates,
Birth Rates for U.S. All Races and U.S. Other Than White,
1955–1982 (Rates per 1,000 Population)

YEAR	INDIAN AND ALASKA NATIVE BIRTHS[1]		U.S. ALL RACES RATE[3]	U.S. OTHER THAN WHITE RATE[3]
	NUMBER	RATE[2]		
1982	38,560	28.5	15.9	21.9
1980	33,937	27.0	15.9	22.5
1975	25,457	26.9	14.6	21.0
1970	22,746	32.0	18.4	25.1
1965	22,370	36.4	19.4	27.6
1960	21,154	42.1	23.7	32.1
1955	17,028	37.5	24.6	33.1

Notes:

[1] Reservation states only
[2] Three year rates centered on year specified
[3] Single year rates

Source: Indian Health Service, Chart Series Book, April 1986
          (Washington, D.C.: U.S. Government Printing Office, 1986),
          p. 19.

Table 5.4
Life Expectancy at Birth, by Sex, American Indians and
Alaska Natives and U.S. White Population, 1940–1980

YEAR	AMERICAN INDIANS AND ALASKA NATIVES[1]			U.S. WHITE POPULATION[2]		
	BOTH SEXES	MALE	FEMALE	BOTH SEXES	MALE	FEMALE
1980	71.1	67.1	75.1	74.4	70.7	78.1
1970	65.1	60.7	71.2	71.6	67.9	75.5
1960	61.7	60.0	65.7	70.7	67.6	74.2
1950	60.0	58.1	62.2	69.0	66.3	72.0
1940	51.0	51.3	51.9	64.9	62.8	67.3

Notes:

1. Life expectancy at birth based upon three years of mortality experience centered in the year specified. Data for 1940 and 1950 are for Continental United States. Data for 1960, 1970, and 1980 are for reservation states.

2. Life expectancy at birth based upon single year specified. Data for 1940 and 1950 are for Continental United States. Data for 1950, 1970, and 1980 are for the fifty states and the District of Columbia.

Source: Indian Health Service, _Chart Series Book_, April 1986 (Washington, D.C.: U.S. Government Printing Office, 1980), p. 49.

Table 5.5
Infant Mortality Rates, American Indians and Alaska Natives in
Reservation States and Selected U.S. Populations, 1944–1982
(Rates per 1,000 Live Births)

YEAR	INDIAN AND ALASKAN NATIVE[1]	INDIAN[1]	ALASKAN NATIVE[1]	U.S. ALL RACES (RATIO[2])	U.S. BLACK[2] (RATIO[2])
1982	11.0	10.6	16.3	11.5 (1.0)	19.6 (0.6)
1980	13.8	13.4	20.4	12.6 (1.1)	21.4 (0.6)
1975	18.7	18.2	25.3	16.1 (1.2)	26.2 (0.8)
1970	24.6	24.3	28.1	20.0 (1.2)	32.6 (0.8)
1965	38.5	40.2	57.3	24.7 (1.6)	41.7 (0.9)
1960	48.0	45.5	72.1	26.0 (1.8)	44.3 (1.1)
1955	62.7	60.9	79.5	26.4 (2.4)	43.1 (1.5)
1950	—	85.1	—	29.2 (2.9)[3]	—
1944	—	135.3	—	41.4[4] (3.3)[3]	—

Notes:

1. Three-year rates centered in year specified for American Indians and Alaska Natives in states served by IHS; all other rates are based on single-year data.
2. Ratio of Indian and Alaska Native rate to rate in column.
3. Ratio of Indian rate to U.S. All Races rate.
4. 1945 rate.

Source: Indian Health Service, Chart Series Book, April 1986 (Washington, D.C.: U.S. Government Printing Office, 1986), p.22; William A, Brophy and Sophie D. Aberle, comp., The Indian: America's Unfinished Business (Norman: University of Oklahoma Press, 1966), p.227.

Table 5.6
Infant Mortality Rates by Age, 1966–1982

	INDIANS AND ALASKA NATIVES*			RATIO TO U.S. ALL RACES RATE		
YEAR	INFANT MORTALITY RATE	NEONATAL (0–27 days) RATE	POSTNEONATAL (28 days – one year) RATE	INFANT MORTALITY	NEONATAL	POSTNEONATAL
1982	11.0	5.0	6.1	1.0	0.7	1.6
1980	13.8	6.6	7.2	1.1	0.8	1.8
1975	18.7	9.2	9.5	1.2	0.8	2.1
1970	24.6	12.2	12.3	1.2	0.8	2.5
1966	36.8	16.1	20.7	1.6	0.9	3.2

Note:

*Three-year rates centered in year specified.

Indian Health Service, Chart Series Book, April 1986 (Washington, D.C.: U.S. Government Printing Office, 1986), p. 23.

Table 5.7

Maternal Deaths and Rates, American Indians and Alaska Natives in
Reservation States, 1958–1982 (Rates per 100,000 Live Births)

YEAR	AMERICAN INDIANS AND ALASKA NATIVES		U.S. ALL RACES RATE	RATIO: INDIAN TO U.S. ALL RACES RATE	U.S. OTHER THAN WHITE RATE	RATIO: INDIAN TO U.S. OTHER THAN WHITE RATE
	NUMBER	RATE[1]				
1982	3	8.9	7.9	1.1	16.4	0.5
1980	3	9.0	9.2	1.0	19.8	0.5
1975	4	11.8	12.8	0.9	29.0	0.4
1970	7	32.3	21.5	1.5	55.9	0.6
1965	12	63.4	31.6	2.0	83.7	0.8
1960	8	67.9	37.1	1.8	97.9	0.7
1958	16	82.6	37.6	2.2	101.8	0.8

Note:

1. Three-year rates centered in year specified; all other rates are for year specified.

Source: Indian Health Service, Chart Series Book, April 1986 (Washington, D.C.: U.S. Government Printing Office, 1986), p. 21.

107

Table 5.8
Ten Leading Causes of American Indian Deaths, Indians in
Twenty-three Reservation States, 1951–1953

CAUSE	PERCENT OF ALL CAUSES
1. Heart Diseases	14.2
2. Accidents	14.1
3. Influenza and Pneumonia	10.5
4. Tuberculosis	8.1
5. Certain Diseases of Early Infancy	7.1
6. Malignant Neoplasms	5.9
7. Gastritis, Duodenitis, Enteritis, and Colitis	5.9
8. Vascular Lesions Affecting the Central Nervous System	4.3
9. Congenital Malformations	1.6
10. Homicide and Legal Execution	1.6

Source: U.S. Congress, Office of Technology Assessment, Indian Health Care
          OTA-H-290 (Washington, D.C.: U.S. Government Printing Office,
          1986), p. 95.

Table 5.9
Ten Leading Causes of Death, American Indians and Alaska Natives in Reservation States, 1972–1974 (Rates per 100,000 Population)

	NUMBER	PERCENT OF ALL CAUSES	RATE
All Causes	13,385	100.0	896.3
1. Accidents	2,972	22.2	199.0
Motor Vehicles	1,663	12.4	114.4
All Other	1,309	9.8	87.7
2. Diseases of the Heart	2,265	16.9	151.7
3. Malignant Neoplasms	1,127	8.4	75.5
4. Cirrhosis of the Liver	738	5.5	49.4
5. Influenza and Pneumonia	687	5.1	46.0
6. Cerebrovascular Diseases	678	5.1	45.4
7. Certain Causes of Mortality in Early Infancy	364	2.7	24.4
8. Homicide	361	2.7	24.2
9. Diabetes Mellitus	354	2.6	23.7
10. Suicide	352	2.6	23.6

Source: Indian Health Service, Selected Vital Statistics for Indian Health Service Areas and Service Units, 1972 to 1977 (Washington, D.C.: U.S. Government Printing Office, 1979), p. 104.

Table 5.10
**Ten Leading Causes of Death, American Indians and Alaska Natives
in Reservation States, 1975–1977 (Rates per 100,000 Population)**

	NUMBER	PERCENT OF ALL CAUSES	RATE	PERCENT CHANGE SINCE 1972–3
All Causes	13,666	100.00	751.2	−16.2
1. Accidents	2,908	21.3	159.9	−19.6
Motor Vehicles	1,670	12.2	91.8	−19.8
All Other	1,238	9.1	68.1	− 0.3
2. Diseases of the Heart	2,322	17.0	127.6	−15.9
3. Malignant Neoplasms	1,244	9.1	68.4	− 9.4
4. Cirrhosis of the Liver	814	6.0	44.7	− 9.5
5. Influenza and Pneumonia	660	4.8	36.3	−21.1
6. Cerebrovascular Disease	658	4.8	36.2	−20.3
7. Suicide	436	3.2	23.9	+ 1.3
8. Homicide	391	2.9	21.5	−11.2
9. Certain Causes of Mortality in Early Infancy	390	2.9	21.4	−12.3
10. Diabetes Mellitus	365	2.7	20.1	−15.2

Source: Indian Health Service. Selected Vital Statistics for Indian Health
Service Areas and Service Units, 1972 to 1977 (Washington, D.C.:
U.S. Government Printing Office, 1979), p. 71.

Table 5.11
Ten Leading Causes of Death, American Indians and Alaska Natives
in IHS Service Area, 1980–1982 (Rates per 100,000 Population)

		NUMBER OF DEATHS	PERCENT OF ALL CAUSES	RATE	RATIO TO U.S. ALL RACES RATE
All Causes		15,321	100.0	778.3	1.4
1.	Diseases of the Heart	3,058	20.0	166.7	0.9
2.	Accidents/Adverse Effects	2,946	19.2	136.3	3.4
3.	Malignant Neoplasms	1,713	11.2	98.4	0.7
4.	Liver Disease/Cirrhosis	801	5.2	48.1	4.2
5.	Cerebrovascular Disease	664	4.3	33.8	0.9
6.	Pneumonia	580	3.8	26.6	2.2
7.	Diabetes Mellitus	470	3.1	27.8	2.8
8.	Homicide	458	3.0	21.2	2.0
9.	Suicide	447	2.9	19.4	1.7
10.	Conditions Arising in Perinatal Period*	331	2.2	9.8	1.1

Note:
*Same as "Certain Causes of Mortality in Early Infancy" in earlier years.

Source: U.S. Congress, Office of Technology Assessment, Indian Health Care, OTA-H-290
(Washington, D.C.: U.S. Government Printing Office, 1986), p. 93.

Table 5.12

Incidence Rates, Fifteen Leading Notifiable Diseases, Indians and
Alaska Natives, 1965–1978 (Rates per 100,000 Population)

	1965	1968	1971	1974	1978	U.S. ALL RACES 1978
Acute Otitis Media	6,170.3	9,115.2	10,742.4	10,958.2	11,099.2	NR
Gastroenterinitis	5,457.0	6,031.2	6,064.2	7,276.7	6,039.5	NR
Impetigo	NR	NR	NR	3,449.2	3,942.1	NR
Pneumonia	3,690.3	3,665.8	3,002.0	3,209.4	3,197.0	NR
Influenza	996.5	3,318.7	3,431.9	3,097.9	2,133.5	NR
Gonococcal Infections	777.4	912.5	1,647.5	1,667.2	1,219.9	468.3
Chickenpox	509.4	411.9	490.9	490.7	547.6	80.4
Scabies	NR	NR	NR	10.0	494.2	NR
Baciliary Dysentary	319.5	213.2	416.0	495.0	441.7	NR
Infectious Hepatitis	146.8	174.0	370.4	376.1	361.0	13.5
Trachoma	1,290.9	871.0	618.8	388.8	119.3	NR
Mumps	308.6	376.2	288.8	187.0	94.4	7.8
Syphillis	101.0	158.0	180.5	148.7	88.9	30.0
Rheumatic Fever	22.1	21.2	43.6	69.4	66.8	0.6
Tuberculosis	218.6	145.0	157.6	79.8	66.0	NR

Note: NR–Not Reported

Source: Division of Indian Health, Illness Among American Indians, 1965-69 (Washington, D.C.:
U.S. Government Printing Office, 1970); Indian Health Service, Illness Among American
Indians and Alaska Natives, 1970-78 (Washington, D.C.: U.S. Government Printing Office,
1979).

Table 5.13

Diabetes Mellitus Deaths and Mortality Rates, American Indians
and Alaska Natives in Reservation States, 1955–1983
(Age-adjusted Rates per 100,000 Population)

YEAR	AMERICAN INDIANS AND ALASKA NATIVES		U.S. ALL RACES RATE	RATIO OF INDIAN TO U.S. ALL RACES RATE	U.S. OTHER THAN WHITE RATE	RATIO OF INDIAN TO U.S. OTHER THAN WHITE RATE
	NUMBER OF DEATHS	RATE				
1983	210	20.5	9.9	2.1	17.8	1.2
1980	204	22.6	10.1	2.2	18.8	1.2
1975	145	20.8	11.6	1.8	21.7	1.0
1970	143	27.1	14.1	1.9	25.2	1.1
1965	110	25.4	13.5	1.9	23.6	1.1
1960	71	20.3	13.6	1.5	21.6	0.9
1955	64	17.0	13.0	1.3	16.5	1.0

Source: Indian Health Service, Chart Series Book, April 1986 (Washington, D.C.: U.S. Government Printing Office, 1986), p. 47.

Table 5.14

Gastrointestinal Disease Deaths and Mortality Rates, American Indians
and Alaska Natives in Reservation States, 1955–1983
(Age-adjusted Rates per 100,000 Population)

YEAR	AMERICAN INDIANS AND ALASKA NATIVES		U.S. ALL RACES RATE	RATIO OF INDIAN TO U.S. ALL RACES RATE	U.S. OTHER THAN WHITE RATE	RATIO OF INDIAN TO U.S. OTHER THAN WHITE RATE
	NUMBER OF DEATHS	RATE				
1983	47	4.2	2.8	1.5	2.9	1.4
1980	44	4.0	3.0	1.3	3.2	1.3
1975	41	3.7	2.2	1.7	3.0	1.2
1970	66	7.8	2.9	2.7	3.5	2.2
1965	111	10.9	3.2	3.4	4.9	2.2
1960	152	14.2	3.4	4.2	6.1	2.3
1955	165	15.4	3.6	4.3	6.8	2.3

Source: Indian Health Service, Chart Series Book, April 1986 (Washington, D.C.: U.S. Government Printing Office, 1986), p. 48.

Table 5.15
Tuberculosis Deaths and Mortality Rates, American Indians and Alaska Natives in Reservation States, 1955–1983
(Age-adjusted Rates per 100,000 Population)

YEAR	AMERICAN INDIANS AND ALASKA NATIVES		U.S. ALL RACES RATE	RATIO OF INDIAN TO U.S. ALL RACES RATE	U.S. OTHER THAN WHITE RATE	RATIO OF INDIAN TO U.S. OTHER THAN WHITE RATE
	NUMBER OF DEATHS	RATE				
1983	36	3.3	0.5	6.6	1.9	1.7
1980	36	3.6	0.6	6.0	2.4	1.5
1975	64	8.6	1.2	7.2	4.0	2.2
1970	63	11.4	2.2	5.2	6.8	1.7
1965	104	27.3	3.6	7.6	10.9	2.5
1960	115	32.3	5.4	6.0	15.1	2.1
1955	253	57.9	8.4	6.9	24.1	2.4

Source: Indian Health Service, Chart Series Book, April 1986 (Washington, D.C.: U.S. Government Printing Office, 1986), p. 46.

Table 5.16
Accident Deaths and Mortality Rates, American Indians and
Alaska Natives in Reservation States, 1955–1983
(Age-adjusted Rates per 100,000 Population)

YEAR	TOTAL DEATHS	AMERICAN INDIAN AND ALASKA NATIVE			U.S. ALL RACES		
		ALL ACCIDENTS RATE	MOTOR VEHICLE RATE	OTHER ACCIDENTS RATE	ALL ACCIDENTS RATE	MOTOR VEHICLE RATE	OTHER ACCIDENTS RATE
1983	1,065	82.9	44.6	38.3	35.3	18.5	16.8
1980	1,225	107.3	61.3	46.0	42.3	22.9	19.5
1975	1,256	143.6	78.5	65.1	44.8	21.3	23.5
1970	1,107	181.8	98.5	83.3	53.7	27.4	26.3
1965	951	186.7	91.9	94.8	53.4	26.6	26.8
1960	773	186.1	91.9	94.6	49.9	22.8	27.1
1955	714	184.0	97.6	90.3	54.3	24.6	29.7

Source: Indian Health Service, Chart Series Book, April 1986 (Washington, D.C.: U.S. Government Printing Office, 1986), p. 37.

Table 5.17
Alcoholism Deaths and Mortality Rates, American Indians and
Alaska Natives in Reservation States, 1970–1983
(Age-adjusted Rates per 100,000 Population)

| YEAR | AMERICAN INDIANS AND ALASKA NATIVES | | U.S. ALL RACES RATE | RATIO OF INDIAN TO U.S. ALL RACES RATE |
	NUMBER OF DEATHS	RATE		
1983	293	28.9	6.1	4.7
1980	382	41.3	7.5	5.5
1975	403	62.2	8.6	7.2
1970	272	56.2	8.1	6.9

Note: For 1970 and 1975 includes deaths due to alcoholism, alcoholic psychosis, and cirrhosis of the liver with mention of alcoholism. For 1980 and 1983 includes deaths due to alcohol dependence syndrome, alcoholic psychosis, and chronic liver disease and cirrhosis, specified as alcoholic.

Source: Indian Health Service, Chart Series Book, April 1986 (Washington, D.C.: U.S. Government Printing Office, 1986), p. 44.

Table 5.18
Homicide Deaths and Mortality Rates, American Indians and Alaska Natives in Reservation States, 1960–1983
(Age-adjusted Rates per 100,000 Population)

YEAR	AMERICAN INDIANS AND ALASKA NATIVES		U.S. ALL RACES RATE	RATIO OF INDIAN TO U.S. ALL RACES RATE	U.S. OTHER THAN WHITE RATE	RATIO OF INDIAN TO U.S. OTHER THAN WHITE RATE
	NUMBER OF DEATHS	RATE				
1983	217	16.4	8.6	1.9	26.4	0.6
1980	212	18.1	10.8	1.7	35.0	0.5
1975	185	21.9	10.5	2.1	41.1	0.5
1970	125	23.8	9.1	2.6	41.3	0.6
1965	102	19.7	6.3	3.1	29.8	0.7
1960	80	19.5	5.3	3.7	25.8	0.8

Source: Indian Health Service, Chart Series Book, April 1986 (Washington, D.C.: U.S. Government Printing Office, 1986), p. 42.

Table 5.19
Suicide Deaths and Mortality Rates, American Indians and Alaska Natives in Reservation States, 1960–1983
(Age-adjusted Rates per 100,000 Population)

YEAR	AMERICAN INDIANS AND ALASKA NATIVES		U.S. ALL RACES RATE	RATIO OF INDIAN TO U.S. ALL RACES RATE	U.S. OTHER THAN WHITE RATE	RATIO OF INDIAN TO U.S. OTHER THAN WHITE RATE
	NUMBER OF DEATHS	RATE				
1983	196	14.7	11.4	1.3	6.4	2.3
1980	173	14.1	11.4	1.2	6.7	2.1
1975	180	21.2	12.6	1.7	7.5	2.8
1970	105	17.9	11.8	1.5	6.5	2.8
1965	65	12.9	11.4	1.1	6.1	2.1
1960	57	16.8	10.6	1.6	5.4	3.1

Source: Indian Health Service, Chart Series Book, April 1986 (Washington, D.C.: U.S. Government Printing Office, 1986), p. 40.

Table 5.20

Suicide Mortality Rates by Race, Age, and Sex, 1982

(Rates per 100,000 Population in Age/Sex Groups Specified)

YEARS	INDIANS AND ALASKA NATIVES*			U.S. ALL RACES			U.S. OTHER THAN WHITE		
	BOTH SEXES	MALE	FEMALE	BOTH SEXES	MALE	FEMALE	BOTH SEXES	MALE	FEMALE
Under 5	—	—	—	—	—	—	—	—	—
5 – 14	1.4	1.8	0.9	0.6	0.9	0.2	0.5	0.8	0.1
15 – 24	27.9	46.2	9.5	12.1	19.8	4.2	7.6	12.3	2.9
25 – 34	25.0	44.4	6.5	16.0	25.2	7.0	11.6	20.0	4.1
35 – 44	18.4	30.9	6.6	15.3	22.5	8.4	8.9	14.5	4.0
44 – 54	13.4	23.8	3.9	16.6	24.1	9.5	7.1	11.7	3.4
55 – 64	7.4	12.8	2.6	16.9	26.2	8.8	6.6	11.0	3.1
65 – 74	9.0	19.9	—	17.4	31.1	6.9	6.7	12.7	2.3
75 – 84	7.0	12.0	3.1	20.3	45.1	5.8	7.0	14.0	2.4
85 and over	—	—	—	17.6	50.2	3.9	6.6	13.6	3.1

Note: * Three-year rate centered on year specified.

Source: Indian Health Service, Chart Series Book, April 1986 (Washington, D.C.: U.S. Government Printing Office, 1986), p. 41.

6

Government Activities

The development of Indian people, communities, and nations has been shaped since the eighteenth century by their interaction with the United States government. The United States government's purpose in dealing with American Indian groups has been at times to exert coercive control, at other times to promote community development, and at times to relocate significant portions of the American Indian population. This chapter presents data that document the efforts of government agencies, principally the Bureau of Indian Affairs, which dealt with Indian groups. Data are also presented that show some of the results of government operations. Data on two significant areas of government activities, education and health care, are presented in Chapter 7.

The United States inherited its formal structure for dealing with American Indian groups from Great Britain. Prior to independence, the British Crown dealt with Indians in the North American colonies through northern and southern superintendents of Indian affairs. These officials were the principal points of contact between Indians and the Crown. The United States adopted this system and between 1802 and 1863 dealt with Indians by creating an increasing number of superintendencies, each dealing with the tribes in a specified geographical region. Working under the superintendents, Indian agents dealt directly with the tribes serving as ambassadors and coordinators of federal efforts.

As the pace and intensity of interaction between American Indians and whites increased during the nineteenth century, Indian agents became more and more significant. After the American Civil War, the superintendencies were gradually eliminated. By 1877 the last superintendencies had been abolished and Indian agents reported directly to Washington. In 1946, a middle level administrative position, the area office, was created in the Bureau of Indian Affairs. When the Indian Health Service was created in 1955, a system of area offices was created in its organizational structure between the local service unit and the headquarters at Washington.[1]

Table 6.1 shows the growth of field units in the Indian Service during the century between 1802 and 1903. Table 6.2 shows the number of employees in the Indian Service between 1843 and 1903. For the early years, the data are somewhat incomplete; in 1873, for example, fifteen of the seventy-eight agencies failed to respond. For other years, the count of employees may have been relatively inaccurate, since the data reflect those employees reported by the agent as working on a particular date rather than the budget allocation of the agency or an average employment level. Several trends are clear, however, beyond the expansion of the total number of employees over the course of the nineteenth century. The headquarters office in Washington grew in the number of employees, but it accounted for a decreasing proportion of the total number of employees. About 5.8 percent of the employees in the Indian Service worked in Washington in 1843, and that proportion had declined to 3.2 percent by 1903. Nor did the middle level officials, inspectors, superintendents, and the like expand in relation to the total number of employees. The largest expansions were in the agency service, particularly in the school service, which was distinguished as a separate unit of the organization after 1883. A final trend is the expansion in the miscellaneous categories of employment, reflecting the increasingly nonroutine and exceptional nature of Indian service work, which required a diverse work force.

Table 6.3 presents data on employees in the Indian Field Service (the agencies and the Indian schools) during the late nineteenth century. The dramatic increase in the importance of education, measured in terms of employment, is documented, as is an expansion in the number of employees devoted to promoting law and order. Principally these positions represent Indian police and judges, members of the tribes who were employed by the Bureau of Indian Affairs as police and judicial officers.[2] Tables 6.2 and 6.3 are based on data compiled from the biannual *Official Registers* of the United States, data that were often incomplete, as noted in the table notes.

The 1903 *Official Register* shows the race of the employees holding positions in the Indian Field Service. A summary of this information is presented in Table 6.4. The largest single occupational category in the Indian agency service was police; the great majority were Indians, as were all judges, interpreters, and teamsters, and most laborers, butchers, and herders. These categories together accounted for nearly 77 percent of employment in the Indian Service in 1903. Whites, who made up a small minority of the employees, were concentrated in such positions as clerks and physicians and made up the majority of such positions as farmer and engineer.

Tables 6.5 and 6.6 display more recent data on American Indians and federal civilian employment. In 1969 and 1977, American Indian employment in the federal civilian service was concentrated in two departments, the Department of the Interior, which included the Bureau of Indian Affairs, and the Department of Health, Education, and Welfare, which included the Office of Education and the Indian Health Service. All three of these agencies had significant responsibility for Indian programs. All three were governed by Indian preference rules in selecting employees. Indian employment in the two departments increased between 1969 and 1977, as it did in the federal establishment as a whole; however, in no department other than Interior and Health, Education, and Welfare, were more than 1 percent of the civilian employees American Indians.

Table 6.6 presents GS (general schedule) levels for all employees and American Indian employees of the Department of Interior for the years 1969 and 1977. Indian employees were concentrated in the lower GS levels in both years. These positions paid less than the higher GS levels, required less education, and provided the occupant with less responsibility and authority.

Tables 6.7 through 6.14 present data on federal expenditures for agencies dealing with American Indians since the eighteenth century. In general, expenditure levels have increased. The areas of greatest expenditure have changed as the objectives of federal Indian policy have changed. Table 6.7 presents data on the annual expenditures of the federal Indian service between 1791 and 1833. Expenditures increased as contacts with Indians increased, particularly as lands were acquired from American Indians and as Indians were removed westward (see Chapter 4). Expenditures were divided into annuities and other treaty stipulations and all other expenditures. Since annuities and treaty payments reflected compensation for lands ceded by the Indians, annuities and other treaty expenditures increased much more rapidly than did the other expenditures of the Indian office. "Other expenditures" also increased during the period, if not as rapidly, reflecting the costs of removing tribes to the West and the government's increasing commitment to "civilization," by which was meant the provision of educational and other services to American Indians which, it was hoped, would result in their assimilation.

Indian Service expenditures during the late nineteenth century are presented in Table 6.8. Total expenditures increased during this period; most dramatic was an increase in expenditures for schools. Education expenditures increased from less than 1 percent of the Indian Service budget in fiscal year 1873-1874 to 37 percent in fiscal year 1892-1893. As is the case with employment data, the expenditure data show the increasing importance placed on education of American Indians by the federal government in the late nineteenth century.[3]

Education continued to be a significant item of Indian expenditure in the early twentieth century, as shown by Table 6.9. Health care became significant as well, as concern grew about the deteriorating health status of the American Indian people (see Chapter 5). Educational expenditures, about 3.7 million dollars in 1903 and 1913, increased to 6.5 million dollars by 1928. During the same period, hospital expenditures increased from $25,000 to $643,000, a much smaller total amount but a much more rapid rate of increase.

Table 6.10 presents data on Indian service expenditures during the second quarter of the twentieth century. The tendency toward placing increased emphasis on spending for health care continued. Education remained a significant budget item in terms of dollars and in terms of the proportion of the budget it accounted for. During the 1930s, a significant proportion of the Indian Affairs budget derived from emergency appropriations, funds from New Deal relief agencies administered by the Bureau of Indian Affairs. These emergency funds amounted to 29 percent of the Indian Service budget in 1934, but declined to only 9 percent of the budget by the end of the decade.

Table 6.11 presents data on 1949 expenditures of the Bureau of Indian Affairs, and Table 6.12 presents data on expenditures between 1954 and 1969. Education remained a significant part of the Bureau of Indian Affairs budget followed by construction and resource management, reflecting an emphasis on reservation economic self-sufficiency. Table 6.13 presents data on expenditures of the Bureau of Indian Affairs between 1974 and 1984. Funds for area and regional economic development continued to increase, reflecting continuing federal efforts to improve the economic level of the American Indian people. (See Chapter 9 for a discussion of the management and development of Indian resources.)

Expenditures for health care are absent from the reports of Bureau of Indian Affairs expenditures for 1954 and later years. In 1955, the responsibility for Indian health was removed from the Bureau of Indian Affairs and transferred to the Public Health Service in the Department of Health, Education, and Welfare (now the Department of Health and Human Services). At first, health services for Indians were provided by a Division of Indian Health within the Public Health Service structure; subsequently, the designation of the agency responsible for Indian health was changed to the present Indian Health Service. Table 6.14 presents data on expenditures for Indian health from 1954, the year before the transfer of Indian health services from the Bureau of Indian Affairs to the Public Health Service, to 1984. Under the Public Health Service, expenditures for Indian health increased dramatically, from 21 million dollars in 1954 to nearly 43 million dollars five years later and 720 million dollars in 1984. A separate item for the construction of Indian health facilities, appropriated for most years between 1954 and 1984, made it possible for the Indian Health Service to replace antiquated hospital facilities. Expenditures for construction increased rapidly between 1954 and 1969.

Transfers from funds held in trust by the United States for Indian tribes made up a significant proportion of government expenditures during the twentieth century. Table 6.15 presents data on expenditures from Indian trust funds between 1969 and 1984. These funds were principally expended by the Bureau of Indian Affairs for economic development projects. (See Chapter 9 for data on Indian trust funds and economic development.)

Tables 6.16 and 6.17 present data on road operations of the Bureau of Indian Affairs at mid-century. Road building and bridge maintenance were significant areas of operations as they improved transportation and increased communication in remote reservation areas, facilitating economic development. In addition to economic development effects, road building improved the access of Indian people to health and educational services and to employment opportunities. Table 6.16 shows data on the road and bridge operations of the Bureau of Indian Affairs in 1939 and 1953. During the 1940s, the miles of roads maintained by the Bureau of Indian Affairs increased by nearly 10,000 miles. However, great needs for additional road construction remained at mid-century. Table 6.17 provides, for selected reservations, data on miles of roads built by the Bureau of Indian Affairs in 1939 and roads maintained in 1939 and 1953.

Throughout the nineteenth and twentieth centuries, federal government activity has been significant for American Indian tribes and individuals. The emphasis of that activity on one kind of enterprise or another, the changing priorities of the federal government, and the changing kinds of service delivery methods used had significant impacts on Indian people and communities. The data in this chapter show some of the ways in which changing priorities were translated into changing services. Chapter 7 focuses on the education and health care activities of the federal government.

Data on governmental activity for the nineteenth century may be found in government documents, particularly the *Annual Reports* of the Commissioner of Indian Affairs and congressional committee reports. The *Official Registers* of the United States, published biannually, and statements of Indian Service appropriations and expenditures are also useful. The *Annual Reports* of the Commissioner of Indian Affairs published before 1906 provide a wealth of data on government activity, including much data on reservation activity. For the twentieth century, a variety of data sources exist including the annual *Budget of the United States Government,* reports of the Civil Service Commission, and publications generated by the Bureau of Indian Affairs and the Indian Health Service.

Discussions of the development of the Bureau of Indian Affairs, the most important federal agency affecting Indian people, are provided by Paul Stuart, "Bureau of Indian Affairs," in Donald R. Whitnah, ed., *Government Agencies* (1983), and "Administrative Reform in Indian Affairs," *Western Historical Quarterly* 16 (April 1985): 133-146. Stuart provides an examination of the Bureau of Indian Affairs in the late nineteenth century in *The Indian Office: Growth and Development of an American Institution, 1865-1900* (1979). Twentieth-century Indian administration is examined in Bureau of Municipal Research, "Administration of the Indian Office," *Municipal Research,* no. 65 (September 1915); Laurence F. Schmeckebier, *The Office of Indian Affairs: Its History, Activities and Organization* (1927); Lewis Meriam and others, *The Problem of Indian Administration* (1928); House Committee on Interior and Insular Affairs, *Investigation of the Bureau of Indian Affairs* (1953), 82d Congress, 2d sess., *House Report* no. 2503, serial 11582; and Warren King and associates, *Bureau of Indian Affairs Management Study* (1976), a report prepared for the American Indian Policy Review Commission. Francis Paul Prucha, in *United States Indian Policy: A Critical Bibliography* (1977), provides an excellent introduction to the secondary literature on United States Indian policy.

NOTES

1. For an overview of the organizational development of the Bureau of Indian Affairs, see two essays by Paul Stuart, "Bureau of Indian Affairs," in Donald R. Whitnah, ed., *Government Agencies* (Westport, Connecticut: Greenwood Press, 1983), pp. 16-20; and "Administrative Reform in Indian Affairs," *Western Historical Quarterly* 16 (April 1985): 133-146.

2. See William T. Hagan, *Indian Police and Judges: Experiments in Acculturation and Control* (New Haven, Connecticut: Yale University Press, 1966).

3. For a discussion of changes in personnel and expenditure allocations during the late nineteenth century and a discussion of the effect of taking into account changes in the value of the dollar on the figures in Table 6.8 see Paul Stuart, *The Indian Office: Growth and Development of an American Institution, 1965-1900* (Ann Arbor, Michigan: UMI Research Press, 1979), pp. 123-133.

TABLES

Table 6.1
Field Units of the Indian Service, 1802–1903

YEAR	SUPERINTENDENCIES		AGENCIES	SUBAGENCIES
	NUMBER	TERRITORIAL GOVERNORS		
1802	4	3	6	—
1818	4	4	15	10
1834	4	3	18	27
1843	5	2	10	14
1853	9	4	25	3
1863	13	5	55	1
1873	4	—	77	1
1883	—	—	65	—
1893	—	—	58	4
1903	—	—	64	—

Source: "Regulating the Indian Department," May 20, 1834, in 23rd Congress, 1st Session, House Reports, no. 474, serial 26, pp. 42–46; Register of Officers and Agents, Civil, Military, and Naval, in the Service of the United States, 1843, 1853, 1863, 1873; and Official Register of the United States, 1883, 1893, 1903.

Table 6.2
Employees in the Indian Service, 1843–1903

YEAR	WASHINGTON OFFICE	INSPECTORS AND SUPERINTENDENTS	AGENCY SERVICE	SCHOOL SERVICE	MISCELLANEOUS	TOTAL EMPLOYEES
1843	16	11[1]	232	—	16	275
1853	19	19[2]	176	—	17	231
1863	34	37[3]	371	—	42	484
1873	44	22	1,037[4]	—	—	1,103
1883	77	11	1,592	59[5]	37	1,776
1893	93	11	1,795	1,384	46	3,329
1903	141	11	1,813	2,222	243[6]	4,430

Notes:

1. Excludes two Territorial governors serving as ex-officio superintendents.

2. Excludes four Territorial governors serving as ex-officio superintendents; includes eight agents, four sub-agents, and one special agent attached to superintendents.

3. Excludes five Territorial governors serving as ex-officio superintendents; includes two "superintending agents" in California and five interpreters, four physicians and two special agents attached to the Southern Superintendency.

4. Incomplete; 15 agencies out of a total of 78 did not report.

5. Includes employees of two off-reservation boarding schools, Carlisle (Pennsylvania) and Forest Grove (Oregon).

6. Includes four members and 160 employees of the Commission to the Five Civilized Tribes.

Sources: Compiled from Register of Officers and Agents, Civil, Military and Naval, in the Service of the United States, 1843, 1853, 1863, 1873; and Official Register of the United States, 1883, 1893, 1903.

Table 6.3

Number and Percentage of Employees in Field (Agency and
School Service), Indian Service, 1865–1897

YEAR	AGENTS AND CLERKS		EDUCATION		LAW AND ORDER		MEDICAL		OTHER		TOTAL
	#	%	#	%	#	%	#	%	#	%	
1865[1]	42	12.6	71	21.3	0	0	12	3.6	208	62.5	333
1867[2]	44	14.7	32	10.7	0	0	13	4.3	210	70.2	299
1869[3]	71	13.2	53	9.8	0	0	26	4.8	389	72.2	539
1871[4]	71	8.5	71	8.5	12	1.4	32	3.8	647	77.7	833
1873[5]	82	7.9	91	8.8	22	2.1	42	4.1	799	77.1	1036
1875	99	14.1	117	16.6	4	0.6	46	6.5	438	62.2	704
1877	98	13.6	114	15.8	9	1.2	41	5.7	461	63.8	723
1879	115	7.9	139	9.5	295	20.2	54	3.7	854[6]	58.6	1457
1881	128	6.1	238	11.3	824	39.2	60	2.9	852	40.5	2102
1883	121	7.4	267	16.3	633	38.5	53	3.2	569	34.6	1643
1885	111	5.9	403	21.3	639	33.8	59	3.1	680	35.9	1892
1887	117	5.3	708	31.8	695	31.2	66	3.0	641	28.8	2227
1889	117	5.0	708	30.3	795	34.0	65	2.8	654	28.0	2339
1891	126	4.3	1088	37.3	930	31.9	77	2.6	696	23.9	2917
1893	128	4.1	1326	42.5	937	30.0	78	2.5	650	20.8	3119
1895	139	3.8	1736	47.6	958	26.3	79	2.2	734	20.1	3646
1897	141	3.6	1936	49.4	954	24.4	86	2.2	800	20.4	3917

Notes:

1. Data incomplete; 41 agencies reported, 18 agency reports missing.
2. Data incomplete; 40 agencies reported, 27 agency reports missing.
3. Data incomplete; 68 agencies reported, 2 agency reports missing.
4. Data incomplete; 61 agencies reported, 15 agency reports missing.
5. Data incomplete; 63 agencies reported, 15 agency reports missing.
6. Excludes 349 Indian freighters at Pine Ridge Agency and 35 "irregular employees" at Rosebud Agency. These personnel performed work which was usually contracted for, and were paid on a piecework basis.

Source: Data compiled from Official Register of the United States, 1865–1897.

129

Table 6.4
The Indian Agency Service, Positions in 1903, with Race of Occupant

POSITION	WHITES	INDIANS	TOTAL
Police	7	776	783
Farmers	106	87	193
Clerks	92	32	124
Judges	—	120	120
Blacksmiths	33	49	82
Laborers	5	77	82
Carpenters	27	30	57
Physicians	51	1	52
Interpreters	—	31	31
Butchers	2	23	25
Teamsters	—	25	25
Herders	1	23	24
Engineers	12	9	21
All Others	100	94	194
TOTAL	436	1,397	1,813

Note:
        Excludes Indian School Service

Source: Compiled from Official Register of the United States, 1903.

Table 6.5

American Indians in Federal Civilian Employment, 1969 and 1977

AGENCY	1969		1977	
	TOTAL EMPLOYEES	AMERICAN INDIANS (% of total)	TOTAL EMPLOYEES	AMERICAN INDIANS (% of total)
Department of Health, Education and Welfare	102,250	2,238 (2.2)	138,507	5,504 (4.0)
Department of The Interior	63,173	8,553 (13.5)	69,524	13,785 (19.8)
All Other Agencies	2,436,188	5,687 (0.2)	2,206,857	5,927 (0.3)
TOTAL	2,601,611	16,478 (0.6)	2,414,888	25,216 (1.0)

Source: U.S. Civil Service Commission, Study of Minority Group Employment in the Federal Government, November 30, 1969 (Washington, D.C.: U.S. Government Printing Office, 1970); U.S. Civil Service Commission, Federal Civilian Workforce Statistics: Equal Employment Opportunity Statistics, November 1977 (Washington, D.C.: U.S. Government Printing Office, 1978).

Table 6.6
GS (General Schedule) Levels, Total Employees, and American Indian Employees, Department of the Interior, 1969 and 1977

GS LEVEL	1969				1977			
	TOTAL EMPLOYEES	%	AMERICAN INDIANS	%	TOTAL EMPLOYEES	%	AMERICAN INDIANS	%
Total on General Schedule	50,257	100.0	5,935	100.0	57,700	100.0	10,445	100.0
1	66	0.1	4	0.1	152	0.3	95	0.9
2	657	1.3	175	2.9	955	1.7	367	3.5
3	2,930	5.8	1,268	21.4	4,224	7.3	1,968	18.8
4	5,226	10.4	1,835	30.9	7,397	12.8	3,289	31.5
5	5,614	11.2	938	15.8	6,428	11.1	1,187	11.4
6	2,328	4.6	134	2.3	2,994	5.2	411	3.9
7	4,858	9.7	428	7.2	4,681	8.1	620	5.9
8	540	1.1	15	0.3	742	1.3	51	0.5
9	7,629	15.2	545	9.2	7,545	13.1	1,093	10.5

10	366	0.7	9	0.2	316	0.5	14	0.1
11	6,969	13.9	280	4.7	7,292	12.6	642	6.1
12	6,113	12.2	146	2.5	7,198	12.5	366	3.5
13	3,644	7.3	88	1.5	4,175	7.2	183	1.8
14	2,060	4.1	54	0.9	2,222	3.9	116	1.1
15	1,064	2.1	12	0.2	1,154	2.0	38	0.4
16	129	0.3	3	0.1	171	0.3	2	*
17	49	0.1	1	*	45	0.1	3	*
18	15	*	—	—	9	*	—	—
Average grade	NA		NA		8.27		5.66	

Notes:
NA – not available.
* Less than 0.1%.

Source: See Table 6.5.

133

Table 6.7
Annual Expenditures of the Indian Department, 1791–1833

CALENDAR YEAR	ANNUITIES AND TREATY STIPULATIONS	ALL OTHER EXPENDITURES	TOTAL EXPENDITURES
1791	$ 27,000	$ —	$ 27,000
1792	529	13,120	13,649
1793	24,000	1,088	25,088
1794	—	13,042	13,042
1795	—	21,220	21,220
1796	55,564	58,000	113,564
1797	23,579	38,817	62,396
1798	15,300	—	15,300
1799	20,080	—	20,080
1800	—	—	—
1801	9,000	—	9,000
1802	20,000	32,000	52,000
1803	—	—	—
1804	53,009	—	53,009
1805	41,000	100,000	141,000
1806	—	75,000	75,000
1807	60,825	44,000	104,825
1808	70,725	2,250	72,975
1809	169,150	43,354	212,504
1810	58,225	23,800	82,025
1811	57,725	4,150	61,875
1812	55,975	—	55,975
1813	55,475	16,883	72,358
1814	—	10,295	10,295
1815	111,750	4,500	116,250
1816	82,075	17,437	99,512
1817	91,276	228,188	319,464
1818	230,410	275,295	505,705
1819	185,523	88,481	274,004
1820	197,278	18,400	215,678
1821	118,050	18,750	136,800
1822	402,497	50,928	453,425
1823	244,518	135,264	379,782
1824	274,780	145,708	420,488
1825	536,740	163,866	700,606
1826	540,183	203,265	743,448
1827	495,886	155,448	651,334
1828	424,542	190,482	615,024
1829	400,625	174,863	575,488
1830	424,363	179,596	603,959
1831	533,514	396,851	930,365
1832	831,399	521,020	1,352,419
1833	1,654,385	158,296	1,812,681

Source: "Regulating the Indian Department," May 20, 1834, in 23rd Congress, 1st Session, House Reports, no 474, serial 26, pp. 49–50.

Table 6.8
Indian Office Expenditures, 1873–1895 (Current Dollars)

FISCAL YEAR	TOTAL EXPENDITURES	SCHOOLS AMOUNT	PERCENTAGE	CIVILIZATION AMOUNT	PERCENTAGE
1873–1874	$4,676,222.90	$ 37,597.31	.804	$ 1,796.12	.038
1874–1875	5,280,122.02	94,320.28	1.786	40,453.99	.766
1875–1876	4,858,653.12	122,920.19	2.530	12,821.77	.264
1876–1877	3,781,948.79	105,172.18	2.781	22,036.60	.583
1877–1878	3,969,749.25	127,649.41	3.216	17,101.75	.431
1878–1879	3,958,373.96	118,928.10	3.004	4,974.87	.126
1879–1880	4,204,271.73	152,411.76	3.625	73,647.88	1.752
1880–1881	4,287,323.74	208,996.47	4.875	117,574.44[3]	2.742
1881–1882	4,897,165.83	244,209.18[2]	4.987	233,364.48[3]	4.765
1882–1883	5,196,218.84	482,336.44	9.282	145,160.25[3]	2.794
1883–1884	5,006,661.49	669,974.21	13.382	92,130.67[3]	1.840
1884–1885	5,192,331.85	887,690.67	17.096	89,215.95[3]	1.718
1885–1886	4,912,736.44	979,716.32	19.942	69,115.76[3]	1.407
1886–1887	5,021,610.13	1,146,773.84	22.837	59,531.68[3]	1.186
1887–1888	4,728,020.01	1,086,259.99	22.975	17,048.89[3]	.361
1888–1889	4,624,817.75	1,149,077.90	24.846	16,143.88[3]	.349
1889–1890	5,188,619.70	1,317,426.35	25.391	16,751.89[3]	.323
1890–1891	5,817,138.11	1,882,471.37	32.361	99,971.93[3]	1.719
1891–1892	8,914,644.28	2,323,284.71	26.061	113,307.20[3]	1.271,
1892–1893	6,128,510.64	2,277,557.15	37.163	119,578.78[3]	1.951
1893–1894[1]	—	—	—	—	—
1894–1895	6,364,494.25	1,961,415.80	30.818	84,373.57	1.326

Notes: 1. Data not published.
2. Does not include amounts paid Indian School employees or subsistence and clothing furnished Indians.
3. Includes Indian labor.

Source: Compiled from "Tabular Statement of Disbursements made from the Appropriations for the Indian Department for the Fiscal Year Ending June 30, 1874–95."

Table 6.9

Indian Service Appropriations, 1903–1928

FISCAL YEARS

PURPOSES	1903	1913	1923	1928
Annuities	$ 187,617.51	$ 44,100.00	$ 44,100.00	$ 44,100.00
Pay of employees	176,248.99	151,220.00	155,220.00	216,266.00
Education	3,771,678.72	3,753,555.00	4,574,445.00	6,495,700.00
Commutation of annuity	999,368.00	—	—	—
Irrigation and water supply	300,000.00	1,133,062.62	1,888,007.00	1,736,625.00
Hospitals	25,000.00	85,000.00	376,000.00	643,500.00
Expenses in connection with affairs of Five Tribes and Osage	310,000.00	215,000.00	395,000.00	247,000.00
Attorneys' fees	43,332.93	—	—	—
Support and civilization	2,428,018.58	1,690,846.00	2,931,030.00	2,129,454.00
Other purposes	1,376,930.10	2,714,374.86	3,467,294.17	3,478,840.00
TOTAL	$9,618,194.83	$9,787,158.48	$13,831,096.17	$14,991,485.00

Source: Lawrence F. Schmeckebier, The Office of Indian Affairs: Its History, Activities and Organization (Baltimore: The Johns Hopkins Press, 1927), p. 516.

Table 6.10
Expenditures, Bureau of Indian Affairs, 1934–1944
(in Thousands of Dollars)

	1934 EXPENDITURES	% OF TOTAL	1939 EXPENDITURES	% OF TOTAL	1944 EXPENDITURES	% OF TOTAL
Salaries, Bureau of Indian Affairs[1]	325	1	520	1	755	3
General Expenses, Indian Service	930	4	1,489	4	1,250	4
Indian Lands	132	1	1,164	3	174	1
Industrial Assistance	1,092	5	2,275	6	1,889	6
Water, Irrigation, and Drainage	2,709	12	1,203	3	1,489	5
Education	8,235	36	10,068	25	10,468	35

Table 6.10
(Continued)

	1934		1939		1944	
	EXPENDITURES	% OF TOTAL	EXPENDITURES	% OF TOTAL	EXPENDITURES	% OF TOTAL
Conservation of Health	3,018	13	5,358	13	5,918	20
Administration of Indian Property	1,819	8	2,719	7	3,849	13
Roads and Bridges	3,780	16	24	*	25	*
Annuities, Claims, and Miscellaneous	1,243	5	14,994	38	3,678	12
TOTAL	23,373	100	39,815	100	29,496	100
Emergency Appropriations[2]	6,873	29	3,714	9	63	*

Notes:
* Less than 1%.
1. Employees in Washington, D.C.
2. Included in total: 1934, National Industrial Recovery funds; 1939, National Industrial Recovery, Emergency Relief, and Public Works Administration funds; 1944, National Defense funds.

Source: The Budget of the United States Government for the Fiscal Year Ending June 30, 1936, 1941, 1946.

Table 6.11
Expenditures, Bureau of Indian Affairs, 1949
(in Thousands of Dollars)

	EXPENDITURES	% OF TOTAL
Salaries and Expenses	3,361	6
Washington, D.C.	749	1
Field Service	2,377	4
District Offices	235	*
Education of Indians	11,043	18
Fulfilling Treaties and Agreements	8,424	14
Conservation of Health	7,452	12
Navajo-Hopi Service	6,155	10
Buildings and Utilities	5,157	9
Power Systems and Irrigation Projects	4,808	8
Alaska Native Service	4,318	7
Roads	3,655	6
Interest on Indian Trust Funds	1,163	2
Forest and Range Management	945	2
Agriculture and Stock Raising	830	1
Welfare of Indians	730	1
Supplies	694	1
Flood and Disaster Relief	527	1
Loans and Land Acquisition	458	1
Law and Order	114	*
Arts and Crafts	41	*
Total	59,875	100

Note:
        * Less than 1%.

Source: The Budget of the United States Government for the Fiscal Year
         Ending June 30, 1951 (Washington, D.C.: U.S. Government Printing
         Office, 1950), pp. A73-A74.

Table 6.12
Expenditures, Bureau of Indian Affairs, 1954–1969
(in Thousands of Dollars)

	1954		1959		1964		1969	
	EXPENDITURES	% OF TOTAL	EXPENDITURES	% OF TOTAL	EXPENDITURES	% OF TOTAL	EXPENDITURES	% OF TOTAL
Education and Welfare Services	49,100	60	58,815	46	89,020	44	147,234	56
Resources Management	12,622	15	19,160	15	37,630	18	54,884	21
Construction	17,087	21	18,447	15	45,634	22	29,266	11
Road Construction and Maintenance	—	—	13,590	11	14,970	7	18,804	7
General Administrative Expenses	3,047	4	3,760	3	4,323	2	5,125	2
Payments to Indians and Miscellaneous	9	*	13,308	10	12,637	6	7,781	3
TOTAL	81,865	100	127,080	100	204,214	100	263,094	100

Note:
  * Less than 1%.

Source: The Budget of the United States for the Fiscal Year Ending June 30, 1956, 1961, 1966, 1971.

140

Table 6.13

Expenditures, Bureau of Indian Affairs, 1974–1984

(in Thousands of Dollars)

	1974		1979		1984	
	EXPENDITURES	% OF TOTAL[1]	EXPENDITURES	% OF TOTAL[1]	EXPENDITURES	% OF TOTAL
Conservation and Land Management	25,809	4	65,161	7	118,635	11
Area and Regional Development	197,551	34	412,955	44	544,050	52
Education	189,193	32	231,815	25	257,760	24
Construction	48,917	8	128,417	14	101,108	10
Road Construction	55,604	10	69,699	7	22,667	2
Loan Funds	156	*	1,453	*	6,388	1
Miscellaneous	65,920	11	30,727	3	2,810	*
TOTAL	582,838	100	940,227	100	1,053,418	100

Note:
* Less than 1%
1. Totals may not add up to 100 because of rounding.

Source: The Budget of the United States for the Fiscal Year Ending June 30, 1976, 1981, 1986.

Table 6.14

Expenditures, Indian Health Service, 1954–1984
(in Thousands of Dollars)

	1954	1959	1964	1969	1974	1979	1984
Indian Health Service Program	21,449	42,946	60,239	92,804	216,056	465,345	720,473
Construction of Indian Health Facilities	57	4,327	5,486	14,604	—	90,110	69,432

Source: The Budget of the United States Government, FY 1961, FY 1966, FY 1971, FY 1976, FY 1981, FY 1986

Table 6.15
Expenditures from Indian Trust Funds, 1969–1984
(in Thousands of Dollars)

YEAR	AMOUNT
1969	113,927
1974	263,656
1979	292,865
1984	433,951

Source: The Budget of the United States Government,
         FY 1971, FY 1976, FY 1981, FY 1986.

Table 6.16
Road Operations, Bureau of Indian Affairs, 1939 and 1953

	1939	1953
Miles of Roads Maintained	6,739	15,191
Primary Roads	NA	6,259
Secondary Roads	NA	8,932
Needed New Roads	6,420	3,401

Source: Statistical Supplement to the Annual Report of the
         Commissioner of Indian Affairs, FY 1939; "Investi-
         gation of the Bureau of Indian Affairs," 1953, 82nd
         Congress, 2nd session, House Reports, no. 2503, serial
         11582, p. 93.

Table 6.17
Roads Built, 1939, and Roads Maintained, 1939 and 1953,
Selected Reservations, Bureau of Indian Affairs (Miles)

	ROADS BUILT FY 1939			ROADS MAINTAINED[1]	
	Graded	Surfaced	Total	1939	1953
Blackfeet, MT	5.7	3.1	8.8	82.9	178
Cherokee, NC	15.1	7.6	22.7	30.0	--
Cheyenne River, SD	19.9	12.6	32.5	79.0	219
Crow, MT	3.5	5.3	8.8	60.0	128
Flathead, MT	3.0	2.0	5.0	80.0	62
Ft. Apache, AZ	16.3	4.3	20.6	125.0	177
Ft. Peck, MT	9.5[2]	.5[2]	10.0[2]	149.0[2]	160
Hopi, AZ	--[2]	--[2]	--[2]	--[2]	114
Menominee, WI	8.4	8.4	16.8	40.5	199
Navajo, AZ-UT-NM,	23.5	--	23.5	1,627.0	2,517
Northern Cheyenne, MT	8.4	8.4	16.8	66.2	71
Papago, AZ	NA	NA	NA	NA	256
Pima, AZ	15.9	16.9	48.7	287.0	236
Pine Ridge, SD	25.5	24.7	50.2	332.1	434
Red Lake, MN	14.2	13.0	27.2	153.0	110
Rosebud, SD	13.8	7.0	20.8	108.0	163
San Carlos, AZ	13.0	--	13.0	55.0	273
Standing Rock, ND-SD	10.3	8.3	18.6	125.7	208
Turtle Mountain, ND	6.5	13.8	20.3	51.7	122
United Peblos, NM	11.2	6.3	17.5	409.0	892
Wind River, WY	22.0	14.0	36.0	44.1	222
Yakima, WA	7.7	--	7.7	31.4	646

Notes:
    NA - not available.
    1. Primary and secondary roads.
    2. Included in Navajo.

Source: Statistical Supplement to the Annual Report of the Commissioner of
         Indian Affairs, FY 1939; "Investigation of the Bureau of Indian
         Affairs," 1953, 82nd Congress, 2nd session, House Reports, no. 2503,
         serial 11582, pp. 93-97.

7

Health Care and Education

As the data on agency budgets and personnel presented in Chapter 6 indicate, the provision of health care and education services became highly significant areas of federal effort in Indian affairs during the twentieth century. Maintaining the health of Indian people in the face of death rates that were higher than those of any other group in the society and providing educational services to the Indian population seemed essential for the accomplishment of any other federal objectives. Health care and education have been controversial areas throughout the twentieth century, but there has been little question about the importance of either. The tables in this chapter present data on the development of Indian health services (Tables 7.1 through 7.12) and on the development of Indian educational services (Tables 7.13 through 7.22).

The provision of health care to American Indians began with European contact. Indeed, showing that European medicine could produce better results than traditional Indian medicine was an important objective of whites who attempted to dominate American Indian communities. The provision of medical service and medicines was often guaranteed to Indians in treaties. The Snyder Act of 1921 designated health care as a service to be provided on a routine basis to Indian people by the federal government.[1] Very little progress was made toward developing a system of health care for Indian people during the nineteenth century. No nationwide Indian medical service was organized; nor was any consistency achieved in the health care provided to the Indian people on the various reservations.

Table 7.1 presents some data on hospitals and health employees in the Indian Service between 1888 and 1926. (Additional data on medical employees in the Indian Service, 1865-1897, may be found in Table 6.3.

Table 6.4 includes data on physicians in the Indian Service in 1903). Despite a fairly large number of physicians, necessitated by the provision of at least one physician at each of the sixty-odd reservations, the government operated few hospitals during the nineteenth century. By 1900, there were only five government hospitals, with a total of twenty-five nurses and fifteen other hospital employees. During the twentieth century, however, the number of hospitals oprerated by the Indian service increased dramatically, reaching eighty-five in 1981. The number of physicians employed doubled, there was a fourfold increase in the number of nurses, and the number of other hospital employees increased ten times. This expansion was in response to the discovery of widespread morbidity in the Indian population in the early twentieth century, particularly the high incidence of tuberculosis and trachoma, diseases that affected all groups in the population but American Indians with much more virulence (see Chapter 5).

By the 1920s, the Bureau of Indian Affairs had begun to cooperate with the United States Public Health Service, which supplied physicians to the Indian Service and provided technical assistance. The number of Indian hospitals and available beds increased. However, the increases did not continue during the 1930s and 1940s. Expenditures for health care rose, but health remained a fairly constant proportion of the Bureau of Indian Affairs budget, around 12 percent to 13 percent (Tables 6.10 and 6.11). In 1955, the responsibility for Indian health care was transferred from the Bureau of Indian Affairs to the Public Health Service. An administrative unit known as the Division of Indian Health was created to provide direct and contract medical care to Indian people. Subsequently, the name of this unit was changed to the present Indian Health Service. Tables 7.2 through 7.12 provide data on Indian Health Service operations.

Table 7.2 presents data on the number of Indian hospitals, the average daily patient load, and the total number of outpatient visits to IHS facilities between 1954 and 1972. The number of hospitals operated by the Indian Health Service declined slightly during this period. The average daily patient load declined rapidly as the result of a successful effort to reduce the average length of hospitalization in IHS hospitals. The total number of outpatient visits to IHS facilities more than doubled, from 491,000 in 1954, the year before the Public Health Service assumed responsibility for Indian health, to over 1,275,000 in 1972. Some of the hospitals included in the data in Table 7.2 were tuberculosis hospitals. Table 7.3 presents data on the number of turberculosis hospitals included in Table 7.2 and the average daily patient load in those hospitals. The average daily patient load declined dramatically and the number of tuberculosis hospitals was reduced from four to two by 1972.

The decline in average daily patient load for tuberculosis patients was largely the result of decreased morbidity and improvements in the outpatient management of tuberculosis achieved during the period.

In addition to hospitals and outpatient clinics operated by the Indian Health Service, a significant part of the Indian Health Service budget has been for contract medical care, care provided by non-IHS physicians and hospitals to Indians living in reservation communities without IHS facilities and to Indians requiring care not provided in IHS facilities. Table 7.4 presents the average daily patient load for Indians hospitalized under the contract care program in three categories, general medical and surgical patients, tuberculosis patients, and neuropsychiatric patients. The use of contract care for general patients increased during the period while there were significant declines achieved in the hospitalization of tuberculosis and neuropsychiatric patients.

Tables 7.5 and 7.6 present data on hospital admissions to Indian Health Service, contract, and tribal hospitals for selected years between 1955 and 1985 and the average daily patient load at these hospitals. The size of the average daily patient load in some cases differs slightly from the figures reported in Tables 7.2 and 7.4 due to corrections made in the data. However, the broad trends are quite similar. Table 7.6 shows that the trend toward reducing the average daily patient load continued after 1972, at both direct and contract hospitals. Beginning in 1975, the Indian Health Service began to contract with tribes to provide health care directly to tribal members under the Indian Self-Determination and Education Assistance Act of 1975.[2] Tables 7.5 and 7.6 include data on hospitalizations in tribal, direct, and contact facilities under these contracts. Table 7.5 shows that, while the average daily patient load at Indian Health Service, direct, and contract hospitals had declined, hospital admissions increased, reaching a maximum in the late 1970s. Thus, shorter patient stays account for most of the decline in the average daily patient load.

Another Indian Health Service program has involved funding urban Indian health projects in urban communities with large numbers of American Indian people. In 1984, the Indian Health Service supported thirty-seven urban Indian Health programs. Table 7.7 presents data on the workload of urban Indian health programs supported by IHS between 1979 and 1985, broken down into the categories of medical services, dental services, community services, and other services. A significant aspect of the urban Indian health program is the provision of a broad range of nonmedical community services, including paralegal counseling and advocacy, housing counseling, food and lodging for the homeless, financial assistance, ex-offender rehabilitation, recreation, and clothing. Thus, urban Indian health programs are important not only because they provide health care but also because of the wide range of social services provided to urban Indian populations. (For data on the urbanization of the Indian population, see Chapter 4.)

Tables 7.8 and 7.9 present data on the dental and sanitation programs of the Indian Health Service. Dental services provided by the Indian Health Service have increased dramatically since the IHS took over responsibility for Indian health in 1955 (Table 7.8). The sanitation program, provided under the Indian Sanitation Act of 1959, supplies water and waste facilities to American Indian homes.[3] Since 1960, the program has had a major role in the reduction of morbidity and mortality from gastrointestinal disease (see Chapter 5). Table 7.9 shows the number of Indian homes receiving sanitation facilities between 1960 and 1985. It shows the number of Indian homes receiving first service sanitation and the number of homes that were upgraded by the sanitation program. In the twenty-five years between 1960 and 1985, nearly 150,000 Indian homes received some service from the sanitation program.

Table 7.10 summarizes data on IHS accomplishments presented in Chapter 5. It shows reductions in Indian death rates for specific causes of death and documents the increased use of health services by American Indians. Table 7.11 provides data on Indian Health Service employees in 1984 and Table 7.12 summarizes data on the hospitals and other facilities operated by the Indian Health Service in 1985.

During the twentieth century, Indian health care expanded from a hospital-based medical model of service to a broad-based program that includes the provision of dental services and sanitation facilities and the provision of services through Indian Health Service facilities, contract care providers, and tribal and urban Indian providers. The number of persons served as a result increased; the impact on the health of Indian people can be traced in the data provided in Chapter 5.

Tables 7.13 through 7.22 present data on Indian educational programs. During the nineteenth century, Indian education was viewed as a significant part of the federal government's effort to acculturate or "civilize" the Indian people. Boarding schools were preferred to day schools because they provided a more comprehensive opportunity to affect the development of Indian children by separating the child from parents and other relatives. During the twentieth century Indian education has been seen as the key to achieving such federal goals as occupational success, urban relocation, and self-determination. Schools have been provided under the auspices of the Bureau of Indian Affairs, local school boards, and tribes.

Table 7.13 presents data on Indian schools operated by mission societies in 1834. Most Indian education was in the hands of Christian mission societies during the first half of the nineteenth century. Much of this activity was supported by allowances from the "Civilization Fund," established by an appropriation in 1819 and renewed annually by Congress until 1873.[4] Table 7.13 shows for each mission society operating Indian schools in 1834 the number of schools supported, the number of teachers and pupils, and the society's allowance from the civilization fund.

Table 7.14 presents data gathered by Alice C. Fletcher on Indian schools and students between 1825 and 1886. The table is incomplete; in particular, Fletcher was unable to find adequate data for the years between 1849 and 1860. In addition, reporting in many of those years left much to be desired. The superintendents of schools sometimes reported children enrolled who were not in attendance; at other times, they failed to make the reports. The Indian school system grew gradually during the nineteenth century, both in number of schools and in number of pupils taught. By the 1880s, large numbers of Indian students were enrolled in reservation boarding schools and in a few boarding schools off the reservation as well.

Enrollments in Indian schools do not give a particularly valid impression of the impact of Indian educational programs, particularly in the nineteenth century. Superintendents of Indian schools complained that students were frequently away from classes, that students did not participate in educational activities, and that parents interfered with the educational program. These problems were thought to be particularly serious in day schools, which accounts in part for the preference of Indian Service educators for boarding schools in the late nineteenth century. Average attendance is a better indicator than enrollment of the effects of nineteenth-century Indian schools. Table 7.15 presents data on the number of schools and the average attendance of Indian students for selected years between 1882 and 1917. Boarding schools and day schools are reported as is the percentage of students attending each type of school. Although the number of boarding schools was approximately equal to the number of day schools, the vast majority of students attended boarding schools, as large a proportion as 85 percent in the first decade of the twentieth century. This was in part because, while day schools may have had higher enrollments, the average attendence was relatively low. It was also in part the result of a decision to construct large and presumably more efficient boarding schools.

By the 1920s, enrolling Indian students in public schools had become a major objective of the Bureau of Indian Affairs. Indian attendance with non-Indians in the public schools, it was thought, would hasten Indian integration into the general society. During the 1920s, the Bureau of Indian Affairs contracted with public school districts to enroll Indian students; this practice was formalized with the passage of the Johnson-O'Malley Act of 1934, which made it possible for the Bureau of

Indian Affairs to contract with a state government for the provision of educational, health, or social services to Indian people within the state.[5] Under Johnson-O'Malley contracts, the state would pass federal funds on to local school districts. Federal funds were to be used to support the education of Indian students.

Table 7.16 presents data on Indian enrollments in Bureau of Indian Affairs schools, public schools, and other schools, primarily mission schools and other private schools, for the years 1912 to 1952. The proportion of students in BIA boarding and day schools declined from more than 50 percent in 1912 to 37 percent in 1952. Indian public school enrollment increased, exceeding 50 percent for most years after 1922. However, the number of students enrolled in BIA boarding schools remained fairly constant in numbers if not in proportions for most of the period. The exception was the years 1938 and 1943, when John Collier, who promoted the expansion of community day schools, was Commissioner of Indian Affairs.[6] In these years, boarding schools enrolled around 20,000 Indian students. Despite efforts to enroll Indian students in the public schools, the number and proportion of Indian students actually attending public schools declined after 1932, while enrollment in mission and other schools was fairly stable.

In large part, increased boarding school enrollments between 1943 and 1952 were the result of efforts to extend educational services to Navajos and Hopis under the Navajo-Hopi Rehabilitation Act, which provided for in the construction of large boarding schools to serve Navajo children, such as the Intermountain School in Brigham City, Utah.[7] Boarding schools seemed essential because of the large size of the Navajo reservation. Table 7.17 presents data on Indian school enrollments in BIA, public, and other schools for selected years between 1957 and 1979. The number of students in BIA boarding schools remained fairly constant, while the proportion declined and public school enrollments mushroomed. By 1979, nearly 90 percent of all Indian students were attending public schools.

Providing postsecondary educational opportunities has become an increasingly significant activity of the Bureau of Indian Affairs. Tables 7.18 and 7.19 present data on postsecondary education activities of the Bureau of Indian Affairs. Table 7.18 presents data on higher education grants awarded by the Bureau of Indian Affairs between 1952 and 1972 as reported in the *Budget of the United States* for selected fiscal years between 1954 and 1974. The number of grants awarded to higher education students increased from fifty-six in 1952 to over 12,000 by 1972, resulting in a large expansion in the Indian college student population and in increased opportunities for Indians to move into occupations requiring a college degree. (Data on training grants awarded during this period under the relocation program are provided in Tables 4.9 and 4.10.) Table 7.19 presents data on career development and continuing education programs of the Bureau of Indian Affairs between 1973 and 1983. Both higher education and adult education grants are reported, along with the funds expended annually under the career development and continuing education programs. Higher education grants continued to increase during the 1970s; by the 1980s, significant numbers of these grants were being provided to students in tribally controlled community colleges. Adult education programs, which continued the vocational education programs of the relocation program, were more stable and by the 1980s had declined somewhat. These programs also included grants for students in tribally controlled programs by 1983.

Tables 7.20 through 7.22 present data on educational accomplishments, based on data gathered at the decennial censuses. Table 7.20 presents data on illiteracy, inability to speak English, and school attendance for American Indians at the decennial censuses of 1910 and 1930. Illiteracy and inability to speak English declined dramatically between those years and the proportion of Indian people attending schools increased from more than 50 percent to slightly more than 60 percent. Table 7.21 shows the median school years completed by American Indians by sex and place of residence at the censuses of 1950, 1960, and 1970. Median educational levels increased for all groups between 1950 and 1970, more rapidly for urban Indians than for those living in rural areas. Since these were also the years of the relocation program and of rapidly increasing Indian urbanization (see Chapter 4), this may reflect the migration of more highly educated persons to cities rather than any effect of urban life. Table 7.22 presents detailed educational characteristics for American Indians, Eskimos, and Aleuts age twenty-five years and over in 1980. The median years of school completed by American Indians had increased from over ten years in 1970 to 12.2 years in 1980. Over half of all American Indian people twenty-five years of age and over in 1980 were high school graduates. In addition, significant numbers of Indian men and women had attended college and had completed at least four years. Educational levels were roughly comparable for Aleuts and somewhat less high for Eskimos.

As in health care, by the 1980s a wide variety of educational services were provided under a variety of auspices including the Bureau of Indian Affairs, contract, grant, and tribal schools. Another development, not shown in the tables, has been the development of urban Indian-controlled schools in cities with large American Indian populations.

Despite advances in Indian health care and educational services, significant problems remain. Many of the issues have to do with the control of health care and educational programs. An underlying problem is the continued lack of equity between American Indians and other Americans in terms of educational accomplishment and health status. To what extent this can be resolved by changes in the health care system and the educational system alone remains to be seen.

Available health care and educational data in the nineteenth century is of doubtful accuracy for many of the reasons discussed in other chapters. Health care and educational data were gathered by Indian agents and agency staffs who often were not in close contact with Indian people and who may have had significant interests in adjusting the data. What data are available can be found in the *Annual Reports* of the Commissioner of Indian Affairs before 1906. The data vary in comprehensiveness and detail but most *Annual Reports* present data for agencies in addition to the aggregate data on health services and education. For the twentieth century, educational statistics are reported in the *Annual Reports* of the Commissioner of Indian Affairs, in the Statistical Supplements to the Commissioner's annual report (1938-1946), and, for recent years, in an annual publication, *Statistics Concerning Indian Education* (1957-1979). All of these sources present reservation-level data.

Health care statistics are inadequate before 1955. Some data may be found in Laurence F. Schmeckebier, *The Office of Indian Affairs* (1927) and Lewis Meriam and others, *The Problem of Indian Administration* (1928). For years after 1955, the publications of the United States Public Health Service are quite valuable, particularly the *Chart Series Books,* published periodically by the Indian Health Service. The report of the Office of Technology Assessment, *Indian Health Care* (1986) contains much valuable data on the IHS program.

The best recent source on Indian health care is the report of the Office of Technology Assessment, *Indian Health Care* (1986), mentioned in the preceding paragraph. Historians have devoted very little attention to the history of Indian health care. An exception is Diane Therese Putney's unpublished dissertation, "Fighting the Scourge: American Indian Morbidity and Federal Indian Policy, 1897-1928," Ph.D. dissertation, Marquette University, Milwaukee, 1980.

Alice C. Fletcher's *Indian Education and Civilization* (1888) is a useful and comprehensive statement. Evelyn C. Adams, *American Indian Education* (1946) is a useful history, supplanted, for the twentieth century, by Margaret Szasz, *Education and the American Indian: The Road to Self-Determination, 1928-1973* (1974). The report of the Special Senate Subcommittee on Indian Education, *Indian Education: A National Tragedy, A National Challenge* (1969), is useful. Brewton Berry completed a survey of the educational literature on American Indians for the subcommittee titled *The Education of American Indians* (1969).

NOTES

1. The Snyder Act of 1921, U.S., *Statutes at Large,* vol. 42, p. 208.

2. The Indian Self-Determination and Education Assistance Act of 1975 (Public Law 93-638), U.S., *Statutes at Large,* vol. 88, p. 2203.

3. The Indian Sanitation Act of 1959 (Public Law 86-121), U.S., *Statutes at Large,* vol. 73, p. 267.

4. Paul Stuart, "Bureau of Indian Affairs," in Donald R. Whitnah, ed., *Government Agencies* (Westport, Connecticut: Greenwood Press, 1983), p. 16.

5. The Johnson-O'Malley Act of 1934, U.S., *Statutes at Large* vol. 48, p. 596.

6. Margaret Szasz, *Education and the American Indian: The Road to Self-Determination, 1928-1973* (Albuquerque: University of New Mexico Press, 1974), p. 61.

7. See Peter Iverson, *The Navajo Nation* (Albuquerque: University of New Mexico Press, 1981), p. 62.

TABLES

Table 7.1
Hosptials and Health Employees, Indian Service, 1888–1926

FISCAL YEAR	HOSPITALS OPERATED	CAPACITY (BEDS)	PHYSICIANS[1]	NURSES	HOSPITAL EMPLOYEES	FIELD MATRONS
1888	4	NR	NR	NR	NR	NR
1900	5	NR	83	25	15	21
1911	50	1268	NR	NR	NR	NR
1916	81	2283	NR	NR	NR	NR
1921	85	NR	168	99	155	75
1926	91[2]	2750	194	132	229	37

Notes:
    NR – Not Reported
    1. Includes contract physicians
    2. Includes Rooms in Dormitories used for ill pupils.

Source: Lawrence F. Schmeckebier, The Office of Indian Affairs: Its
         History, Activities, and Organization (Baltimore: The Johns
         Hopkins Press, 1927), p. 232.

Table 7.2
Hospitals and Outpatient Visits, Indian Health Service, 1954–1972

FISCAL YEAR	NUMBER OF HOSPITALS	AVERAGE DAILY PATIENT LOAD (inpatient)	TOTAL OUTPATIENT VISITS
1954	---	2,530	491,107
1955	56	2,534	496,853
1956	56	2,663	563,589
1957	56	2,785	657,474
1958	54	2,573	574,235
1959	54	2,264	605,677
1960	50	2,232	659,410
1961	50	2,120	686,551
1962	50	2,334	673,192
1963	50	2,377	721,678
1964	49	2,316	742,383
1965	49	2,244	757,512
1966	51	2,149	788,466
1967	51	2,057	849,807
1968	51	2,003	926,640
1969	51	1,849	982,187
1970	51	1,729	1,068,820
1971	51	1,627	1,202,027
1972	51	1,626	1,275,726

Note:
  Includes tuberculosis hospitals and tuberculosis inpatients. For
  separate tuberculosis hospitalization statistics, see Table 7.3.

Source: The Budget of the United States Government of the Fiscal
  Year Ending June 30, 1956–1974.

Table 7.3
Tuberculosis Hospitals and Patients, Indian Health Service, 1954–1972

FISCAL YEAR	NUMBER OF TUBERCULOSIS HOSPITALS	AVERAGE DAILY PATIENT LOAD
1954	—	1,223
1955	4	509
1956	4	535
1957	4	555
1958	4	484
1959	3	784
1960	2	618
1961	3	509
1962	3	499
1963	3	488
1964	2	412
1965	2	353
1966	2	258
1967	2	173
1968	2	152
1969	2	125
1970	2	107
1971	2	63
1972	2	40

Source: The Budget of the United States Government for the Fiscal Year Ending June 30, 1956–1974.

Table 7.4
Contract Care, Average Daily Patient Load, Indian Health Service, 1954–1972

FISCAL YEAR	AVERAGE DAILY PATIENT LOAD (INPATIENTS)			
	GENERAL PATIENTS	TUBERCULOSIS PATIENTS	NEUROPSYCHIATRIC PATIENTS	TOTAL
1954	100	600	214	914
1955	152	810	203	1,165
1956	278	1,052	204	1,534
1957	302	899	219	1,420
1958	372	475	219	1,066
1959	414	279	221	914
1960	430	265	215	910
1961	418	215	222	855
1962	464	231	210	905
1963	491	184	223	898
1964	504	172	219	895
1965	490	183	210	883
1966	473	227	188	888
1967	449	203	161	813
1968	418	167	159	744
1969	425	117	162	704
1970	398	98	128	624
1971	390	50	110	550
1972	440	20	86	546

Source: The Budget of the United States Government for the Fiscal Year Ending June 30, 1956–1974.

Table 7.5
Hospital Admissions, IHS and Tribal Direct and Contract Hospitals,
Fiscal Years 1955–1985

Fiscal Year	INDIAN HEALTH SERVICE Total	Direct	Contract [1]	Tribal	Total IHS and Tribal Admissions
1955	50,143	42,762	7,381	–	50,143
1960	76,754	56,874	19,880	–	76,754
1965	91,744	67,744	24,000	–	91,744
1970	92,710	67,877	24,833	–	92,710
1971	94,945	70,729	24,216	–	94,945
1972	102,472	76,054	26,418	–	102,472
1973	102,350	75,245	27,105	–	102,350
1974	103,853	73,402	30,451	–	103,853
1975	105,735	74,594	31,141	–	105,735
1976	106,461	76,382	30,079	–	106,461
1977	110,025	78,424	31,601	–	110,025
1978	112,203	77,567	34,636	–	112,203
1979	106,329	75,174	31,155	940	107,269
1980	106,992	77,798	29,194	1,250	108,242
1981	107,087	81,387	25,700	2,266	109,353
1982	102,343	77,070	25,273	2,075	104,418
1983	102,961	78,027	24,934	1,845	104,806
1984	99,849	77,522	22,327	2,994	102,843
1985	98,245	78,423	19,822	10,532[2]	108,777

Notes: 1. Number of discharges used as estimate for number of admissions.
       2. Includes 6,854 contract admissions.

Source: Indian Health Service, Chart Series Book, April 1986 (Washington, D.C.: U.S. Government Printing Office, 1986) p. 54.

Table 7.6
**Average Daily Patient Load, Indian Health Service and Tribal Direct
and Contract Hospitals, Fiscal Years 1955–1985**

INDIAN HEALTH SERVICE

Fiscal Year	Total	Direct	Contract	Tribal	Grand Total ADPL
1955	3,711	2,531	1,180	–	3,711
1960	3,142	2,232	910	–	3,142
1965	3,127	2,244	883	–	3,127
1970	2,353	1,729	624	–	2,353
1971	2,177	1,627	550	–	2,177
1972	2,172	1,626	546	–	2,172
1973	2,013	1,499	514	–	2,013
1974	1,840	1,376	464	–	1,840
1975	1,768	1,330	438	–	1,768
1976	1,736	1,299	437	–	1,736
1977	1,710	1,302	408	–	1,710
1978	1,723	1,256	467	–	1,723
1979	1,569	1,192	377	17	1,586
1980	1,576	1,178	398	18	1,594
1981	1,550	1,194	356	25	1,575
1982	1,460	1,121	339	28	1,488
1983	1,449	1,119	330	28	1,477
1984	1,353	1,072	281	39	1,392
1985	1,286	1,052	234	118[1]	1,404

Notes: 1. Includes 77 patients in tribal contract hospitals.

Source: Indian Health Service, Chart Series Book, April 1986 (Washington, D.C.: U.S. Government Printing Office, 1986), p. 55.

Table 7.7
Urban Indian Health Program Workload[1] and Appropriation, Fiscal Years 1979–1985

FISCAL YEAR	TOTAL WORKLOAD	COMMUNITY SERVICES	MEDICAL	DENTAL	OTHER[2]	APPROPRIATION (MILLIONS)
1985	509,607	145,068	175,536	53,369	135,634	$9,800
1984	507,055	106,191	162,563	51,800	186,501	$9,000
1983	534,157	126,814	165,747	52,905	188,691	$6,000
1982	582,567	142,233	185,502	65,043	189,789	$8,160
1981	665,980	209,207	185,053	57,887	213,883	$8,900
1980	564,451	236,383	153,402	54,843	119,823	$8,000
1979	374,673	154,947	108,654	33,893	77,188	$7,270

Notes:

1. Number of services provided – Fiscal Years 1979–1983, number of patient encounters – Fiscal Years 1984–1985.

2. Includes family planning, mental health and alcoholism counseling, health and nutrition education, social services, etc.

Source: Indian Health Service, Chart Series Book, April 1986 (Washington, D.C.: U.S. Government Printing Office, 1986), p. 53.

Table 7.8
Dental Services Provided to Indians, Indian Health Service, Fiscal Years 1955-1985

NUMBER OF SERVICES PROVIDED

Fiscal Year	Total	INDIAN HEALTH SERVICE Direct	Contract[1]	Tribal & Urban
1955	180,000	180,000	–	–
1956	219,353	219,353	–	–
1957	249,048	249,048	–	–
1958	282,372	282,372	–	–
1959[2]	328,613	283,206	45,407	–
1960[2]	364,423	307,248	57,175	–
1961	403,528	348,776	54,752	–
1962	421,597	364,988	56,609	–
1963	453,906	398,452	55,454	–
1964	525,010	462,981	62,029	–
1965[2]	572,079	495,006	77,073	–
1966[2]	570,779	502,710	68,069	–
1967	626,458	545,509	80,949	–
1968	681,745	613,084	68,661	–
1969	703,232	634,479	68,753	–
1970	737,206	646,580	90,626	–
1971	776,168	684,612	91,556	–
1972	844,724	718,176	126,548	–
1973	863,057	728,909	134,148	–
1974	927,701	775,747	151,954	–
1975	946,722	745,831	200,891	–
1976	975,647	798,709	176,938	–
1977	1,037,640	823,328	214,312	–
1978[2]	1,099,019	885,019	214,000	–
1979[2]	1,618,383	1,239,108	215,997	163,278
1980	1,833,206	1,357,809	216,574	258,823
1981	1,801,982	1,319,913	182,880	299,189
1982	1,666,263	1,202,422	153,030	311,341
1983	1,907,336	1,325,187	149,741	432,408
1984	2,011,326	1,348,599	224,918	437,809
1985	1,914,820	1,276,623	210,508	427,689

Notes: 1. Beginning with FY 1979 this category excludes contract services purchased from the private sector by Tribes.

2. Data systems were modified in 1960, 1966 and 1978. In 1978 the IHS began to use the dental services coding list adopted by the American Dental Association (ADA). The ADA list identified individual clinical services. Previously the IHS had reported specified clinical services combined into major dental service groupings. Excluded from the 1978 count are diagnostic and adjunctive services. Excluded from the 1979-1985 clinical counts are diagnostic services other than examinations, revisits and non-clinical adjunctive services. The new coding procedure was used throughout the IHS during only the last nine months of FY 1978 but during all of FY 1979-1985. By January 1979, the personnel completing the new forms were thoroughly familiar with the revised procedure and thus their reporting is considered to be more accurate and complete.

Source: Indian Health Service, Chart Series Book, April 1986 (Washington, D.C.: U.S. Government Printing Office, 1986), p. 64.

Table 7.9
Indian Homes Receiving Sanitation Facilities, Indian Health Service,
Fiscal Years 1960-1985

Fiscal Year	Total First Service	Total Upgrade	First Service & Upgrade
1960	60	—	60
1961	2,607	26	2,633
1962	3,450	5	3,455
1963	5,488	376	5,864
1964	6,089	291	6,380
1965	4,075	386	4,461
1966	4,155	265	4,420
1967	4,064	1,099	5,163
1968	4,984	37	5,021
1969	6,377	700	7,077
1970	6,792	936	7,728
1971	5,142	1,735	6,877
1972	8,976	1,958	10,934
1973	8,141	1,536	9,677
1974	6,069	2,356	8,425
1975	6,043	2,506	8,549
1976	7,410	2,456	9,866
1977	14,275	7,860	22,135
1978	3,235	288	3,523
1979	7,539	1,340	8,879
1980	6,465	2,550	9,015
1981	6,200	2,692	8,892
1982	7,709	887	8,596
1983	5,251	4,600	9,851
1984	3,588	3,717	7,305
1985	4,868	3,936	8,804
TOTAL	149,052	44,538	193,590

Source: Indian Health Service, Chart Series Book, April 1986 (Washington, D.C.: US. Government Printing Office, 1986), p. 65.

Table 7.10
Program Accomplishments, Indian Health Service, 1955–1982

	1955 RATE[1]	1982 RATE[1]	% DECREASE
HEALTH IMPROVEMENTS			
Death Rates:			
Infant[2]	62.7	11.0	82
Neonatal[2]	23.1	5.0	78
Postneonatal[2]	39.7	6.1	85
Maternal[3]	82.6	8.9	89
Pneumonia and influenza[4]	89.8	16.2	82
Certain conditions originating in the perinatal period[4]	67.6	9.7	86
Tuberculosis, all forms[4]	55.1	2.3	96
Gastrointestinal diseases[4]	39.2	2.9	93
Congenital malformations[4]	19.0	6.8	64
Accidents[4]	155.6	84.4	46

	FY 1955	FY 1985	% INCREASE
INCREASED USE OF SERVICES			
Hospital Admissions	50,143	108,777	117
Outpatient Visits	455,000	4,411,597	870
Dental Services	180,000	1,914,820	964

Notes:

1. Three-year rates centered in year specified.
2. Rates per 1,000 live births.
3. Rates per 100,000 live births, for 1957–1959 and 1981–1983.
4. Rates per 100,000 population.

Source: Indian Health Service, Chart Series Book, April 1986 (Washington, D.C.: U.S. Government Printing Office, 1986), p. 50.

Table 7.11
Indian Health Service Employees, Fiscal Year 1984

	INDIAN	NON-INDIAN	TOTAL
MEDICAL OFFICERS	23	666	689
DENTAL OFFICERS	9	260	269
PHYSICIAN ASSISTANTS	72	11	83
NURSES (HOSPITALS AND CLINICS)	514	1,381	1,895
NURSES (COMMUNITY AND PUBLIC HEALTH)	808	59	867
CLINICAL SUPPORT	886	847	1,733
ADMINISTRATIVE SUPPORT	3,824	982	4,806
TOTAL	6,136	4,206	10,342

Source: U.S. Congress, Office of Technology Assessment, Indian Health Care, OTA-H-290 (Washington, D.C.: U.S. Government Printing Office, 1986), p. 163.

Table 7.12
Health Facilities Operated by Indian Health Service and Tribes, 1985

	IHS	TRIBES
Hospitals	46	5
Outpatient Facilities	137	284
Health Centers	65	62
School Health Centers	6	1
Health Stations	66	48
Alaska Village Clinics	—	173
Treatment Locations*	201	36

Note:
*Places where clinical services are provided but no fixed IHS or tribal health care facility is available.

Source: Indian Health Service, Chart Series Book, April 1986 (Washington, D.C.: U.S. Government Printing Office, 1986), p. 11.

Table 7.13

Mission Societies and Indian Schools in 1834

MISSION SOCIETY	NUMBER OF SCHOOLS	NUMBER OF TEACHERS	NUMBER OF PUPILS	ALLOWANCE FROM CIVILIZATION FUND
United Bretheren	1	3	20	—
American Board of Commissioners for Foreign Missions	35	98[1]	1,317	$1,690
Methodist Society	2	1[2]	47	$550
Baptist General Convention	14	17[3]	300[4]	$2,810[5]
Methodist Episcopal Church	3	7	85	—
Protestant Episcopal Church	2	7	160	$1,700[6]
Roman Catholic Church	3	4	120	$1,300
TOTAL	60	137[7]	2,049[7]	$8,950[8]

Notes:

1. Information not supplied for two out of thirty-five schools.
2. Information not supplied for one out of two schools.
3. Information not supplied for four out of fourteen schools.
4. Information not supplied for three out of fourteen schools.
5. Includes $810 for Choctaw Academy in Kentucky.
6. For buildings at Green Bay.
7. Incomplete.
8. Includes $900 paid to Indian tribes and individuals.

Source: "Regulating the Indian Department," May 20, 1834, in 23rd Congress, 1st session, House Reports, no. 474, serial 26, pp. 69-70.

Table 7.14
Indian Schools and Indian Pupils, 1825–1886

Year	Number of Schools	Number of Pupils
1825	38	1,159
1826	40	1,248
1827	40	1,291
1828	40	1,291
1828	45	1,460
1830	52	1,601
1831	43	1,215
1832	51	1,979
1833	58	1,835
1836	52	1,381
1838	46	1,425
1839	44	2,104
1840	29	975
1842	52	2,132
1844	45	2,644
1845	58	2,508
1848	103	3,682
1861	162	5,950
1862	75	2,776
1863	89	2,643
1864	47	1,458
1865	48	2,165
1866	69	2,872
1867[1]	90	4,041
1868[2]	109	4,633
1869	20	1,200
1870	60	3,095
1871	256	5,981
1872	260	6,180
1873	285	9,026
1874	345	10,958
1875	329	10,501
1876	344	11,328
1877	330	11,515
1878	366	12,222
1879	354	13,443
1880	393	13,338
1881	383	14,292
1882[3]	391	14,394
1883	284	15,118
1884[4]	433	19,593
1885	261	9,314
1886	531	21,231

Notes: 1. New York schools not included.
2. New York and five civilized tribes schools not included.
3. Creek day schools not included.
4. Five civilized tribes schools not included.

Source: Alice C. Fletcher, Indian Education and Civilization, 48th Congress, 2nd Session, Senate Executive Document No. 95, serial 2264 (Washington, D.C.: U.S. Government Printing Office, 1888), p. 197.

Table 7.15
Indian Service Schools and Average Attendance, Selected Years, 1882–1917

YEAR	BOARDING SCHOOLS			DAY SCHOOLS			TOTAL AVERAGE ATTENDANCE
	NUMBER	AVERAGE ATTENDANCE	PERCENT OF TOTAL	NUMBER	AVERAGE ATTENDANCE	PERCENT OF TOTAL	
1882	71	3,077	65	76	1,637	35	4,714
1887	117	8,020	76	110	2,500	24	10,520
1892	149	12,422	82	126	2,745	18	15,167
1897	145	15,026	80	143	3,650	20	18,676
1902	163	20,576	85	136	3,544	15	24,120
1907	173	21,825	85	168	3,977	15	25,802
1912*	170	20,973	80	242	5,308	20	26,281
1917*	160	20,368	81	234	4,925	19	25,294

Note: *Includes schools of the Five Civilized Tribes

Source: Secretary of the Interior, Annual Reports, 1913, 1917.

Table 7.16

Indian School Enrollment: Indian, Public, and Other Schools,
Selected Years, 1912–1952

| YEAR | BIA SCHOOLS | | | | PUBLIC SCHOOLS | | OTHER SCHOOLS[1] | | TOTAL |
| | BOARDING | | DAY | | | | | | |
	NUMBER	PERCENT	NUMBER	PERCENT	NUMBER	PERCENT	NUMBER	PERCENT	
1912	17,924	39	6,417	14	17,011	37	4,779	10	46,131
1917	22,200	35	6,558	10	29,173	46	5,837	9	63,768
1922	18,674	29	5,548	9	34,301	53	6,420	10	64,943
1927	21,232	32	4,390	7	34,124	51	7,321	11	67,067
1932	21,756	26	5,250	6	48,834	59	7,570	9	83,410
1938	10,181	16	13,797	21	33,645[2]	52	7,543	12	65,166
1943[3]	11,664	15	21,559	29	34,613	46	7,409	10	75,245
1952[3]	19,739	20	16,957	17	52,854	53	10,162	10	99,712

Notes:

1. Mission and other private schools.
2. Excludes an estimated 10,000 Indian students enrolled in off-reservation public schools.
3. Children 6 to 18 years of age only.

Source: Secretary of the Interior, Annual Reports, 1912, 1917, 1922, 1927 1932, 1938; Statistical Supplement to the Annual Report of the Commissioner of Indian Affairs, 1943; "Investigation of Bureau of Indian Affairs," 1953, House Report No. 2503, 82nd Congress, 2nd Session, Serial 11582, p.58.

Table 7.17
Indian School Enrollment: BIA, Public, and Other Schools, Selected Years, 1957–1979

INDIAN SCHOOL ENROLLMENT: BUREAU OF INDIAN AFFAIRS (BIA), PUBLIC, AND OTHER SCHOOLS SELECTED YEARS, 1957-1979

YEAR	BIA SCHOOLS				PUBLIC SCHOOLS		OTHER SCHOOLS		TOTAL
	BOARDING		DAY						
	NUMBER	PERCENT	NUMBER	PERCENT	NUMBER	PERCENT	NUMBER	PERCENT	
1957	21,665	17	16,630	13	76,250	61	11,010	9	125,555
1960	21,352	16	16,025	12	84,650	63	11,289	8	133,316
1965	24,481	18	18,641	14	82,302	61	8,640	6	134,064
1970	28,794	15	20,365	11	126,859	68	10,850	6	186,869
1974	25,841	14	21,792	11	131,912	69	10,558	6	190,103
1979	20,192	9	21,406	10	171,920	78	6,413*	3	219,300

Note: * Excludes students in noncontract mission and other private schools.

Source: Bureau of Indian Affairs, Statistics Concerning Indian Education, FY 1957, FY 1960, FY 1965, FY 1970, FY 1974, FY 1979.

Table 7.18
Higher Education Grants, Bureau of Indian Affairs, 1952–1972

FISCAL YEAR	NUMBER OF GRANTS AWARDED
1952	56
1953	54
1954	149
1955	214
1956	326
1957	390
1958	624
1959	731
1960	857
1961	623
1962	936
1963	963
1964	1,327
1965	1,718
1966	1,949
1967	2,040
1968	2,468
1969	3,430
1970	4,278
1971	6,447
1972	12,229

Note:
For Fiscal Years 1952–1960, grants are designated for "other institutions." For Fiscal Years 1961–1972, grants are designated for "higher education."

Source: The Budget of the United States Government for the Fiscal Year Ending June 30, 1954–1974.

Table 7.19
Career Development[1]—Higher Education and Adult Education Grants,
Bureau of Indian Affairs, 1973–1983

FISCAL YEAR	FUNDS EXPENDED (000's)	GRANTS AWARDED	
		HIGHER EDUCATION	ADULT EDUCATION
1973	7,561[2]	13,387	16,040
1974	45,941	13,717	18,949
1975	52,776	14,256	13,875
1976	34,160	15,000	18,000
1977	36,792	17,000	18,350
1978	35,308	20,000	18,350
1979	35,533	21,000	18,350
1980	45,272	20,000	18,500
1981	49,484	16,574	18,500
1982	N.R.	16,800	13,859
1983	N.R.	18,138[3]	14,592[4]

Notes:

N.R. — not reported
1. Program designated "Career Development," 1973–1975, "Continuing Education," 1976–1983.
2. An additional $50,990,000 expended for Direct Indian Education operations.
3. Includes 3,080 grants for students in tribally controlled community colleges.
4. Includes 1,701 grants for students in post-secondary education programs.

Source: The Budget of the United States Government, FY 1975 through FY 1985.

Table 7.20

Illiteracy, Inability to Speak English, and School Attendance,
American Indians, 1910–1930

| | PERCENT OF AMERICAN INDIANS 10 YEARS OLD AND OVER | | | | PERCENT OF AMERICAN INDIANS 5 TO 20 YEARS OLD | |
| | ILLITERATE | | UNABLE TO SPEAK ENGLISH | | ATTENDING SCHOOL | |
YEAR	U.S.	ALASKA	U.S.	ALASKA	U.S.	ALASKA
1910	45.3	N.R.	31.3	56.3	50.8	N.R.
1930	25.7	44.8	17.0	30.8	60.2	48.0

Note:
    N.R. – not reported

Source: U.S. Bureau of the Census, The Indian Population of the United States
    and Alaska, 1930 (Washington, D.C.: U.S. Government Printing
    Office, 1937), pp. 130, 143, 155, 232, 236–237.

Table 7.21

Median School Years Completed, by Sex, American Indians, 1950–1970

| | Median School Years Completed | | | | | | | |
| | Male | | | | Female | | | |
	Total	Urban	Rural Nonfarm	Rural Farm	Total	Urban	Rural Nonfarm	Rural Farm
1950[1]	7.3	8.8	7.1	6.3	7.4	8.9	7.3	6.4
1960[1]	8.4	9.4	8.1	7.1	8.5	9.5	8.1	7.4
1970[2]	10.4	11.5	9.5	8.9	10.5	11.4	9.7	9.4

Notes: 1. American Indians 14 years and over
        2. American Indians 16 years and over

Source: U.S. Bureau of the Census, U.S. Census of Population: 1950. Special Reports. Nonwhite
         Population by Race, P-E No. 3B (Washington, D.C.: U.S. Government Printing Office, 1953),
         p. 3B-32; U.S. Bureau of the Census, U.S. Census of Population: 1960. Subject Reports. Nonwhite
         Population by Race, Final Report PC (2)-1C (Washington, D.C.: U.S. Government Printing Office,
         1963), p. 12; U.S. Bureau of the Census, Census of Population: 1970. Subject Reports. American
         Indians, Final Report PC (2)-1F (Washington, D.C.: U.S. Government Printing Office, 1973), pp. 36-
         39.

Table 7.22
Educational Characteristics, American Indians, Eskimos, and Aleuts, 1980 (Persons Twenty-five Years Old and Over)

Years of School Completed	American Indians	Eskimos	Aleuts
Males, 25 and over	331,081	8,599	3,304
Elementary: 0 to 4 years	26,978	2,066	272
5 to 7 years	27,860	1,014	314
8 years	26,790	770	463
High School: 1 to 3 years	59,634	841	412
4 years	100,385	2,425	1,032
College: 1 to 3 years	58,879	1,010	329
4 or more years	30,555	473	482
Percent High School Graduates	57.3	45.4	55.8
Females, 25 and over	360,371	8,722	3,381
Elementary: 0 to 4 years	28,695	1,758	246
5 to 7 years	28,498	1,243	318
8 years	30,197	949	356
High School: 1 to 3 years	77,238	1,005	398
4 years	116,453	2,490	1,274
College: 1 to 3 years	56,389	915	500
4 or more years	22,901	362	289
Percent High School Graduates	54.3	43.2	61.0
Persons, 25 years and over	691,452	17,321	6,685
Percent High School Graduates	55.8	44.3	58.4
Median years of school completed	12.2	10.4	12.2

Source: U.S Bureau of the Census, 1980 Census of the Population, Characteristics of the Population. U.S. Summary, PC80-1-C1 (Washington, D.C.: U.S Government Printing Office, 1983), p. 157.

8

Employment, Earnings, and Income

The most significant resource of any community is its people; the men and women who, through productive work, create wealth as well as continuity in community life. The potential value of individuals cannot be measured by employment earnings or income alone; indeed, these are culturally bound measures of values upheld by Western industrial societies. The economic value of workers is affected by their education, health, and geographical location. Much of United States Indian policy in the last forty years has been directed toward enhancing the economic productivity of American Indians by improving their education levels and health status and by developing economic opportunities in Indian areas or moving Indian people closer to the location of jobs and training programs.

The tables in this chapter provide statistics on the employment, earnings, and income of American Indian individuals and families. The data presented in the tables were gathered by the Bureau of the Census and by the Bureau of Indian Affairs. The data are not without problems: the Bureau of Indian Affairs gathered data somewhat inconsistently during the twentieth century. BIA data are available only for Indians living on or near recognized reservations. Census bureau data, while not confined to reservation Indians, are limited by the shifting methods employed by the Bureau of the Census for determining the ethnic status of respondents during the twentieth century. Still, the broad outlines of the picture presented by the data in this chapter are clear. American Indians have lower rates of labor force participation than other Americans, their earnings and income fall behind those of other groups, and these deficits are more pronounced for American Indians living in reservation areas than for Indians living off-reservation. These general statements must be qualified, however, because of the wide local and individual variations which occur.

Although labor force participation and the coming of a wage income and a cash economy has been a significant element in the twentieth century of history of many American Indian communities, many American Indian persons participated in the labor force throughout the twentieth century.[1] Table 8.1 shows the number and proportion of American Indians ten years of age and older who were gainfully employed at the censuses of 1910 and 1930. Labor force participation, particularly of males, was relatively high, exceeding 60 percent in each year. Female labor force participation was much lower. While both male and female Indian rates were lower than the corresponding white rates in both years, the relationship of male to female Indian labor force participation was similar to that prevailing in the general population. Table 8.2 presents labor force participation data for American Indians at the decennial censuses between 1950 and 1980. Interpretation of these data is complicated since the age of persons under examination changes from persons fourteen years of age and older in 1950 and 1960 to persons sixteen years of age and older in 1970 and 1980. However, labor force participation of American Indian males appears to have increased, with the proportion of unemployed males remaining fairly high—more than 10 percent in each census year. For females, labor force participation increased dramatically between 1950 and 1980, mirroring national trends. While female unemployment was generally lower than male unemployment, female unemployment rates were high and increased during the period.

Tables 8.3 through 8.7 present data on the occupations of American Indian workers between 1910 and 1980. Perhaps the most dramatic development during this period has been the decline in farming occupations for American Indians. Indians participated heavily in agricultural occupations, as proprietors and as agriculture laborers, in 1910 and 1930. Around 30 percent of all employed American Indians were farm proprietors in 1910 and 1930; an additional 30 percent were agricultural laborers. The overwhelming Indian participation in agriculture in the early twentieth century was particularly pronounced among men. Table 8.4 presents data on Indian farming operations in 1930. More than 25,000 Indian farm operators farmed more than three million acres, for an average farm size of more than 115 acres. Land, buildings, implements, and machinery were valued at over eighty million dollars. After mid-century, the number of farmers and farm managers, farm laborers, and farm foremen declined, while the number of American Indians in the labor force increased. The decline was quite precipitous;

by 1980, only about 6 percent of Indian males were involved in farming, forestry, and fishing occupations (Table 8.6).

In part, the decline of Indian participation in agricultural occupations was a result of Indian migration to urban areas and the resulting urbanization of the Indian population (see Chapter 4). In part, it was the result of increasing opportunities in government employment and successful economic development efforts on reservations (see chapters 6 and 9). The decline in Indian participation in agriculture mirrored general trends in the society as well. The mechanization of agriculture eliminated many farm labor jobs, which Indians, along with other disadvantaged groups in the society, had held. The decline in the number of farms in the twentieth century hit Indian farm operators harder than non-Indians because they operated smaller farms and lacked ready access to credit.[2] Urbanization is reflected in the increasing Indian participation in manufacturing occupations, while educational improvements are reflected in the increasing representation of Indians in managerial and professional specialty occupations.

Tables 8.8, 8.9, and 8.10 present data on the industry of employed American Indians by sex. Table 8.8 reports data on the employment of American Indians in the United States and Alaska in 1930 by industry and sex. A significant proportion of Indian males—nearly two-thirds—were employed in agriculture; however, 15 percent of employed Indian males worked in manufacturing in 1930. This proportion was exceeded by employed American Indian females, over 35 percent of whom worked in manufacturing in 1930. Employment of American Indians in manufacturing increased between 1960 and 1980 (Table 8.9), while employment in agriculture, forestry, and fishing declined. Indian employment in wholesale and retail trades, professional and related services, and public administration also increased during this period.

Table 8.11 and 8.12 present data on income and sources of income on reservations in the years 1933, 1939, and 1944. The most dramatic development of this decade, which includes most of the depression and World War II years, is the dramatic increase in salaries and wages as a source of income, from four and half million dollars in 1933 to nearly twenty-three million dollars eleven years later. Even so, salaries and wages accounted for 31 percent of reservation income in 1933 and less than 30 percent in 1944. Increases in income from agriculture and "unearned income," principally income from annuities, land sales, and land and mineral leases, accounted for the decline in the relative importance of wage work. The depression and war years were watershed years in Indian affairs; reservation Indians emerged from the war with increased wage-earning power, a significant stake in agriculture, and increased "unearned" income from land and mineral leases. (Data on income from land and mineral leases are presented in Chapter 9.) Table 8.13 presents data on sources of reservation earned income for the years 1969 and 1972. The data shown are for selected reservations. Unfortunately, which reservations are being included is not specified.

Data on Indian income in the post–World War II period are presented in Tables 8.14 through 8.17. Based upon data gathered by the Bureau of the Census, median incomes for individuals and families are presented. Tables 8.14 and 8.15 present data for American Indian personal income for the years 1949 through 1979. For comparative purposes, data for persons of all races are also presented. Indian income lagged significantly below the income for all persons in each of the census years, although less so for females in 1969 and 1979 than for males. Indian income was higher for urban Indian males and females than for Indian males and females living in rural farm and rural nonfarm areas.

Tables 8.16 and 8.17 present data on Indian family income for the years 1969 and 1979. Like personal income, median family income was low; the incomes of 33 percent of American Indian families in 1969 and nearly 24 percent in 1979 placed them below the poverty line.[3] These proportions were higher for rural people than for uban people, although the differences were not as great in 1979 as they had been a decade earlier. Table 8.17 provides comparable data for American Indians, Eskimos, and Aleuts by place of residence in 1979. American Indian, Eskimo, and Aleut families residing on reservations had lower incomes in 1979 than the average income for all such families or for such families living in the historic areas of Oklahoma or in the state of Alaska. However, female-headed families, which in every case had received lower family incomes than all families had lower incomes in the historic areas of Oklahoma than on reservations, although the difference was not great. In every case, American Indian, Eskimo, and Aleut families residing in the state of Alaska received higher incomes than others. Fully 42 percent of all American Indian, Eskimo, and Aleut families living on reservations had incomes below the poverty level.

The last two tables in this chapter present data on reservation unemployment. Table 8.18 presents reservation unemployment rates published by the Bureau of Indian Affairs, by BIA area, for selected years in the mid-1960s and early 1980s. Despite considerable fluctuations and inconsistencies between areas, reservation unemployment, as estimated by Bureau of Indian Affairs staff, was consistently very high. The high unemployment rate helped to explain the rather high rates of in- and out-migration on reservations. Table 8.19 presents similar data for selected reservations. Again, the reservation picture is characterized by inconsistency across reservations and by considerable fluctuation from year to year.

In conclusion, despite improvements in labor force participation, in the range of occupations and industries represented, and in earnings, American Indians remain relatively unrewarded in the employment market. Unemployment rates are high, and are much higher on reservations than in urban areas. Earnings are relatively low and the rate of poverty for American Indian families continues to be very high. Another source of income for American Indian people has been income from natural resources and from trust funds that were set up to compensate Indian people for the loss of lands ceded to the United States. These sources of income are discussed in Chapter 9.

Major sources of data on Indian employment, earnings, and income include the reports of the United States Census referred to earlier and publications of the Bureau of Indian Affairs, particularly the Bureau's *Local Estimates of Resident Indian Population and Labor Force Status*, issued periodically by the Bureau. Henry W. Hough presented some data on earnings and income in his monograph, *Development of Indian Resources* (1967) as did Keith L. Fay in *Developing Indian Employment Opportunities* (n.d. [1973?]).

The monographs by Hough and by Fay, mentioned above, provide interesting views of the thinking of Bureau of Indian Affairs and the Office of Economic Opportunity officials in the 1960s and 1970s. Alan L. Sorkin, *American Indians and Federal Aid* (1971), Sar A. Levitan and Barbara Hetrick, *Big Brother's Indian Program—With Reservations* (1971), and Sar Levitan and William P. Johnston, *Indian Giving: Federal Programs for Native Americans* (1975), discuss Indian economic development programs, including programs designed to increase employment and earnings. The problem of Indian unemployment is discussed in Lewis Meriam and others, *The Problem of Indian Administration* (1928), and by the report of the Commission on the Rights, Liberties, and Responsibilities of the American Indian, *The Indian: America's Unfinished Business* (1966), compiled by William A. Brophy and Sophie D. Aberle.

NOTES

1. For example, the work relief programs of the 1930s introduced wages and a cash economy to remote regions of the Navajo Reservation. See Donald L. Parman, *The Navajos and the New Deal* (New Haven, Connecticut: Yale University Press, 1976), p. 35.

2. Russel Lawrence Barsh, in "The Rise and Fall of Indigenous Agrarian Democracy," an unpublished paper presented at the symposium "Plains Indian Cultures: Past and Present Meanings," Lincoln, Nebraska, March 1986, suggests that federal policy, particularly the programs of the Indian New Deal, played a role in the decline of Indian agriculture.

3. On the poverty line, see Diana Karter Applebaum, "The Level of the Poverty Line: A Historical Survey," *Social Service Review* 51 (September 1977): 514-523.

TABLES

Table 8.1
Indians Gainfully Employed, 1910–1930
(Persons Ten Years of Age and Over)

	1910	1930
TOTAL		
Total 10 years and over	188,758	238,981
Gainfully employed	73,916	98,148
Percent of total	39.2	41.1
MALES		
Males 10 years and over	96,582	123,469
Gainfully employed	59,206	80,306
Percent of total	61.3	65.0
FEMALES		
Females 10 years and over	92,176	115,512
Gainfully employed	14,710	17,842
Percent of total	16.0	15.4

Source: U.S. Bureau of the Census, The Indian Population of the United States and Alaska, 1930 (Washington, D.C.: U.S. Government Printing Office, 1937), p. 199.

Table 8.2
Labor Force Participation of American Indians,[1] 1950–1980

	1950[2]	1960[2]	1970[2]	1970[3]	1980[4]
MALES					
Total	110,451	163,337	239,005	219,672	497,737
In labor force	69,619	97,197	140,880	139,339	346,419
% in labor force	63.0	59.5	58.9	63.4	69.6
Civilian labor force	68,019	93,178	133,310	131,775	333,841
Employed	59,209	78,100	117,683	116,467	286,687
Unemployed	8,810	15,078	15,627	15,308	46,884
% unemployed	13.0	16.2	11.7	11.6	14.0
Not in labor force	40,832	66,140	98,125	80,333	151,318
FEMALES					
Total	100,158	162,952	252,112	233,266	524,674
In labor force	17,016	41,495	83,372	82,394	252,207
% in labor force	17.0	25.5	33.1	35.3	48.1
Civilian labor force	16,977	41,367	83,100	82,122	250,908
Employed	15,488	36,900	74,582	73,766	220,927
Unemployed	1,489	4,467	8,518	8,356	29,981
% unemployed	8.8	10.8	10.3	10.2	11.9
Not in labor force	83,142	121,457	168,740	150,872	272,467

Notes:
1. Data based on sample.
2. American Indians, 14 years of age and over.
3. American Indians, 16 years of age and over.
4. American Indians, Eskimos, and Aleuts, 16 years of age and over

Source: U.S. Bureau of the Census, U.S. Census of Population: 1950. Special Reports. Nonwhite Population by Race, P–E No. 3B (Washington, D.C.: U.S. Government Printing Office, 1953), p. 3B–32; U.S. Bureau of the Census, U.S. Census of Population: 1960. Subject Reports. Nonwhite Population by Race, Final Report PC (2)–1C (Washington, D.C.: U.S. Government Printing Office, 1963), p. 104; U.S. Bureau of the Census, Census of Population: 1970. Subject Reports. American Indians, Final Report PC (2)–1F (Washington, D.C.: U.S. Government Printing Office, 1973), p. 86; U.S. Bureau of the Census, 1980 Census of Population. Characteristics of the Population. United States Summary, Vol. 1, pt. 1, PC 80–1–C1. (Washington, D.C.: U.S. Government Printing Office, 1983), p. 1–100.

Table 8.3
Occupations of Indian Workers, Ten Years Old and Over, 1910–1930

	1910		1930	
	Number	%	Number	%
TOTAL	73,916	100.0	98,148	100.0
Professional persons	1,284	1.7	2,355	2.4
Proprietors, managers, and officials	23,013	31.1	29,280	29.8
Farmers (owners and tenants)	21,997	29.8	28,038	28.6
Wholesale and· retail dealers	520	0.7	625	0.6
Other proprietors, managers, and officials	496	0.7	617	0.6
Clerks and kindred workers	1,027	1.4	2,494	2.5
Skilled workers and foremen	2,056	2.8	4,228	4.3
Semiskilled workers	8,052	10.9	11,755	12.0
Semiskilled workers in manufacturing	6,728	9.1	8,016	8.2
Other semiskilled workers	1,342	1.8	3,739	3.8
Unskilled workers	38,484	52.1	48,036	46.9
Agricultural laborers	26,490	35.8	28,245	28.8
Factory and building construction laborers	3,656	4.9	7,084	7.2
Other laborers	4,873	6.6	8,323	8.5
Servant classes	3,465	4.7	4,384	4.5
MALES	59,206	100.0	80,306	100.0
Professional persons	927	1.6	1,531	1.9
Proprietors, managers, and officials	21,765	36.8	27,615	34.4
Farmers (owners and tenants)	20,841	35.2	26,521	33.0
Wholesale and retail dealers	482	0.8	569	0.7
Other proprietors, managers, and officials	442	0.7	525	0.7
Clerks and kindred workers	859	1.5	1,630	2.0
Skilled workers and foremen	2,021	3.4	4,204	5.2
Semiskilled workers	1,511	2.6	4,278	5.3
Semiskilled workers in manufacturing	673	1.1	1,632	2.0
Other semiskilled workers	838	1.4	2,646	3.3
Unskilled workers	32,123	54.3	41,048	51.1
Agricultural laborers	23,293	39.3	25,124	31.3
Factory and building construction laborers	3,571	6.0	6,973	8.7
Other laborers	4,772	8.1	8,277	10.3
Servant classes	487	0.8	674	0.8
FEMALES	14,710	100.0	17,842	100.0
Professional persons	357	2.4	824	4.6
Proprietors, managers, and officials	1,248	8.5	1,665	9.3
Farmers (owners and tenants)	1,156	7.9	1,517	8.5
Wholesale and retail dealers	38	0.3	56	0.3
Other proprietors, managers, and officials	54	0.4	92	0.5
Clerks and kindred workers	168	1.1	864	4.8
Skilled workers and foremen	35	0.2	24	0.1
Semiskilled workers	6,541	44.5	7,477	41.9
Semiskilled workers in manufacturing	6,055	41.2	6,384	35.8
Other semiskilled workers	486	3.3	1,093	6.1
Unskilled workers	6,361	43.2	6,988	39.2
Agricultural laborers	3,197	21.7	3,121	17.5
Factory and building construction laborers	85	0.6	111	0.6
Other laborers	101	0.7	46	0.3
Servant classes	2,978	20.2	3,710	20.8

Source: U.S. Bureau of the Census, The Indian Population of the United States and Alaska, 1930 (Washington, D.C.: U.S. Government Printing Office, 1937), p. 202.

Table 8.4
Indian Farming Operations, 1930

	1930
Number of Indian Farm Operators	26,817
Land in Farms (acres)	3,130,478
Value of Land	$60,199,627
Value of Buildings	17,311,985
Value of Implements and Machinery	5,817,729
TOTAL	$83,329,341

Source: U.S. Bureau of the Census, The Indian Population of the United States and Alaska: 1930 (Washington, D.C.: U.S. Government Printing Office, 1937), pp. 228-229.

Table 8.5

Major Occupation Groups, Employed American Indians, by Sex,
1950–1970

	1950	1960	1970
MALES	59,209	78,100	116,467
Professional, technical, and kindred workers	1,148	3,270	10,754
Farmers and farm managers	13,499	6,247	2,645
Managers, officials, and proprieters, except farm	1,090	1,859	5,871
Clerical and kindred workers	1,754	2,222	6,609
Sales workers[1]	----	989	2,798
Craftsmen, foremen, and kindred workers	6,129	10,214	25,725
Operatives and kindred workers	7,289	14,491	15,327
Private household workers	141	211	164
Service workers, except private household	2,020	3,952	12,047
Farm laborers, unpaid family workers[2]	4,599	----	----
Farm laborers and farm foremen	7,854	9,279	6,655
Laborers, except farm and mine	9,902	13,334	15,327
Occupation not reported[3]	3,514	12,032	----
FEMALES	15,488	36,900	73,766
Professional, technical, and kindred workers	807	2,553	8,184
Farmers and farm managers	828	752	439
Managers, officials, and proprieters, except farm	216	547	1,752
Clerical and kindred workers	1,376	3,963	18,523
Sales workers[1]	----	1,013	2,914
Craftsmen, foremen, and kindred workers	247	343	1,578
Operatives and kindred workers	3,968	4,260	13,759
Private household workers	2,200	4,697	4,955
Service workers, except private household	2,860	7,224	19,401
Farm laborers, unpaid family workers[2]	1,177	----	----
Farm laborers and farm foremen	465	2,183	1,270
Laborers, except farm and mine	150	464	991
Occupation not reported[3]	1,194	8,901	----

Notes: 1. Included in "Clerical and kindred workers" in 1950.
        2. Included in "Farm laborers and farm foremen" in 1960 and 1970.
        3. All occupations reported in 1970.

Source: U.S. Bureau of the Census, U.S. Census of Population: 1950. Special Reports.
         Nonwhite Population by Race, P-E No. 3B (Washington, D.C.: U.S. Government
         Printing Office, 1953), p. 3B-32; U.S. Bureau of the Census, U.S. Census of
         Population: 1960. Subject Reports. Nonwhite Population by Race, Final Report
         PC(2)-1C (Washington, D.C.: U.S. Government Printing Office, 1963), p. 104; U.S.
         Bureau of the Census, Census of Population: 1970. Subject Reports. American
         Indians, Final Report PC(2)-1F (Washington, D.C.: U.S. Government Printing
         Office, 1973), p. 86.

Table 8.6
Major Occupation Groups, Employed American Indians,
Eskimos, and Aleuts, by Sex, 1980

	Male	Female
Employed persons, 16 years and over	286,687	220,927
Managerial & Professional Specialty Occupations	42,517	39,323
Technical, Sales, and Administrative Support Occ.	37,480	85,196
Service Occupations	36,050	55,763
Farming, Forestry, & Fishing Occupations	16,066	2,548
Precision Production, Craft, & Repair Occupations	69,074	7,033
Construction Trades	30,757	1,054
Extractive Occupations	3,026	155
Precision Production Occupations	15,890	4,977
Operators, Fabricators and Laborers	85,500	31,064
Transportation and Material Moving Occupations	27,195	2,825
Handlers, Equipment Cleaners, Helpers & Laborers	27,545	5,922

Source: U.S. Bureau of the Census, 1980 Census of Population.
         Characteristics of the Population, Detailed Population
         Characteristics, U.S. Summary, PC80-1-D1-A (Washington, D.C.: U.S.
         Government Printing Office, 1984) Table 278, pp. 196-205.

Table 8.7

Detailed Occupations of American Indians, Eskimos, and Aleuts, United States, Reservations, Historic Areas of Oklahoma, and Alaska, 1980

	UNITED STATES	ON IDENTIFIED RESERVATIONS	IN HISTORIC AREAS OF OKLAHOMA	IN THE STATE OF ALASKA
Employed persons 16 years and over	507,614	79,698	32,259	15,762
Managerial and professional specialty occupations	81,840	11,884	4,597	2,965
Executive, administrative, and managerial occupations	36,776	4,964	1,863	1,374
Officials and administrators, public administration	3,565	1,259	257	174
Management related occupations	9,385	1,137	466	278
Professional specialty occupations	45,064	6,920	2,733	1,591
Engineers and natural scientists	5,804	395	182	88
Engineers	3,274	157	149	29
Health diagnosing occupations	863	29	45	8
Health assessment and treating occupations	5,364	477	309	82
Teachers, librarians, and counselors	20,607	3,778	1,450	1,079
Teachers, elementary and secondary	13,906	2,531	1,040	899
Technical, sales, and administrative support occupations	122,676	20,256	7,509	4,512
Health technologists and technicians	5,250	900	491	72
Technologists and technicians, except health	8,786	1,544	481	409
Sales occupations	31,100	2,264	1,965	762
Supervisors and proprietors, sales occupations	4,985	404	415	164
Sales representatives, commodities and finance	7,048	214	272	99
Other sales occupations	19,067	1,646	1,279	499
Cashiers	8,174	846	523	201

Administrative support occupations, including clerical	77,540	15,547	4,572	3,269
Computer equipment operators	1,873	118	62	26
Secretaries, stenographers, and typists	21,210	4,919	1,421	888
Financial records processing occupations	8,333	1,023	398	334
Mail and message distributing occupations	2,998	201	154	164
Service occupations	91,813	19,436	6,579	3,499
Private household occupations	3,350	480	188	108
Protective service occupations	10,224	2,412	557	287
Police and firefighters	4,043	1,254	194	165
Service occupations, except protective and household	78,239	16,545	5,834	3,104
Food service occupations	27,597	4,144	1,593	850
Cleaning and building service occupations	23,463	5,976	1,788	1,295
Farming, forestry, and fishing occupations	18,614	6,230	2,004	649
Farm operators and managers	3,639	1,631	626	3
Farm workers and related occupations	11,220	4,599	1,378	37
Precision production, craft, and repair occupations	76,107	10,414	5,973	1,791
Mechanics and repairers	20,248	2,130	1,324	474
Construction trades	31,811	5,488	2,845	864
Precision production occupations	20,867	1,830	1,275	380

Table 8.7
(Continued)

	UNITED STATES	ON IDENTIFIED RESERVATIONS	IN HISTORIC AREAS OF OKLAHOMA	IN THE STATE OF ALASKA
Operators, fabricators, and laborers	116,564	17,358	9,999	2,346
Machine operators and tenders, except precision	32,990	2,628	2,800	327
Fabricators, assemblers, inspectors, and samplers	20,087	1,716	1,686	78
Transportation occupations	20,611	4,940	2,289	491
Motor vehicle operators	19,005	2,856	1,381	381
Material moving equipment operators	9,409	2,017	860	270
Handlers, equipment cleaners, helpers, and laborers	33,467	8,073	3,224	1,180
Construction laborers	7,035	2,252	826	266
Freight, stock, and material handlers	7,376	879	568	353
Traditional occupations[1]	—	4,120	176	—
Tribal government occupations	—	834	53	—
Officials and administrators	—	563	43	—
Legislators	—	200	7	—
Judicial administrators	—	71	3	—
Native healers	—	31	—	—
Sheep workers	—	276	1	—
Artists and performers	—	290	44	—
Dancers	—	6	—	—
Drummers and singers	—	3	—	—
Painters	—	70	43	—
Potters	—	211	1	—

Jewelers	—	1,323	26	—
Handworking occupations	—	1,365	51	—
Basket makers	—	156	1	—
Beaders	—	193	26	—
Bustle makers	—	2	—	—
Carvers	—	54	5	—
Fan makers	—	2	—	—
Moccasin makers	—	20	1	—
Quilters	—	47	7	—
Rattle makers	—	—	—	—
Weavers	—	806	7	—
Other handworking occupations	—	85	4	—

Note:

1. Data gathered on identified reservations and in the historic areas of Oklahoma only. Individuals with traditional Indian occupations included in computation of non-traditional occupations also.

Source: U.S. Bureau of the Census, 1980 Census of Population. Characteristics of the Population. U.S. Summary, PC 80-1-C-1 (Washington, D.C.: U.S. Government Printing Office, 1983), p. 1-102; Characteristics of the Population. Alaska, PC 80-1-C-3, p. 3-45; Subject Reports. American Indians, Eskimos, and Aleuts on Identified Reservations and in the Historic Areas of Oklahoma (Excluding Urbanized Areas), PC 80-2-1D, Part 2 (Washington, D.C.: U.S. Government Printing Office, 1986), pp. 482, 1040.

Table 8.8
Employment by Industry and Sex, Indians in the
United States and Alaska, 1930

	INDIANS IN THE UNITED STATES		INDIANS IN ALASKA	
	MALES	FEMALES	MALES	FEMALES
Agriculture	51,771	4,640	384	10
Forestry and Fishing	3,566	25	2,361	104
Extraction of Minerals	1,482	—	133	2
Manufacturing and Mechanical Industries	12,278	6,521	371	556
Transportation and Communication	3,872	128	256	6
Trade	2,018	366	122	26
Public Service	1,223	20	18	—
Professional Service	1,781	854	77	54
Domestic and Personal Service	1,739	4,817	3,955	246
Clerical Occupations	576	471	81[1]	8[1]
Gainful Workers	80,306	17,842	7,758	1,012
Population, 10 Years and Older	123,469	115,512	10,616	10,046

Notes:
    1. Industry not specified.

Source: U.S. Bureau of the Census, The Indian Population of the United
          States and Alaska, 1930 (Washington, D.C.: U.S. Government
          Printing Office, 1937), pp. 208-219, 237-238.

Table 8.9
Industry of Employed American Indians, 1960–1980[1]

	1960	1970	1980[2]
Agriculture, Forestry and Fisheries	20,241	13,612	17,839
Mining	2,208	2,832	11,133
Construction	9,254	15,425	42,592
Durable Goods Manufacturing	11,990	27,079	97,913
Nondurable Goods Manufacturing	5,946	17,281	—[3]
Transportation, Communication, and Other Public Utilities	5,792	10,859	35,483
Wholesale and Retail Trade	9,478	26,495	79,655
Finance, Insurance, and Real Estate	839	4,160	17,129
Business and Repair Services	1,509	5,470	20,583
Personal Services	8,684	12,620	18,363
Entertainment and Recreation Services	617	1,416	5,057
Professional and Related Services	12,359	36,175	102,589
Public Administration	5,921	16,764	59,278
Industry Not Reported	20,162	—	—
Total Employed	115,000	190,233	507,614

Notes:
1. Data include all workers, 14 years of age and above, for 1960, and all workers, 16 years of age and above, for 1970 and 1980.
2. Includes American Indians, Eskimos, and Aleuts. Other years, American Indians only.
3. Included in Durable Goods Manufacturing.

Source: U.S. Bureau of the Census, U.S. Census of Population: 1960. Subject Reports. Nonwhite Population by Race. Final Report PC(2)-1C (Washington, D.C.: U.S. Government Printing Office, 1963), p. 104; U.S. Bureau of the Census, U.S. Census of Population: 1970. Subject Reports. American Indians. Final Report PC(2)-1F (Washington, D.C.: U.S. Government Printing Office, 1973), p. 86; U.S. Bureau of the Census, 1980 Census of Population. Detailed Population Characteristics, U.S. Summary, PC80-1-D1-1 (Washington, D.C.: U.S. Government Printing Office, 1984), pp. 372-374.

Table 8.10
Industry of Employed American Indians, Eskimos, and Aleuts, by Sex, 1980

	MALE	FEMALE
Agriculture, Forestry, and Fisheries	14,631	3,208
Mining	9,780	1,353
Construction	39,618	2,974
Manufacturing	63,763	34,150
Transportation, Communications, and Other Public Utilities	27,082	8,401
Wholesale Trade	10,472	3,801
Retail Trade	30,357	35,025
Finance, Insurance, and Real Estate	6,399	10,730
Business and Repair Services	13,454	7,129
Personal Services	4,762	13,601
Entertainment and Recreation Services	2,956	2,101
Professional and Related Services	31,727	70,862
Public Administration	31,686	27,592
Total Employed Persons, 16 Years and Over	286,687	220,927

Source: U.S. Bureau of the Census, 1980 Census of Population. Detailed
          Population Characteristics, U.S. Summary, PC80-1-D1-1 (Washington,
          D.C.: U.S. Government Printing Office, 1984), pp. 372-374.

Table 8.11
Income on Selected Indian Reservations, Eighty Reservations, 1933

UNEARNED INCOME	$ 4,416,923
Annuities, Interest, etc.	1,924,234
Land Leases	1,881,601
Land Sales	354,356
Mineral Leases	256,732
EARNED INCOME	6,595,694
Employment at Wages	4,524,596
Relief work[1]	1,529,329
Livestock sold	685,301
Value of farm & garden produce consumed	629,536
Crops sold	540,399
Farm and garden produce sold	151,060
Arts and crafts sold	45,899
Miscellaneous	18,903
TOTAL INCOME	$11,012,617

Note: 1. Work relief programs: Civil Works Administration,
           Public Works Administration, etc.

Source: National Resources Board, Report on National Planning and Public
         Works. Part II, Report of the Land Planning Committee (Washington,
         D.C.: U.S. Government Printing Office, 1935), p. 227.

Table 8.12
Sources of Income, Indian Reservation Residents, 1939 and 1944

SOURCE	1939	1944
Native Products	$759,706	$1,424,632
Arts and Crafts	937,880	460,088
Agriculture	9,248,255	22,038,111
Private Business	400,791	503,690
Salaries and Wages	13,618,586	22,997,414
Other Earned Income	253,961	555,866
Total Earned	25,219,179	47,979,801
Total Unearned	11,052,843	30,298,888
Grand Totals	$36,272,022	$78,278,689

Source: Bureau of Indian Affairs, reproduced in Henry W. Hough, Development of Indian Resources (Denver: World Press, 1967), p. 10.

Table 8.13
Indian Employment and Earnings, by Source,
Selected Reservations, 1969–1972

Source	1969 Employment	1969 Earnings	1972 Employment	1972 Earnings
FEDERAL GOVERNMENT (TOTAL)	(17,828)	($75,188,600)	(36,504)	($159,019,600)
Bureau of Indian Affairs	NA	NA	7,324	51,920,500
Indian Health Service	NA	NA	1,684	19,129,200
O.E.O. Programs	NA	NA	5,193	23,589,400
Other Federal Government	NA	NA	3,706	19,648,000
TRIBAL GOVERNMENT	NA	NA	4,736	44,732,500
OTHER GOVERNMENT[1]	NA	NA	18,597	44,063,600
COMMERCIAL AND INDUSTRIAL (TOTAL)	(7,456)	(30,752,000)	(17,964)	(90,766,000)
Bureau of Indian Affairs assisted	NA	NA	8,018	44,510,400
Tribal Developments	NA	NA	940	3,981,900
Non-Bureau Commercial[2]	NA	NA	9,006	42,273,700
AGRICULTURE (TOTAL)	(12,485)	(39,358,700)	(23,116)	(42,839,400)
Rangeland	11,174	28,943,800	NA	NA
Dry Farming and Pasture	1,311	10,414,900	NA	NA
FORESTRY	2,247	14,730,000	1,781	12,720,300
MINERALS	577	6,663,800	1,122	11,965,500
OUTDOOR RECREATION	255	1,306,200	401	1,454,400

Notes:
NA – Not available.
1. Includes state, county, and local governments.
2. Includes employment in industry and commerce not induced by bureau or tribal funding.

Source: Keith L. Fay, Developing Indian Employment Opportunities (Washington, D.C.: Bureau of Indian Affairs, n.d. [1973?]), p. 100.

Table 8.14
Median Income, American Indians with Income, 1949–1959
(Persons Fourteen Years of Age and Over) (in Dollars)

	1949		1959	
	AMERICAN INDIAN	U.S. ALL RACES	AMERICAN INDIAN	U.S. ALL RACES
United States, age 14 and older	725	1,917	1,792	4,791
Urban	1,240	2,162	2,759	5,199
Rural Nonfarm	695	1,553	1,493	4,013
Rural Farm	551	1,099	1,045	2,951

Source: U.S. Bureau of the Census, U.S. Census of Population: 1950. Special
Reports, Nonwhite Population by Race, vol. 4, P–E, No. 3B
(Washington, D.C.: U.S. Government Printing Office, 1953), p. 32;
U.S. Bureau of the Census, U.S. Census of Population: 1950.
Characteristics of the Population, U.S. Summary, vol. 2, Part 1
(Washington, D.C.: U.S. Government Printing Office, 1953), p. 1–298;
U.S. Bureau of the Census, U.S. Census of Population: 1960. Subject
Reports. Nonwhite Population by Race. Final Report PC(2)–1C.
(Washington, D.C.: U.S. Government Printing Office, 1963), p. 104;
U.S. Bureau of the Census, Census of Population: 1960.
Characteristics of the Population, U.S. Summary, vol. 1, Part 1
(Washington, D.C.: U.S. Government Printing Office, 1964), p. 225.

Table 8.15
Median Income, American Indians with Income, by Sex, 1969–1979
(in Dollars)

	1969[1]		1979[2]	
	AMERICAN INDIANS	U.S. ALL RACES	AMERICAN INDIANS, AND ALEUTS	U.S. ALL RACES
MALES				
United States	3,509	6,444	8,077	12,192
Urban	4,568	6,860	9,320	12,526
Rural Nonfarm	2,768	5,591	6,660[3]	11,329[3]
Rural Farm	2,460	4,509	7,075	11,057
FEMALES				
United States	1,697	2,328	4,263	5,263
Urban	2,023	2,514	4,744	5,527
Rural Nonfarm	1,397	1,838	3,609[3]	4,473[3]
Rural Farm	1,043	1,534	3,969	4,379

Notes:
1. Persons 16 years and over, with income.
2. Persons 15 years and over, with income.
3. Includes farm and nonfarm.

Source: U.S. Bureau of the Census, Census of Population: 1970. Subject
Reports. American Indians. Final Report PC(2)-1F (Washington,
D.C.: U.S. Government Printing Office, 1973), pp. 61–64; U.S.
Bureau of the Census, Census of Population: 1970. Characteristics
of the Population. U.S. Summary, vol. 1, Part 1, section 2
(Washington, D.C.: U.S. Government Printing Office, 1973),
p. 1–833; U.S. Bureau of the Census, 1980 Census of Population,
General Social and Economic Characteristics, U.S. Summary, vol. 1,
Chapter C, Part 1, PC80-1-C1 (Washington, D.C.: U.S. Government
Printing Office, 1983), pp. 1–78, 1–112.

Table 8.16

Family Income and Poverty Status, American Indians, 1969-1979

FARM	1969				1979[1]			
	TOTAL	URBAN	RURAL NONFARM	RURAL FARM	TOTAL	URBAN	RURAL[2]	RURAL FARM
Median income, all families (in dollars)	5,832	7,323	4,691	4,319	13,724	15,160	12,091	15,672
Median income, families with female head (in dollars)	3,198	3,695	2,730	2,435	7,231	7,459	6,876	8,544
Percent of families below poverty level	33.3	21.0	45.1	40.9	23.7	19.5	29.2	19.0

Notes:

1. Includes American Indians, Eskimos, and Aleuts.
2. Includes rural nonfarm and rural farm.

Source: U.S. Bureau of the Census, Census of Population: 1970. Subject Reports. American Indians. Final Report PC(2)-1F. (Washington, D.C.: U.S. Government Printing Office, 1973), p. 120; U.S. Bureau of the Census, 1980 Census of Population. Characteristics of the Population, U.S. Summary, PC80-1-C1 (Washington, D.C.: U.S. Government Printing Office, 1983), pp. 1-112, 1-114.

Table 8.17

Family Income and Poverty Status, American Indians,
Eskimos, and Aleuts, by Place of Residence, 1979

	United States	On Reservations	In Historic Areas Of Oklahoma	In State of Alaska
Median Income, all families (in dollars)	13,724	9,666	10,571	15,921
Median Income, families with female head (in dollars)	7,231	6,411	6,328	9,034
Percent of Families below poverty level	23.7	42.0	29.6	25.3

Source: U.S. Bureau of the Census, 1980 Census of Population. Characteristics of the Population. U.S. Summary, PC80-1-C1 (Washington, D.C.: U.S. Government Printing Office, 1983), pp. 1-112, 1-114; Characteristics of the Population. Alaska, PC80-1-C3 (Washington, D.C.: U.S. Government Printing Office, 1983), pp. 3-51, 3-53; Subject Reports. American Indians, Eskimos, and Aleuts on Identified Reservations and in the Historic Indian Areas of Oklahoma (Excluding Urbanized Areas), PC80-2-1D, Part 2 (Washington, D.C.: U.S. Government Printing Office, 1986), pp. 521, 560, 1050, 1060.

Table 8.18

Reservation Unemployment Rates, by Bureau of
Indian Affairs Area, 1965–1983

AREA	DECEMBER 1965	SEPTEMBER 1966	DECEMBER 1967	DECEMBER 1981[1]	JANUARY 1983[1]
Aberdeen	63%	49%	43%	44%	55%
Albuquerque	NA	43	44	27	45
Anadarko	NA	NA	NA	32	32
Billings	50	32	25	32	46
Eastern	46	11	24	36	39
Juneau	NA	NA	NA	52	52
Minneapolis	38	31	28	41	53
Muskogee	NA[2]	NA	NA[2]	11	9
Navajo	44[2]	32	32[2]	29	45
Phoenix	53	47	38	24	29
Portland	34	34	28	45	52
Sacramento	45	31	22	43	56

Notes:

NA – not available.
1. Persons 16 and over, not employed, able to work, and seeking work.
2. Gallup Area.

Source: Keith L. Fay, Developing Indian Employment Opportunities (Washington, D.C.: Bureau of Indian Affairs, n.d. [1973?]), pp. 95, 97, 98; Bureau of Indian Affairs, Local Estimates of Resident Indian Population and Labor Force Status, January 1982 and August 1983.

Table 8.19
Reservation Unemployment Rates, Bureau of Indian Affairs Estimates, Selected Reservations, 1972–1983

RESERVATION	1972	1981[1]	1983[2]
Blackfeet, MT	37%	22%	22%
Cherokee, NC	21	23	38
Cheyenne River, SD	27	54	50
Crow, MT	27	44	59
Flathead, MT	34	23	29
Ft. Apache, AZ	59	21	20
Ft. Peck, MT	48	12	43
Gila River, AZ	18	19	27
Hopi, AZ	51	32	33
Laguna, NM	35	36	68
Menominee, WI	—	17	39
Navajo, AZ-UT-NM	43	29	45
Northern Cheyenne, MT	27	34	48
Papago, AZ	25	17	17
Pine Ridge, SD	42	44	49
Red Lake, MN	39	24	42
Rosebud, SD	26	26	52
San Carlos, AZ	19	17	46
Standing Rock, ND-SD	34	76	76
Turtle Mountain, ND	42	24	50
Wind River, WY	47	44	61
Yakima, WA	32	51	61
Zuni, NM	29	35	50

Notes:

1. Percent 16 years and over able to work, not employed, and actively seeking work in December 1981.
2. Percent 16 years and over able to work, not employed and actively seeking work in January 1983.

Source: Department of Commerce, Federal and State Reservations and Indian Trust Areas (Washington, D.C.: U.S. Government Printing Office, 1974); Bureau of Indian Affairs, Local Estimates of Resident Indian Population and Labor Force Status, January 1982 and August 1983.

9

Indian Resources and Economic Development

In addition to human capital, the resource represented by the Indian people themselves, American Indian tribes and communities own a variety of natural resources. These include the lands owned by American Indian tribes and individuals outlined in Chapter 2, the mineral resources found in the lands, and the trust funds held by the federal govenment on the behalf of Indian tribes. The trust funds represent natural resources as well, as these include monies paid by the government of the United States to the tribes in compensation for lands ceded to the United States by the tribes. The funds were either paid at the time of the cession and held in trust for the tribe by the federal government or paid as a result of a successful claim pursued by the tribe. Other economic resources derived from the use of land include revenues from land leases, mineral leases and royalties, timber permits and fees, and direct income paid to tribes and individuals as a result of the operation of tribal and individual enterprises on Indian land.

A significant problem in the utilization of allotted Indian lands has been the heirship land problem. When the original allottee died, his or her interest in the allotment was divided between the heirs, resulting, after several generations, in the ownership of small allotments by a relatively large number of persons. This problem, which was recognized as significant as early as the 1930s, will also be discussed in this chapter.

Indian trust funds represent a substantial economic resource to Indian tribes. As noted in Chapter 6 (Table 6.15), trust funds have been used to finance substantial government services to Indian tribes. The sources of trust funds include payments made to Indian tribes in compensation for lands ceded to the United States, income from leases, royalties, and other fees for use of Indian lands paid to the United States as a trustee for the Indian tribe, and awards received by Indian tribes as the result of claims successfully pursued in the United States Court of Claims (1881-1946) or the Indian Claims Commission (1946-1978).

Table 9.1 shows the amount of trust funds held for Indian tribes by the United States government for selected years between 1840 and 1965. The total amount of trust obligations of the federal government to the tribes increased from four and a half million dollars in 1840 to over 268 million dollars by 1965. Trust funds represent a significant economic resource for Indian communities. Tables 9.2 and 9.3 summarize the claims experience of Indian tribes in the United States Court of Claims and the Indian Claims Commission. While not all of the claims money was paid into trust funds (some was distributed to tribal members in per capita distributions or used to finance particular projects desired by the tribes), much of the increase in the value of trust funds after 1946 was the result of claims awards.

Land leases, from the late nineteenth century on, provided another source of income resource for Indian tribes and individuals. Tables 9.4 and 9.5 show the results of land leasing in the early twentieth century. Three kinds of leases were made by the Bureau of Indian Affairs on behalf of Indian tribes and individuals. These included agricultural leases, grazing leases, and mineral leases. Table 9.4 shows the number of leases awarded and the acreage leased for the years 1911, 1917, and 1925. Agricultural and grazing leases are divided into leases of allotted and tribal lands. Table 9.5 shows the income from these leases for each of the three years. Lease income increased from 3.8 million dollars in 1911 to nearly 33.8 million dollars in 1926, largely due to increases in the revenues from mineral leases.

Indian timber and lumber operations, particularly on reservations in the Northwest and North Central states, provided another significant source of revenue for Indian tribes and individuals. Table 9.6 summarizes a variety of data on Indian timberlands and lumber operations between 1912 and 1925. Based on data gathered by the Bureau of Indian Affairs, the table shows that timber provided a substantial annual revenue to reservations with significant timber holdings during these years. Table 9.7 presents data on receipts from timber operations over the fifty-year period from 1910 to 1966. Timber revenues fluctuated during the period, declining precipitously during the depression years of the 1930s both in total receipts and in receipts per 1,000 board feet, but increasing in the late 1930s and accelerating during the postwar construction boom.

Table 9.8 summarizes data on surface leases and permits on Indian lands for recent years. The income from leasing Indian lands increased dramatically in recent years. Surface leases, as distinguished from mining leases, were classified as agriculture leases, business leases, and other leases, principally leases for residential and other nonagricultural and nonbusiness purposes. While all types of leases increased during the period, the increase in rentals received for business and other leases was particularly dramatic, with income from business leases increasing from 10.7 million to 20.3 million dollars between 1978 and 1984 and income from other leases increasing from 1.2 million dollars in 1978 to 92.6 million dollars in 1984. Both of these dramatic increases were largely the result of business and other leases on the Agua Calente Reservation, located in Palm Springs, California. In 1984, the Agua Calente Reservation accounted for over 20.7 million dollars in business leases and 90.0 million dollars in other leases. In 1982, the reservation accounted for only 6.2 million dollars in business leases and 0.5 million dollars in other leases. Consequently, much of the increase in the value of business and other leases was the result of the growth of the community of Palm Springs during the 1980s.[1]

Mineral leases and royalties have been a much-discussed source of Indian income in recent years. Table 9.9 presents data on royalty revenues for all leasable minerals on Indian lands between 1948 and 1971. Royalties from subsurface operations, particularly oil and gas operations, increased dramatically between 1946 and 1971. Other mining operations increased as well, although oil and gas operations accounted for the majority of royalty income to tribes for each of the years reported. Table 9.10 presents data on income from mining operations on Indian lands between 1949 and 1978. For tribes with significant mineral wealth, oil and gas revenues provided substantial amounts of income. Revenues from other minerals, particuarly uranium, were substantial as well. Table 9.11 continues the data presented in Table 9.10, showing the volume, value, and revenues produced from Indian mineral leases for oil, gas, and coal, and the value and revenues produced from other production on Indian lands between 1979 and 1984. Revenues from oil and gas production grew in the late 1970s, declining somewhat in the early 1980s as a result of the energy glut. Still, oil, gas, and other production provided significant sources of income for Indian tribes.

In addition to royalties based on the value of minerals actually extracted from the land, Indian tribes realized income from rents and bonuses. These are payments to tribes and individuals for the right to explore and attempt to extract minerals. The amounts were, in general, less than the amounts paid as royalties, but were considerable in some years. Table 9.12 presents data on income from rents and bonuses on Indian lands for the years 1982, 1983, and 1984. The decline in the value of bonuses reflects the decline in energy prices during the 1980s.

A significant problem in the development of Indian resources has been the amount of Indian land that is not used. Table 9.13 presents the results of a land survey completed in 1934 on the potential use of Indian lands, together with data gathered in 1953 and 1966 on the actual use of Indian lands. The lands in the "miscellaneous and unused" category accounted for a substantial proportion of Indian lands (around 10 percent in 1966) in both of the latter years, indicating that much potentially useful Indian land was idle. In addition, the amount of land used for farming declined and was much less than the amount of land found to be potentially useful for farming in 1934, even though the Indian land base was larger. (In part, this reflects the decline in Indian agriculture discussed in Chapter 8.)

Unused land is, in part, the result of what has become known as the heirship land problem. First documented in 1934, the heirship land problem resulted from the practice of the Bureau of Indian Affairs of dividing the lands of deceased allottees in equal shares among the surviving heirs. After several generations, the result was tracts of lands having several owners, and, in some cases, many hundreds of owners. Table 9.14 shows the distribution of Indian lands in 1934 by ownership and character. By 1934, nearly 40 percent of the allotted tracts of Indian land were "deceased allotments," meaning that the original allottee had died and the land was in heirship status. A significant proportion of these "deceased" allotments (43 percent) were in farming land, reflecting the tendency of the government to allot reservations having large amounts of farm land earlier than other reservations. Table 9.15, based on the same survey, provides the information for selected reservations. A number of these reservations were never allotted, including some with timberlands, such as the Menominee Reservation in Wisconsin, and reservations in the southwest, like the Hopi and San Carlos Reservations in Arizona. For reservations that were allotted, such as Pine Ridge, Rosebud, and Standing Rock in the Dakotas, the heirship land problem had already become significant, with half or more of reservation allotments in heirship status by 1934.

Table 9.16 and 9.17 present the results of a 1953 land survey. By 1953, a minority of allotments, accounting for less than 40 percent of the total acreage, were still held by the living original allottee. Nearly 47 percent of all allotted Indian land was owned by two or more owners and over three million acres was owned by six or more persons. Table 9.17 presents this information for selected reservations.

By 1959, more than half of all allotments were in heirship status, as shown in Table 9.18. Of the total acreage of heirship land, 59 percent was used by non-Indians and nearly 9 percent was unused (Table 9.19). Heirship land was difficult for Indian heirs to utilize since the number of heirs that would have to agree on the use of the land was often very large. The Bureau of Indian Affairs managed the tracts for the owners, leasing the tracts and paying the heirs the appropriate fraction of the proceeds. By 1965, as shown in Table 9.20, the majority of heirship tracts, 37,339 out of 61,778, had two or more owners. This amounted to 60 percent of the allotments remaining in trust on a sample of fifty-two reservations. Seventeen percent of the tracts had eleven or more owners, making management and consolidation difficult. On some reservations, such as the Rosebud Reservation in South Dakota, tribal land enterprises were developed in an attempt to consolidate in tribal ownership the heirship lands that had become economically meaningless to the owners during this period.

Indian land and natural resources found on the land provide significant sources of wealth for Indian tribes and individuals. The management of that wealth has been a significant problem in the late twentieth century, a problem that continues to plague Indian tribes and the federal government to this date. The problems include the questions of how much management assistance should be provided to the tribes by the Bureau of Indian Affairs and other federal agencies such as the Minerals Management Service, how much tribal autonomy should be permitted, and how to strike a balance between tribal and individual interests in the management of natural resources.

Data on Indian resources and economic development can be found in a variety of sources. The *Annual Reports* of the Commissioner of Indian Affairs before 1906 present detailed data on Indian trust funds, agricultural production, and, for some years, lease income. Both Laurence F. Schmeckebier, *The Office of Indian Affairs* (1927), and Lewis Meriam and others, *The Problem of Indian Administration* (1928) contain some data on economic development, as does the report of the National Resources Board, *Indian Land Tenure, Economic Status, and Population Trends* (1935). For the more recent period, the Bureau of Indian Affairs published an *Annual Report of Indian Lands and Income from Surface and Subsurface Leases* in the 1970s; much resource information is included in the Bureau's *Annual Report of Indian Lands* published in the 1980s. Data on income from mineral leases may be found in the U.S. Geological Survey's *Federal and Indian Lands: Coal, Phosphate, Potash, Sodium, and Other Mineral Production Royalty Income and Related Statistics, 1920-1972* (1973). More recent information is published in an annual report on receipts from federal and Indian leases, published by the U.S. Minerals Management Service, titled *Mineral Revenues.*

The Schmeckebier volume, the Meriam Report, and the report of the National Resources Board, mentioned in the preceding paragraph, provide useful perspectives on the resource development problem as it was perceived in the early part of the twentieth century. Henry Hough's *Development of Indian Resources* (1967) provides useful information on economic development efforts during the 1960s. The report of the Joint

Economic Committee, *Toward Economic Development of Native American Communities* (1969), contains many useful papers on various aspects of economic development. *The Final Report* of the Indian Claims Commission (1979) summarizes claims awarded by the Indian Claims Commission between 1947 and 1978. The report of the Task Force on Reservation Resource Development and Protection to the American Indian Policy Review Commission, *Report on Reservation Resource Development and Protection* (1976) includes useful information on a range of resource management problems facing Indian tribes. Sam Stanley, ed., *American Indian Economic Development* (1978), includes a number of useful essays on specific Indian communities from across the country.

NOTE

1. U.S. Bureau of Indian Affairs, *Annual Report of Indian Lands, September 30, 1982* (Washington, D.C.: U.S. Department of the Interior, 1982), p. 86; U.S. Bureau of Indian Affairs, *Annual Report of Indian Lands, September 30, 1984* (Washington, D.C.: U.S. Department of the Interior, 1984), p. 88.

TABLES

Table 9.1
Trust Funds of Indian Tribes, 1840–1965

FISCAL YEAR	BONDS HELD IN TRUST	CAPITAL SUM ON WHICH INTEREST WAS PAID BUT WHICH HAD NOT BEEN DEPOSITED IN TREASURY	FUNDS HELD IN TRUST	TOTAL AMOUNT OF TRUST AND CAPITAL OBLIGATION OF THE GOVERNMENT	INTEREST ACCOUNT
1840	$1,897,321.76	$2,580,100.00	$ —	$4,477,321.76	NA
1850	2,251,959.83	5,273,100.00	—	7,525,059.83	NA
1860	3,396,241.82	—	—	3,396,241.82	NA
1870	4,608,366.66	—	—	4,608,366.66	NA
1880	4,664,216.83	—	11,010,923.39	15,675,140.22	NA
1890	—	—	23,760,413.00	23,760,413.00	NA
1900	—	—	34,317,955.09	34,317,955.09	NA
1911	—	—	41,843,830.00	41,843,830.00	NA
1921	—	—	26,590,306.00	26,590,306.00	NA
1925	—	—	32,544,972.00	32,544,972.00	NA
1947	—	—	28,497,080.00	28,497,080.00	$1,112,453.00
1950	—	—	42,224,129.00	42,224,129.00	3,335,822.00
1955	—	—	84,949,383.00	84,949,383.00	2,933,818.00
1960	—	—	157,757,238.00	157,757,238.00	2,875,978.00
1965	—	—	268,470,447.00	268,470,447.00	2,921,327.00

Source: Laurence F. Schmeckebier, The Office of Indian Affairs: Its History, Activities, and Organization (Baltimore: The Johns Hopkins Press, 1927), p. 191; Alan L. Sorkin, "Indian Trust Funds," in U.S. Congress, Joint Economic Committee, Toward Economic Development for Native American Communities (Washington, D.C.: U.S. Government Printing Office, 1969), p. 250.

Table 9.2
Indian Claims Decided by the U.S. Court of Claims, 1881–1946

YEAR	NUMBER OF DOCKETS COMPLETED			TOTAL AMOUNT OF AWARDS	CUMULATIVE TOTAL OF AWARDS
	BY DISMISSALS	BY DECISIONS[1]	BY AWARDS		
1881	–	–	–	$ –	$ –
1882	–	–	–	–	–
1883	1	–	–	–	–
1884	1	–	–	–	–
1885	1	–	–	–	–
1886	–	–	1	2,858,798.62	2,858,798.62
1887	–	–	1	240,164.58	3,098,963.20
1888	–	–	–	–	3,098,963.20
1889	–	–	–	–	3,098,963.20
1890	–	–	–	–	3,098,963.20
1891	–	–	2	816,113.23	3,915,076.43
1892	–	–	1	104,626.00	4,019,702.43
1893	–	–	1	205,265.00	4,224,967.43
1894	–	–	1	168,604.54	4,393,571.97
1895	–	–	1	903,365.00	5,296,936.97
1896	–	–	–	–	5,296,936.97
1897	–	–	–	–	5,296,936.97
1898	–	–	–	–	5,296,936.97
1899	1	–	–	–	5,296,936.97
1900	–	–	1	15,144.85	5,312,081.82
1901	1	–	–	–	5,312,081.82
1902	–	1	–	–	5,312,081.82
1903	1	–	–	–	5,312,081.82
1904	–	–	2	4,371,597.89	9,683,679.71
1905	–	1	1	1,134,248.23	10,817,927.94
1906	–	–	1	1,998,844.46	12,816,772.40
1907	–	–	1	131,188.94	12,947,961.34
1908	–	–	–	–	12,947,961.34
1909	1	–	–	–	12,947,961.34
1910	–	–	1	3,516,231.05	16,464,192.39
1911	–	–	–	–	16,464,192.39
1912	1	–	–	–	16,464,192.39
1913	–	–	–	–	16,464,192.39
1914	–	–	–	–	16,464,192.39
1915	–	–	–	–	16,464,192.39
1916	–	–	1	711,828.47	17,176,020.86
1917	1	1	–	–	17,176,020.86
1918	–	–	1	117,735.31	17,293,756.17
1919	–	–	–	–	17,293,756.17
1920	–	–	1	312,811.27	17,606,567.44
1921	–	–	–	–	17,606,567.44
1922	–	–	–	–	17,606,567.44
1923	1	–	–	–	17,606,567.44
1924	1	–	–	–	17,606,567.44
1925	–	–	–	–	17,606,567.44

Table 9.2
(Continued)

YEAR	NUMBER OF DOCKETS COMPLETED			TOTAL AMOUNT OF AWARDS	CUMUALTIVE TOTAL OF AWARDS
	BY DISMISSALS	BY DECISIONS[1]	BY AWARDS		
1926	1	–	–	–	17,606,567.44
1927	2	–	–	–	17,606,567.44
1928	2	–	1	100,000.00	17,706,567.44
1929	–	–	1	254,632.59	17,961,200.03
1930	3	–	1	2,169,168.58	20,130,368.61
1931	5	–	–	–	20,130,368.61
1932	8	–	–	–	20,130,368.61
1933	4	–	2	766,571.58	20,896,940.19
1934	2	–	–	–	20,896,940.19
1935	7	–	2	4,418,543.48	25,315,483.67
1936	7	–	–	–	25,315,483.67
1937	6	–	1	5,313,347.32	30,628,830.99
1938	9	1	1	372,816.93	31,001,647.92
1939	5	1	–	–	31,001,647.92
1940	16	–	–	–	31,001,647.92
1941	14	2	2	2,022,367.47	33,024,015.39
1942	13	–	1	5,024,847.34	38,048,862.73
1943	3	–	–	–	38,048,862.73
1944	5	–	–	–	38,048,862.73
1945	5	–	–	–	38,048,862.73
1946	9	1	–	–	38,048,862.73
Total	137	8	30		

Dockets not completed as of December, 1946 – 27

Note:
1. Decisions with no monetary compensation stated.

Source: Compiled from data in U.S. Congress, House of Representatives, Committee on Interior and Insular Affairs, "Investgation of the Bureau of Indian Affairs" 83rd Congress, 2nd session, House Report, no. 2608, serial 11747, pp. 1563-1571.

Table 9.3
Indian Claims Decided by the Indian Claims Commission, 1947–1978

FISCAL YEAR	NUMBER OF DOCKETS COMPLETED		NUMBER OF AWARDS	TOTAL AMOUNT OF AWARDS	CUMULATIVE TOTAL OF AWARDS
	BY DISMISSALS	BY AWARDS			
1947	---	---	---	$ ---	$ ---
1948	---	---	---	---	---
1949	7	---	---	---	---
1950	12	---	---	---	---
1951	7	2	2	3,489,843.58	3,489,843.58
1952	8	3	3	2,998,220.02	6,488,063.60
1953	7	---	---	---	6,488,063.60
1954	8	1	1	927,688.04	7,415,731.64
1955	4	1	1	864,107.55	8,279,839.19
1956	1	3	3	1,515,494.95	9,795,334.14
1957	12	1	1	433,013.60	10,228,347.74
1958	10	4	4	6,860,238.54	17,088,586.28
1959	12	2	1	3,288,974.90	20,377,561.18
1960	7	13	8	21,588,007.51	41,965,658.69
1961	5	5	5	14,926,255.11	56,891,823.80
1962	5	2	3	18,063,859.65	74,955,683.45
1963	9	8	9	18,319,187.20	93,274,870.65
1964	7	9	11	15,796,254.69	109,071,125.34
1965	7	27	17	57,019,352.93	166,090,478.27
1966	2	12	11	38,701,569.58	204,792,047.85
1967	2	7	6	21,497,766.74	226,289,814.59
1968	3	23	16	43,576,732.73	269,866,547.32
1969	23	24	20	32,025,817.01	301,892,364.33
1970	2	14	13	44,254,099.43	346,146,463.76
1971	4	20	16	46,621,560.61	392,768,024.37
1972	11	14	10	33,078,111.56	425,846,135.93
1973	11	32	18	40,837,122.35	466,683,258.28
1974	11	24	20	46,409,564.06	513,092,822.34
1975	3	9	7	35,945,458.57	549,038,280.91
1976	---	15	11	63,055,867.25	612,094,148.16
Jul. – Sep. '76	---	5	4	27,825,465.90	639,919,614.06
1977	---	11	12	67,604,270.07	707,523,884.13
1978	4	31	24	110,648,772.51	818,172,606.64
	204	342	274		

Dockets not completed by September 30, 1978 – 68 (transferred to U.S. Court of Claims).

Source: U.S. Indian Claims Commission, Final Report: August 13, 1946 – September 30, 1978 (Washington, D.C.: U.S. Government Printing Office, 1979), p. 125.

Table 9.4
Number of Leases and Area Leased, Indian Lands, 1911–1925

CLASS OF LAND	1911	1917	1925
AGRICULTURAL LAND			
Allotted			
Leases...................number	19,753[1]	20,561	NR
Area.......................acres	2,528,495	2,023,788	1,710,218
Tribal			
Leases...................number	1,706	1,063	NR
Area.......................acres	183,528	434,961	11,596
Total			
Leases...................number	21,459	21,624	NR
Area.......................acres	2,712,023	2,458,749	1,721,814
GRAZING LAND			
Allotted			
Leases...................number	—	17,693	NR
Area.......................acres	—	3,627,193	5,689,407
Tribal			
Leases...................number	5,584	340	NR
Area.......................acres	5,859,325	9,042,869	4,350,938
Total			
Leases...................number	5,584	18,033	NR
Area.......................acres	5,859,325	12,310,062	10,040,345
MINERAL LAND			
Leases...................number	NR	NR	12,026
Area.......................acres	NR	2,191,011	1,549,951

Notes:

NR – not reported
1. Figure given for agricultural leases includes grazing leases.

Source: Laurence F. Schmeckebier, The Office of Indian Affairs: Its History, Activities, and Organization (Baltimore: The Johns Hopkins Press, 1927), p. 184.

Table 9.5
Income from Leasing Indian Lands, 1911–1926

CLASS OF LAND	1911	1917	1926
AGRICULTURAL LEASES			
Allotted.............................	$ —	$2,615,639	$2,898,595
Tribal..............................	230,901	44,270	10,966
Total.............................	230,901	2,659,909	2,909,561
GRAZING LEASES			
Allotted.............................	—	970,529	612,746
Tribal..............................	316,755	714,884	368,641
Total.............................	316,755	1,685,413	981,387
AGRICULTURAL AND GRAZING LEASES			
Allotted.............................	1,844,370	—	161,583
Tribal..............................	—	—	13,212
Total.............................	1,844,370	—	174,795
MINERAL LEASES			
Allotted.............................	1,396,234	—	7,304,622
Tribal..............................	9,767	10,083,028	22,385,317
Total.............................	1,406,001	10,083,028	29,689,939
Grand Total.........................	$3,798,027	$14,428,350	$33,755,682

Source: Laurence F. Schmeckebier, The Office of Indian Affairs: Its
History, Activities, and Organization, (Baltimore: The Johns
Hopkins Press, 1927), p. 183.

Table 9.6
Indian Timberlands and Lumber Operations, 1912–1925

ITEMS	1912	1916	1920	1925
AREA OF TIMBER LAND				
Allotted lands – acres.............	1,555,571	1,442,043	1,102,197	867,993
Unallotted lands – acres...........	5,295,868	6,080,541	5,287,849	5,829,808
Total..........................	6,851,439	7,522,584	6,390,046	6,697,801
ESTIMATED AMOUNT OF TIMBER				
Allotted lands – M board feet........	6,775,767	6,754,175	5,145,443	4,447,644
Unallotted lands – M board feet......	32,909,805	35,461,107	30,645,056	32,100,068
Total..........................	39,685,572	42,215,282	35,890,499	36,547,712
ESTIMATED STUMPAGE VALUE				
Allotted lands....................	$11,745,511	$11,093,545	$10,445,622	$11,746,517
Unallotted lands..................	72,011,067	73,682,815	73,366,901	91,484,073
Total..........................	$83,756,578	$84,776,360	$83,812,523	$103,230,590
SAWMILLS ON RESERVATIONS				
Number				
Private......................	41	31	59	37
Government...................	36	42	28	21
Total..........................	77	73	87	58

Table 9.6
(Continued)

COST OF SAWMILLS ON RESERVATIONS			
Private............................	$314,000	$242,500	$655,800	$ 2,144,057
Government.........................	313,180	337,680	307,230	140,402
Total.......................	$627,180	$580,180	$963,030	$2,284,459
TIMBER CUT			
Quantity			
By the government — M board feet..	33,603	28,816	26,965	13,218
By Indians — M board feet..........	50,248	36,318	44,877	14,334
By contractors — M board feet......	283,877	177,589	361,267	454,885
Total.......................	367,728	242,723	453,109	482,437
VALUE OF LUMBER CUT			
By government......................	$580,142	$103,196	$381,161	$87,907
By Indians.........................	287,192	190,156	223,397	74,690
By contractors.....................	2,000,337	843,709	1,456,001	1,821,965
Total.......................	$2,867,671	$1,137,061	$2,060,559	$1,984,562

Source: Laurence F. Schmeckebier, The Office of Indian Affairs: Its History, Activities, and Organization (Baltimore: The Johns Hopkins Press, 1927), p. 189.

Table 9.7
Income from Timber Cut from Indian Reservation Lands, 1910–1966
(All Cutting: Paid, Free Use, and Used by Tribal Sawmills)

YEAR	THOUSANDS OF BOARD FEET	RECEIPTS	PER THOUSAND BOARD FEET
1910	141,532	$ 900,612	$ 6.36
1911	137,208	752,303	5.48
1912	123,472	739,699	5.99
1913	170,766	1,028,184	6.02
1914	143,426	780,856	5.44
1915	138,624	773,483	5.58
1916	167,602	726,483	4.33
1917	205,312	715,453	3.48
1918	323,131	1,253,651	3.88
1919	291,164	1,303,840	4.48
1920	398,485	1,585,812	3.98
1921	348,300	1,390,436	3.99
1922	216,583	808,551	3.73
1923	493,563	1,856,323	3.76
1924	510,314	1,937,245	3.80
1925	467,779	1,921,157	4.11
1926	579,958	2,446,455	4.22
1927	627,365	2,953,752	4.71
1928	639,244	2,676,779	4.19
1929	660,257	2,818,317	4.27
1930	541,014	2,273,820	4.20
1931	315,366	1,240,817	3.93
1932	121,509	393,151	3.24
1933	99,047	290,292	2.93
1934	167,992	452,195	2.69
1935	277,795	903,933	3.25
1936	337,951	1,056,042	3.12
1937	493,493	1,604,737	3.25
1938	457,504	1,239,456	2.71
1939	510,957	1,437,610	2.81
1940	531,965	1,423,627	2.68
1941	608,366	1,792,951	2.95
1942	577,360	1,890,767	3.27
1942 (7/1–12/31)	297,167	1,163,839	3.92
1943	504,117	1,905,047	3.78
1944	528,472	2,326,228	4.40
1945	475,662	2,113,884	4.44
1946	497,972	2,262,791	4.54
1947	512,469	2,574,117	5.02
1948	597,662	4,816,437	8.06
1949	573,236	5,411,061	9.44
1950	688,791	6,067,847	8.81
1951	719,076	7,720,989	10.74
1952	658,728	8,369,011	12.71
1953	696,189	9,567,608	13.74
1954	638,156	9,002,699	14.11
1955	778,413	11,715,027	15.05
1956	740,033	14,430,583	19.50
1957	539,628	9,234,767	17.11
1958	620,770	11,106,861	17.89
1959	715,997	12,633,751	17.64
1960	669,333	11,649,548	17.40
1961	625,483	8,466,873	13.54
1962	651,447	8,616,658	13.23
1963	764,947	10,429,272	13.63
1964	885,739	13,023,283	14.70
1965	922,906	13,398,940	14.52
1966	889,819	15,596,609	17.53

Note:
    Fiscal years, 1910 to 1942; calendar years, 1943–1966.

Source: Bureau of Indian Affairs, reprinted in Henry W. Hough, Development of Indian Resources (Denver: World Press, 1967), pp. 143–144.

Table 9.8
Surface Leases and Permits on Indian Lands, 1978–1984

YEAR	AGRICULTURAL LEASES			BUSINESS LEASES		
	NUMBER	ACRES	RENTAL	NUMBER	ACRES	RENTAL
1978	33,064	4,279,119.69	$35,430,568.64	3,792	102,393.32	$10,774,621.16
1982	45,095	5,348,218.26	$36,046,538.45	4,447	94,130.56	$16,020,856.44
1984	33,262	7,051,560.73	$48,361,924.72	4,958	86,239.86	$20,299,440.39

YEAR	OTHER LEASES			TOTAL		
	NUMBER	ACRES	RENTAL	NUMBER	ACRES	RENTAL
1978	22,478	145,698.43	$1,251,099.10	59,334	4,527,211.44	$47,456,288.90
1982	24,650	140,125.71	$2,580,720.10	74,192	5,582,474.53	$54,648,114.99
1984	29,072	134,401.01	$92,581,004.98	67,292	7,272,201.60	$161,242,370.09

Source: Office of Trust Responsibilities, Bureau of Indian Affairs, Annual Report of Indian Land and Income From Surface and Subsurface Leases as of September 30, 1978 (Washington, D.C.: U.S. Department of the Interior, n.d. [1979?]), p. 95; Annual Report of Indian Lands, September 30, 1982 (n.d. [1983?]), p.53; Annual Report of Indian Lands, September 30, 1984 (n.d. [1984?]), p. 54.

Table 9.9

Royalty Revenues, All Leasable Minerals, Indian Lands, 1946–1971

YEAR	OIL AND GAS OPERATIONS		MINING OPERATIONS		TOTALS	
	VALUE	ROYALTY	VALUE	ROYALTY	VALUE	ROYALTY
1937–1945	$126,576,610	$14,697,376	$188,929,966	$15,881,455	$315,506,576	$30,578,831
1946	19,549,681	2,257,035	9,550,340	527,727	29,100,021	2,784,762
1947	31,519,492	3,640,684	12,059,039	677,091	43,578,531	4,317,775
1948	46,672,972	5,361,384	14,985,509	850,729	61,658,481	6,212,113
1949	37,474,196	4,287,522	6,442,466	530,303	43,916,662	4,817,825
1950	38,281,811	4,392,287	11,044,509	876,861	49,326,320	5,269,148
1951	41,843,174	4,749,297	13,473,295	1,063,926	55,316,469	5,813,223
1952	40,654,689	4,612,642	13,029,351	1,092,324	53,684,040	5,704,966
1953	48,038,668	5,522,898	11,497,837	1,122,258	59,536,505	6,645,456
1954	50,931,731	5,958,121	14,377,733	1,442,981	65,309,464	7,401,102
1955	51,276,267	5,854,292	21,409,729	2,217,440	72,685,996	8,071,732
1956	55,971,039	6,418,870	31,133,250	3,393,677	87,104,289	9,812,547
1957	69,479,204	7,989,914	28,394,080	3,028,839	97,873,284	11,018,753
1958	126,341,443	15,167,706	28,308,060	2,887,912	154,649,503	18,055,618
1959	176,850,081	21,589,345	27,042,582	2,800,437	203,892,663	24,389,782
1960	168,509,591	21,151,044	28,177,253	2,951,776	196,686,844	24,102,820
1961	147,742,396	19,117,152	27,355,670	2,720,116	175,098,066	21,837,268
1962	136,512,664	18,002,610	22,518,923	2,262,281	159,031,587	20,264,891
1963	134,779,958	17,833,451	25,877,671	2,471,804	160,657,629	20,305,255
1964	115,521,788	15,013,867	27,430,112	2,615,437	142,951,900	17,629,304
1965	109,663,086	14,593,704	25,326,714	2,307,152	134,989,800	16,900,856
1966	106,826,872	14,272,026	27,540,962	2,330,874	134,367,834	16,602,900
1967	126,638,644	16,952,321	34,019,142	3,014,550	160,657,786	19,966,871
1968	110,940,205	15,159,309	32,399,750	2,925,829	143,339,955	18,085,138
1969	111,859,351	15,220,945	38,144,651	3,445,622	150,004,002	18,666,567
1970	120,457,129	16,105,829	48,891,162	4,483,122	169,348,291	20,588,951
1971	123,900,674	16,854,455	56,205,477	5,123,086	180,106,151	21,977,541
THROUGH 1971	$2,474,813,416	$312,776,086	$825,565,233	$75,045,609	$3,300,378,649	$387,821,695

Note: Excludes income from rents and bonuses.

Source: Conservation Division, U.S. Geological Survey, Federal and Indian Lands: Coal, Phosphate, Potash, Sodium, and Other Mineral Production, Royalty Income, and Related Statistics, 1920–1972 (Washington, D.C.: U.S. Department of the Interior, 1973), p. 36.

Table 9.10
Income from Petroleum, Natural Gas, and Other Minerals on
Indian Lands, 1949–1978

YEAR		TRIBAL	ALLOTTED	TOTAL
1949	O & G	$ 6,794,101	$ 4,709,351	$11,503,452
	Other	228,943	623,222	852,452
1950	O & G	6,691,228	4,388,153	11,079,381
	Other	133,708	387,439	521,147
1951	O & G	8,893,638	4,339,477	13,233,115
	Other	194,497	574,850	769,347
1952	O & G	13,565,491	5,560,109	19,125,600
	Other	382,094	1,286,019	1,668,113
1953	O & G	18,855,144	5,763,740	24,618,884
	Other	595,925	541,441	1,137,366
1954	O & G	23,040,900	10,636,789	33,677,689
	Other	920,121	299,130	1,219,251
1955	O & G	18,901,034	9,472,583	28,373,617
	Other	1,253,413	346,902	1,600,315
1956	O & G	33,681,456	7,325,620	41,007,076
	Other	2,127,949	753,583	2,881,532
1957	O & G	63,619,649	8,996,400	72,616,049
	Other	2,459,596	749,396	3,208,992
1958	O & G	46,837,566	8,372,901	55,210,467
	Other	2,812,298	1,595,589	4,407,887
1959	O & G	38,586,073	8,001,385	46,587,458
	Other	2,700,648	325,514	3,026,162
1960	O & G	41,505,232	6,200,266	47,705,498
	Other	2,129,062	531,972	2,661,034
1961	O & G	35,963,989	8,443,653	44,407,642
	Other	2,812,298	1,595,589	4,407,887
1962	O & G	32,392,150	5,758,964	38,151,114
	Other	2,108,304	1,088,311	3,196,615
1963	O & G	32,099,912	5,308,264	37,408,176
	Other	1,681,843	1,065,394	2,747,237
1964	O & G	60,517,310	5,493,175	66,010,485
	Other	1,501,766	1,265,234	2,767,000
1965	O & G	36,386,475	5,154,035	41,540,510
	Other	1,725,599	1,334,825	3,060,424
1966	O & G	24,595,881	5,002,101	29,597,982
	Other	1,860,293	932,352	2,792,645
1978	O & G	NA	NA	101,189,295
	Other	NA	NA	34,650,956
Ten-Year Average 1957–1966				
	O & G	41,250,424	6,673,114	47,923,538
	Other	2,108,867	995,853	3,104,720

Notes:

    O & G – Income from petroleum and natural gas leases.
    Other – Income from minerals other than petroleum and natural gas.
    NA – Not available.

Source: Bureau of Indian Affairs, reprinted in Henry Hough, Development of
       Indian Resources (Denver: World Press, 1967), p. 118; Bureau of
       Indian Affairs, Annual Report of Indian Land and Income From Surface
       and Subsurface Leases (Washington, D.C.: Bureau of Indian Affairs,
       1978), p. 95.

Table 9.11
Royalty Revenues,[1] Indian Mineral Leases, 1979–1984

YEAR	OIL PRODUCTION VOLUME[3]	OIL PRODUCTION VALUE[4]	OIL PRODUCTION REVENUES[4]	GAS PRODUCTION VOLUME[5]	GAS PRODUCTION VALUE[4]	GAS PRODUCTION REVENUES[4]	COAL PRODUCTION VOLUME[6]	COAL PRODUCTION VALUE[4]	COAL PRODUCTION REVENUES[4]	OTHER MINERAL PRODUCTION[2] VALUE[4]	OTHER MINERAL PRODUCTION[2] REVENUES[4]	TOTAL PRODUCTION VALUE[4]	TOTAL PRODUCTION REVENUES[4]
1937–1978	1,063	$3,432	$468	2,783	$679	$90	156	$633	$35	$1,252	$127	$5,996	$720
1979	24	288	43	118	177	24	25	247	10	67	12	779	89
1980	22	449	67	115	220	31	24	249	8	84	13	1,002	119
1981	22	705	104	119	268	37	22	265	9	99	12	1,337	162
1982	20	612	92	133	375	54	29	409	9	60	7	1,456	162
1983	20	593	90	116	350	50	25	406	9	97	7	1,446	156
1984	22	585	76	100	310	37	20	262	8	76	7	1,233	128
1920–1984	1,193	$6,664	$940	3,484	$2,379	$323	301	$2,471	$88	$1,735	$185	$13,249	$1,536

Notes:

1. Excludes income from rents and bonuses.
2. Other mineral production includes the following solid and fluid minerals: barite, bentonite, carbon dioxide, chat, clay, copper, feldspar, flourspar, gas lost, gasoline and LPG, geothermal energy, gilsonite, gypsum, iron ore, lead, limestone, molybdenum, oil lost, oil shale, phosphate, potash, quartz crystals, salt, sand-gravel, silica sand, sodium, sulfur, uranium, wavellite, and zinc.
3. In millions of barrels (42 U.S. gallons).
4. In millions of dollars.
5. In millions of mcf (thousand cubic feet).
6. In millions of short tons (2,000 pounds).

Source: Minerals Management Service, U.S. Department of the Interior, Mineral Revenues: The 1982 Report on Receipts From Federal and Indian Leases (Washington, D.C.: U.S. Government Printing Office, 1983), pp. 4–5; Mineral Revenues: The 1984 Report From Federal and Indian Leases (Washington, D.C.: U.S. Department of the Interior, n.d. [1985?]), pp. 6–7.

Table 9.12
Income from Rents and Bonuses, Indian Lands
in Eighteen States, 1982–1984

YEAR	RENTS	BONUSES	TOTAL
1982	$4,656,065	$35,455,416	$40,111,481
1983	3,621,550	15,418,356	19,039,906
1984	3,576,549	6,330,451	9,907,000

Note:
Excludes royalty income.

Source: Minerals Management Service, U.S. Department of the Interior, Mineral Revenues: The 1982 Report on Receipts From Federal and Indian Leases (Washington, D.C.: U.S. Government Printing Office, 1983), p. 51; Mineral Revenues: The 1983 Report on Receipts From Federal and Indian Leases (Washington, D.C.: U.S. Government Printing Office, 1984), p. 51; Minerals Revenues: The 1984 Report on Receipts From Federal and Indian Leases (Washington, D.C.: U.S. Department of the Interior, n.d. [1985?]), p. 57.

Table 9.13

Potential Use of Indian Lands, 1934, and Use of Indian Lands, 1953 and 1966

	1934 ACRES	1934 PERCENT	1953 ACRES	1953 PERCENT	1966[1] ACRES	1966[1] PERCENT
Farming	4,119,153	8	3,479,013	6	2,281,000	4
Irrigated lands	277,960	*	443,113	1	447,000	1
Susceptible, not irrigated	384,815	*	---	---	---	---
Dry farm lands	3,456,378	7	3,035,900	5	1,834,000	3
Grazing	35,755,732	69	37,655,394	67	33,185,000	60
Timber	10,237,856	20	10,036,233	18	14,522,000	26
Miscellaneous and Unused	1,514,352	3	4,970,809	9	5,348,000	10
Total	51,627,352	100	56,141,449	100	55,336,000	100

Notes:

* Less than 1%.
1. Includes lands in Alaska. Acres rounded to nearest thousand.

Sources: National Resources Board, Report on Land Planning, Part X: Indian Land Tenure, Economic Status, and Population Trends (Washington, D.C.: U.S. Government Printing Office, 1935), Table I; U.S. Congress, House of Representatives, Committee on Interior and Insular Affairs, Investigation of the Bureau of Indian Affairs, 82nd Congress, 2nd Session, House Report No. 2503, Serial 11582 (Washington, D.C.: U.S. Government Printing Office, 1953), pp. 75-78; Henry W. Hough, Development of Indian Resources (Denver: World Press, 1967), p. 76.

Table 9.14

Indian Lands in 1934, by Ownership and Character

OWNERSHIP	NUMBER OF TRACTS	FARMING (acres)	IRRIGABLE (acres)	FOREST AND GRAZING (acres)	TOTAL (acres)
Living Allotments	63,360	1,905,242	309,520	9,155,212	11,369,974
Deceased Allotments[1]	41,087	1,436,617	215,386	4,600,723	6,252,726
Tribal[2]	—	114,519	137,871	34,034,946	34,287,336
Reserves[3]	—	24,358	9,449	199,092	232,899
TOTAL	104,447	3,480,736	672,226	47,989,973	52,142,935

Notes:

1. Heirship lands. Incomplete; not all reservations distinguished between living and deceased allotments.
2. Unallotted lands.
3. Reserved for agency, school, etc.

Source: National Resources Board, Indian Land Tenure, Economic Status, and Population Trends, Report on Land Planning, Part X (Washington, D.C.: U.S. Government Printing Office, 1935), p. 27.

Table 9.15

Indian Lands in 1934, Selected Reservations, by Type of Ownership

AREA	LIVING ALLOTMENTS		DECEASED ALLOTMENTS		TRIBAL (ACRES)	RESERVES (ACRES)	TOTAL (ACRES)
	NUMBER	ACRES	NUMBER	ACRES			
Blackfeet, MT	4,914[1]	1,161,140[1]	—	—	54,465	1,726	1,217,331
Cherokee, NC	—	—	—	—	62,930	330	63,260
Cheyenne River, SD	3,062	492,942	1,180	424,357	378,329	40,842	1,336,470
Crow, MT	1,850	1,229,141	2,319	606,778	279,838	4,306	2,120,063
Flathead, MT	1,320	107,206	634	64,683	388,246	23,493	583,628
Ft. Apache, AZ	—	—	—	—	1,662,569	2,330	1,664,899
Ft. Peck, MT	2,435	813,522	1,272	311,732	45,449	3,329	1,174,032
Gila River, AZ	3,268	65,800	1,630	31,795	251,821	621	350,037
Hopi, AZ	—	—	—	—	2,472,220	100	2,472,320
Laguna, NM	—	—	—	—	253,490	—	253,490
Menominee, WI	—	—	—	—	231,018	505	231,523
Navajo, AZ–UT–NM	3,855[1]	764,486[1]	—	—	12,296,732	5,939	13,071,012
Northern Cheyenne, MT	1,205	192,800	252	40,320	205,320	4,400	442,840
Papago, AZ	—	—	—	—	2,663,874	—	2,663,874
Pine Ridge, SD	2,529	820,484	2,430	904,321	146,633	12,116	1,883,554
Red Lake, MN	—	—	—	—	406,890	350	407,240
Rosebud, SD	2,398	464,823	2,201	535,787	3,089	25,558	1,029,257
San Carlos, AZ	—	—	—	—	1,587,706	119	1,587,825
Standing Rock, ND–SD	1,442[1]	358,204[1]	1,780	511,406	92,836	7,387	969,833
Turtle Mountain, ND	252[1]	27,072[1]	—	—	—	160	27,232
Wind River, WY	892	84,042	1,262	143,242	2,019,603	2,689	2,249,576
Yakima, WA	1,842	201,911	1,544	157,043	749,129	3,688	1,113,771
Zuni, NM	—	—	—	—	332,326	770	333,096

Notes: 1. Living Allotments and deceased allotments not distinguished; figure represents all allotments on reservation.

Source: National Resources Board, Indian Land Tenure, Economic Status, and Population Trends, Report on Land Planning, Part X (Washington, D.C.: U.S. Government Printing Office, 1935), pp. 28–35.

Table 9.16
Ownership Status of Allotted Indian Trust Lands,
United States and Alaska, 1953

OWNERSHIP	NUMBER OF TRACTS	ACRES
Living Original Allottee	43,537	5,793,016.48
Other single owner	16,919	2,009,012.54
Joint ownership, 2 to 5 owners	31,212	3,805,815.11
Joint ownership, 6 or more owners	23,462	3,067,900.78
TOTAL	115,130	14,675,744.91

Source: U.S. Congress, House of Representatives, Committee on Interior and
          Insular Affairs, Investigation of the Bureau of Indian Affairs, 82nd
          Congress, 2nd session, House Reports, no. 2503, serial 11582
          (Washington, D.C.: U.S. Government Printing Office, 1953), p. 79.

Table 9.17
Ownership Status of Allotted Indian Trust Lands, Selected Reservations, 1953

AREA	LIVING ORIGINAL ALLOTTEE		OTHER SINGLE OWNER		JOINT OWNERSHIP, 2 TO 5	
	NO. OF TRACTS	ACRES	NO. OF TRACTS	ACRES	NO. OF TRACTS	ACRES
Blackfeet, MT	3,113	547,880	219	66,917	789	238,229
Cheyenne River, SD	992	201,376	30	4,800	775	157,325
Crow, MT	984	743,012	1,457	376,895	778	342,862
Flathead, MT	758	91,799	298	31,361	512	51,980
Ft. Peck, MT	2,898	700,160	234	28,320	1,912	172,000
Gila River, AZ	2,041	4,082	229	7,510	1,257	41,306
Laguna, NM	30	4,331	1	160	2	310
Navajo, AZ–UT–NM	2,000	320,000	100	16,000	917	146,720
Northern Cheyenne, MT	737	119,347	—	—	564	90,240
Papago, AZ	—	—	1	160	—	—
Pine Ridge, SD	2,682	429,175	473	75,737	1,058	562,615
Red Lake, MN	2	142	1	101	1	41
Rosebud, SD	1,890	265,000	360	63,000	1,170	21,000
San Carlos, AZ	1	160	1	40	4	520
Standing Rock, ND–SD	1,224	139,674	918	233,040	1,338	224,771
Turtle Mountain, ND	35	3,300	157	12,985	24	2,571
Wind River, WY	222	19,956	478	30,139	430	38,924
Yakima, WA	1,051	110,733	538	56,684	1,144	120,523
Zuni, NM	8	1,121	—	—	3	480

Table 9.17
(Continued)

AREA	JOINT OWNERSHIP, 6 OR MORE		ALL TYPES OF OWNERSHIP	
	NO. OF TRACTS	ACRES	NO. OF TRACTS	ACRES
Blackfeet, MT	687	212,888	4,808	1,065,914
Cheyenne River, SD	220	46,238	2,017	409,739
Crow, MT	846	273,932	4,065	1,736,701
Flathead, MT	256	24,868	1,824	200,008
Ft. Peck, MT	943	90,845	5,987	991,325
Gila River, AZ	1,371	45,062	4,898	97,960
Laguna, NM	1	160	34	4,961
Navajo, AZ-UT-NM	1,120	179,141	4,137	661,861
Northern Cheyenne, MT	156	24,960	1,457	234,547
Papago, AZ	—	—	1	160
Pine Ridge, SD	800	375,076	5,013	1,442,603
Red Lake, MN	—	—	4	284
Rosebud, SD	1,440	280,078	4,800	629,078
San Carlos, AZ	2	240	8	960
Standing Rock, ND-SD	918	195,652	4,398	793,137
Turtle Mountain, ND	152	17,380	368	36,236
Wind River, WY	540	54,002	1,670	143,021
Yakima, WA	980	103,247	3,713	391,187
Zuni, NM	2	332	13	1,933

Source: U.S. Congress, House of Representatives, Committee on Interior and Insular Affairs, Investigation of the Bureau of Indian Affairs, 82nd Congress, 2nd session, House Reports, no. 2503, serial 11582 (Washington, D.C.: U.S. Government Printing Office, 1953), pp. 79-83.

Table 9.18
Individual Allotments in Trust Status, by BIA Area,
Number, and Acreage, 1959

AREA OFFICE	ALL ALLOTMENTS[1]		ALLOTMENTS IN HEIRSHIP STATUS	
	NUMBER	ACREAGE	NUMBER	ACREAGE
Aberdeen	22,128	4,405,020	11,898	2,457,376
Anadarko	7,951	972,388	3,963	432,335
Billings	14,567	3,921,604	6,860	1,699,903
Gallup	5,033	791,693	2,143	340,380
Minneapolis	2,573	169,816	1,855	130,784
Muskogee	259[2]	855,712	192[2]	337,236
Phoenix	9,849	326,384	5,803	222,115
Portland	12,444	1,409,549	7,085	809,641
Sacramento	1,917	63,709	988	36,778
TOTAL	76,721	12,915,875	40,787	6,466,548

Notes:
1. Still in trust status.
2. Five Civilized Tribes Agency is not included under "number" but
    is under "acreage."

Source: Stephen A. Langone, "The Heirship Land Problem and Its Effect On the
         Indians, the Tribe, and Effective Utilization," in U.S. Congress,
         Joint Economic Committee, Toward Economic Development for Native
         Communities (Washington, D.C.: U.S. Government Printing Office,
         1969), p. 529.

Table 9.19
Indian Heirship Land, by Use and Classification, 1960 (Acres)

CLASSIFICATION	USED BY INDIANS	USED BY NON-INDIANS	NOT USED	TOTAL[1]
Irrigated	34,157	107,512	69,675	211,344
Dry farm	79,187	725,044	60,208	869,037
Grazing	1,688,461	2,548,385	150,245	4,381,109
Forest	210,922	111,067	127,871	405,312
Other	40,994	137,844	133,306	309,225
TOTAL	2,053,721	3,629,852	541,305	6,176,027

Note:
1. This total does not agree necessarily with a total for the first
    three columns. Some tracts are partly one type of land and partly
    another, e.g., forestry and grazing.

Source: Stephen A. Langone, "The Heirship Land Problem and Its Effect On the
         Indian, the Tribe, and Effective Utilization," in U.S. Congress,
         Joint Economic Committee, Toward Economic Development for Native
         American Communities (Washington, D.C.: U.S. Government Printing
         Office, 1953), p. 532.

Table 9.20

Heirship Lands on Fifty-two Reservations, by Number of Owners, 1965

AREA	NUMBER OF RESERVATIONS	TOTAL TRACTS	SINGLE OWNER	2 TO 5 OWNERS	6 TO 10 OWNERS	11 OR MORE OWNERS
Gallup	2	346	244	30	31	41
California	4	342	256	70	11	5
Anadarko	2	3,443	1,321	1,044	457	621
Aberdeen	3	11,043	4,753	2,862	1,338	2,090
Portland	28	18,162	7,255	4,958	2,467	3,482
Phoenix	2	5,835	2,030	1,683	936	1,186
Billings	11	22,607	8,580	8,530	2,256	3,241
TOTAL	52	31,778	24,439	19,177	7,496	10,666

Source: Stephen A. Langone, "The Heirship Land Problem and Its Effect On the Indian, the Tribe, and Effective Utilization," in U.S. Congress, Joint Economic Committee, Toward Economic Development for Native American Communities (Washington, D.C.: U.S. Government Printing Office, 1953), p. 529.

Bibliography

Adams, Evelyn C. *American Indian Education: Government Schools and Economic Progress.* New York: King's Crown Press, 1946.

Applebaum, Diana Karter. "The Level of the Poverty Line: A Historical Survey." *Social Service Review* 51 (September 1977): 514-523.

Barsh, Russel Lawrence. "The Rise and Fall of Indigenous Agrarian Democracy." Paper presented at the symposium "Plains Indian Cultures: Past and Present Meanings," sponsored by the Center for Great Plains Studies, University of Nebraska–Lincoln, March 1986.

Berry, Brewton. *The Education of American Indians: A Survey of the Literature.* Committee print, prepared for the Special Subcommittee on Indian Education, Committee on Labor and Public Welfare, U.S. Senate. Washington, D.C.: U.S. Government Printing Office, 1969.

Bureau of Municipal Research. "Administration of the Indian Office." *Municipal Research,* no. 65 (September 1915).

Burt, Larry W. *Tribalism in Crisis: Federal Indian Policy, 1953-1961.* Albuquerque, N.M.: University of New Mexico Press, 1982.

Commission on the Rights, Liberties, and Responsibilities of the American Indian. *The Indian: America's Unfinished Business.* Compiled by William A. Brophy and Sophia D. Aberle. Norman: University of Oklahoma Press, 1966.

Crosby, Alfred W., Jr. *The Columbian Exchange: Biological and Social Consequences of 1492.* Westport, Connecticut: Greenwood Press, 1972.

Deloria, Vine, Jr. "The Twentieth Century." In *Red Men and Hat-Wearers: Viewpoints in Indian History,* edited by Daniel Tyler. Boulder, Colorado: Pruett Publishing Company, 1976, pp. 155-166.

Deloria, Vine, Jr., and Clifford Lytle. *The Nations Within: The Past and Future of American Indian Sovereignty.* New York: Pantheon, 1984.

Dobyns, Henry F. "Estimating Aboriginal American Population: An Appraisal of Techniques with a New Hemispheric Estimate." *Current Anthropology* 7 (1966): 395-416.

_____. *Native American Historical Demography: A Critical Bibliography.* Blooming-
ton: Indiana University Press, 1976.

_____. *Their Number Become Thinned: Native American Population Dynamics in
Eastern North America.* Knoxville: University of Tennessee Press, 1983.

Doran, Michael F. "Population Statistics of Nineteenth Century Indian Territory."
Chronicles of Oklahoma 53 (1975): 492-515.

Fay, Keith L. *Developing Indian Employment Opportunities.* Washington, D.C.:
U.S. Government Printing Office, n.d. [1973].

Fletcher, Alice C. *Indian Education and Civilization.* Washington, D.C.: U.S.
Government Printing Office, 1888. 48th Congress, 2nd session. *Senate
Executive Documents,* no. 95, serial 2264.

Gibson, Arrell Morgan. "The Great Plains as a Colonization Zone for Eastern
Indians." In *Ethnicity on the Great Plains,* edited by Frederick C. Luebke.
Lincoln: University of Nebraska Press and Center for Great Plains Studies,
1980, pp. 19-37.

_____. ed. *America's Exiles: Indian Colonization in Oklahoma.* Oklahoma City:
Oklahoma Historical Society, 1976.

Greenbaum, Susan D. "In Search of Lost Tribes: Anthropology and the Federal
Acknowledgement Process." *Human Organization* 44 (Winter 1985): 361-367.

Gundlach, James H.; P. Nelson Reid; and Alden E. Roberts. "Migration, Labor
Mobility, and Relocation Assistance: The Case of the American Indian."
Social Service Review 51 (September 1977): 464-473.

Hadley, J. Nixon. "Demography of the American Indians." *Annals of the American
Academy of Political and Social Science* 311 (May 1957): 23-30.

Hagan, William T. *Indian Police and Judges; Experiments in Acculturations and
Control.* New Haven, Connecticut: Yale University Press, 1966.

_____. "The Reservation Policy: Too Little and Too Late." In *Indian-White
Relations: A Persistent Paradox,* edited by Jane F. Smith and Robert M.
Kvasnicka. Washington, D.C.: Howard University Press, 1976, pp. 157-169.

Hough, Henry W. *Development of Indian Resources.* Denver: World Press, 1967.

Iverson, Peter. *The Navajo Nation.* Albuquerque: University of New Mexico
Press, 1981.

Johnson, Steven L., comp. *Guide to American Indian Documents in the Congressional
Serial Set: 1817-1899.* New York: Clearwater Publishing Company, 1977.

Kickingbird, Kirke, and Karen Ducheneaux. *One Hundred Million Acres.* New
York: Macmillan, 1973.

Kinney, Jay P. *A Continent Lost—A Civilization Won: Indian Land Tenure in America.*
Baltimore: The Johns Hopkins Press, 1937.

Langone, Stephen A. "The Heirship Land Problem and Its Effect upon the Indian,
the Tribe, and Effective Utilization." In U.S. Congress, Joint Economic
Committee, *Toward Economic Development for Native American
Communities,* vol. 2. Washington, D.C.: U.S. Government Printing Office,
1969, pp. 519-548.

_____. "A Statistical Profile of the Indian: The Lack of Numbers." In U.S. Con-
gress, Joint Economic Committee, *Toward Economic Development for Native
American Communities,* vol. 1. Washington, D.C.: U.S. Government
Printing Office, 1969, pp. 1-18.

Levitan, Sar A., and Barbara Hetrick. *Big Brother's Indian Program—With
Reservations.* New York: McGraw-Hill, 1971.

Levitan, Sar A., and William B. Johnston. *Indian Giving: Federal Programs and Native Americans*, Policy Studies in Employment and Welfare, no. 20. Baltimore: The Johns Hopkins University Press, 1975.

Lowry, Ira S. "The Science and Politics of Ethnic Enumeration." In *Ethnicity and Public Policy*, edited by Winston A. Van Horne. Milwaukee: University of Wisconsin System American Ethnic Studies Coordinating Committee, 1982, pp. 42-61.

Madigan, LaVerne. *The American Indian Relocation Program*. New York: Association on American Indian Affairs, 1956.

Meriam, Lewis, and others. *The Problem of Indian Administration*, Institute for Government Research, Studies in Administration. Baltimore: The Johns Hopkins Press, 1928.

Morse, Jedidiah. *A Report to the Secretary of War of the United States, on Indian Affairs, Comprising a Narrative of a Tour Performed in the Summer of 1820 . . . for the Purpose of Ascertaining, for the Use of the Government, the Actual State of the Indian Tribes in Our Country*. New Haven, Connecticut: S. Converse, 1822.

Nagler, Mark. *Indians in the City: A Study of the Urbanization of Indians in Toronto*. Ottawa: Canadian Research Centre for Anthropology, Saint Paul University, 1970.

Neils, Elaine M. *Reservation to City: Indian Migration and Federal Relocation*. University of Chicago, Department of Geography, Research Paper no. 131. Chicago: Department of Geography, University of Chicago, 1971.

Parman, Donald L. *The Navajos and the New Deal*. New Haven, Connecticut: Yale University Press, 1976.

Philip, Kenneth R. "Stride toward Freedom: The Relocation of Indians to Cities, 1952-1960." *Western Historical Quarterly* 16 (April 1985): 175-190.

Prucha, Francis Paul. *American Indian Policy in the Formative Years: The Indian Trade and Intercourse Acts, 1790-1834*. Cambridge, Massachusetts: Harvard University Press, 1962.

_____. "Andrew Jackson's Indian Policy: A Reassessment." *Journal of American History* 56 (December 1969): 527-539.

_____. *A Bibliographical Guide to the History of Indian-White Relations in the United States*. Chicago: University of Chicago Press, 1977.

_____. "Federal Indian Policy in the Twentieth Century." *Western Historical Quarterly* 15 (January 1985): 5-18.

_____. "Indian Removal and the Great American Desert." *Indiana Magazine of History* 59 (December 1963): 299-322.

_____. *Indian-White Relations in the United States: A Bibliography of Works Published 1975-1980*. Lincoln: University of Nebraska Press, 1982.

_____. *United States Indian Policy: A Critical Bibliography*. Bloomington: Indiana University Press, 1977.

Putney, Diane Therese. "Fighting the Scourge: American Indian Morbidity and Federal Indian Policy, 1897-1928." Ph.D. dissertation, Marquette University, 1980.

Satz, Ronald N. *American Indian Policy in the Jacksonian Era*. Lincoln: University of Nebraska Press, 1975.

_____. "Indian Policy in the Jacksonian Era: The Old Northwest as a Test Case." *Michigan History* 60 (Spring 1976): 71-93.

_____. "Thomas Hartley Crawford, 1838-45." In *The Commissioners of Indian Affairs, 1824-1977,* edited by Robert M. Kvasnicka and Herman J. Viola. Lincoln: University of Nebraska Press, 1980, pp. 23-27.

Schmeckebier, Laurence F. *The Office of Indian Affairs: Its History, Activities, and Organization,* Institute for Government Research, Service Monographs of the United States Government, no. 48. Baltimore; The Johns Hopkins Press, 1927.

Schoolcraft, Henry R. *Historical and Statistical Information Respecting the History, Conditions, and Prospects of the Indian Tribes of the United States,* 6 volumes. Philadelphia: Lippincott, Grambo, and Company, 1851-1857.

Sorkin, Alan L. *American Indians and Federal Aid.* Washington, D.C.: Brookings Institution, 1971.

_____. "Indian Trust Funds." In U.S. Congress, Joint Economic Committee, *Toward Economic Development for Native American Communities,* vol. 2. Washington, D.C.: U.S. Government Printing Office, 1969, pp. 449-459.

Stanley, Sam, ed. *American Indian Economic Development.* T ie Hague: Mouton Publishers, 1978.

Stanley, Sam, and Robert K. Thomas. "Current Social and Demographic Trends among North American Indians." *Annals of the American Academy of Political and Social Science* 436 (March 1978): 111-120.

Statistics Canada. *Canada Yearbook, 1985.* Ottawa: Minister of Supply and Services, 1985.

Stuart, Paul. "Administrative Reform in Indian Affairs." *Western Historical Quarterly* 16 (April 1985): 133-146.

_____. "Bureau of Indian Affairs." In *Government Agencies,* edited by Donald R. Whitnah. The Greenwood Encyclopedia of American Institutions, no. 7. Westport, Connecticut: Greenwood Press, 1983, pp. 16-20.

_____. *A History of the Flandreau Santee Sioux Tribe.* Flandreau, South Dakota: Flandreau Santee Sioux Tribe, 1971.

_____. *The Indian Office: Growth and Development of an American Institution, 1865-1900,* Studies in American History and Culture, no. 12. Ann Arbor, Michigan: UMI Research Press, 1979.

_____. "United States Indian Policy: From the Dawes Act to the American Indian Policy Review Commission." *Social Service Review* 51 (September 1977): 451-463.

Sutton, Imre. *Indian Land Tenure: Bibliographical Essays and a Guide to the Literature.* New York: Clearwater Publishing Company, 1975.

Swanton, John R. *The Indian Tribes of North America,* Smithsonian Institution, Bureau of American Ethnology, Bulletin 145. Washington, D.C.: U.S. Government Printing Office, 1952.

Szasz, Margaret. *Education and the American Indian: The Road to Self-Determination, 1928-1973.* Albuquerque: University of New Mexico Press, 1974.

Taylor, Theodore W. *American Indian Policy.* Mt. Airy, Maryland: Lomond Publications, 1983.

_____. *The Bureau of Indian Affairs,* Westview Library of Federal Departments, Agencies, and Systems. Boulder, Colorado: Westview Press, 1984.

Thornton, Russell. "Cherokee Population Losses during the Trail of Tears: A New Perspectiv⌣ and a New Estimate." *Ethnohistory* 31 (November 1984): 289-300.

Thornton, Russell, and Jeanne Marsh-Thornton. "Estimating Prehistoric American Indian Population Size for the United States: Implications of the Nineteenth Century Population Decline and Nadir." *American Journal of Physical Anthropology* 55 (1981): 47-53.

Tyler, S. Lyman. *A History of Indian Policy.* Washington, D.C.: U.S. Government Printing Office, 1973.

Ubelaker, Douglas H. "Prehistoric New World Population Size: Historical Review and Current Appraisal of New World Estimates." *American Journal of Physical Anthropology* 45 (1976): 661-666.

U.S. Bureau of Indian Affairs. *Annual Report of Indian Lands and Income from Surface and Subsurface Leases as of September 30, 1978.* Washington, D.C.: U.S. Department of the Interior, n.d. [1979?].

———. *Annual Report of Indian Lands, September 30, 1982.* Washington, D.C.: Department of the Interior, 1982.

———. *Annual Report of Indian Lands, September 30, 1983.* Washington, D.C.: Department of the Interior, 1983.

———. *Annual Report of Indian Lands, September 30, 1984.* Washington, D.C.: Department of the Interior, 1984.

———. *BIA Profile: The Bureau of Indian Affairs and American Indians.* Washington, D.C.: U.S. Government Printing Office, 1981.

———. *Indian Land and Its Care.* Lawrence, Kansas: The Haskell Press, 1953.

———. *Local Estimates of Resident Indian Population and Labor Force Status, January 1982.* Washington, D.C.: U.S. Department of the Interior, 1982.

———. *Local Estimates of Resident Indian Population and Labor Force Status, August 1983.* Washington, D.C.: U.S. Government Printing Office, 1983.

———. *Statistics Concerning Indian Schools,* FY 1957-1979. Washington, D.C.: U.S. Department of the Interior, 1958-1982.

———. "Tabular Statement of Disbursements Made from the Appropriations for the Indian Department for the Fiscal Year Ending July 30, 1874 . . . " 43rd Congress, 2nd Session, *House Executive Documents,* no. 6, serial 1341.

———. "Tabular Statement of Disbursements, 1875," 44th Congress, 1st Session, *House Executive Documents,* no. 6, serial 1685.

———. "Tabular Statement of Disbursements, 1876," 44th Congress, 2nd Session, *House Executive Documents,* no. 6, serial 1754.

———. "Tabular Statement of Disbursements, 1877," 45th Congress, 2nd Session, *House Executive Documents,* no. 6, serial 1805.

———. "Tabular Statement of Disbursements, 1878," 45th Congress, 2nd Session, *House Executive Documents,* no. 6, serial 1855.

———. "Tabular Statement of Disbursements, 1879," 46th Congress, 2nd Session, *House Executive Documents,* no. 6, serial 1916.

———. "Tabular Statement of Disbursements, 1880," 46th Congress, 3rd Session, *House Executive Documents,* no. 6, serial 1965.

———. "Tabular Statement of Disbursements, 1881," 47th Congress, 1st Session, *House Executive Documents,* no. 6, serial 2024.

———. "Tabular Statement of Disbursements, 1882," 47th Congress, 2nd Session, *House Executive Documents,* no. 6, serial 2106.

———. "Tabular Statement of Disbursements, 1883," 48th Congress, 1st Session, *House Executive Documents,* no. 6, serial 2193.

————. "Tabular Statement of Disbursements, 1884," 48th Congress, 2nd Session, *House Executive Documents*, no. 6, serial 2290.

————. "Tabular Statement of Disbursements, 1885," 49th Congress, 1st Session, *House Executive Documents*, no. 6, serial 2387.

————. "Tabular Statement of Disbursements, 1886," 49th Congress, 2nd Session, *House Executive Documents*, no. 6, serial 2477.

————. "Tabular Statement of Disbursements, 1887," 50th Congress, 1st Session, *House Executive Documents*, no. 8, serial 2550.

————. "Tabular Statement of Disbursements, 1888," 50th Congress, 2nd Session, *House Executive Documents*, no. 8, serial 2645.

————. "Tabular Statement of Disbursements, 1889," 51st Congress, 1st Session, *House Executive Documents*, no. 8, serial 2739.

————. "Tabular Statement of Disbursements, 1890," 51st Congress, 2nd Session, *House Executive Documents*, no. 8, serial 2855.

————. "Tabular Statement of Disbursements, 1891," 52nd Congress, 1st Session, *House Executive Documents*, no. 8, serial 2949.

————. "Tabular Statement of Disbursements, 1892," 52nd Congress, 2nd Session, *House Executive Documents*, no. 239, serial 3107.

————. "Tabular Statement of Disbursements, 1893," 53rd Congress, 2nd Session, *House Executive Documents*, no. 36, serial 3223.

————."Tabular Statement of Disbursements, 1895" 54th Congress, 1st Session, *House Executive Documents*, no. 36, serial 3414.

————. *U.S. Indian Population and Land, 1962.* Washington, D.C.: U.S. Department of the Interior, 1962.

U.S. Bureau of the Census. *Census of Population: 1950. Characteristics of the Population, United States Summary,* vol. 2, pt. 1. Washington, D.C.: U.S. Government Printing Office, 1953.

————. *Census of Population: 1950. Special Reports. Non-white Population by Race,* P-E No. 3B. Washington, D.C.: U.S. Government Printing Office, 1953.

————. *Census of Population: 1960. Characteristics of the Population, United States Summary,* vol. 1, pt. 1. Washington, D.C.: U.S. Government Printing Office, 1964.

————. *Census of Population: 1960. Subject Reports. Non-white Population by Race,* Final Report PC(2)-1C. Washington, D.C.: U.S. Government Printing Office, 1963.

————. *Census of Population: 1970. Characteristics of the Population, United States Summary,* vol. 1, part 1, section 2. Washington, D.C.: U.S. Government Printing Office, 1973.

————. *Census of Population: 1970. Subject Reports. American Indians,* Final Report PC(2)-1F. Washington, D.C.: U.S. Government Printing Office, 1973.

————. *1980 Census of Population. Characteristics of the Population. General Social and Economic Characteristics. United States Summary,* vol. 1, chapter C, part 1, PC80-1-C1. Washington, D.C.: U.S. Government Printing Office, 1983.

————. *1980 Census of Population. General Population Characteristics. Alaska,* PC80-1-C3. Washington, D.C.: U.S. Government Printing Office, 1983.

————. *1980 Census of Population. Characteristics of the Population, Detailed Population Characteristics, United States Summary,* PC80-1-D1-A. Washington, D.C.: U.S. Government Printing Office, 1984.

_____. *1980 Census of Population. Subject Reports. American Indians, Eskimos, and Aleuts on Identified Reservations and in the Historic Indian Areas of Oklahoma (Excluding Urbanized Areas)*, PC80-2-ND, parts 1 and 2. Washington, D.C.: U.S. Government Printing Office, 1986.

_____. *1980 Census of Population. Supplementary Report. American Indian Areas and Alaska Native Villages*, PC80-S1-13. Washington, D.C.: U.S. Government Printing Office, 1984.

_____. *Report on Indians Taxed and Indians Not Taxed in the United States (Excluding Alaska) at the Eleventh Census: 1890*. Washington, D.C.: U.S. Government Printing Office, 1894.

_____. *The Indian Population of the United States and Alaska: 1910*. Washington, D.C.: U.S. Government Printing Office, 1915.

_____. *The Indian Population of the United States and Alaska: 1930*. Washington, D.C.: U.S. Government Printing Office, 1937.

U.S. Commissioner of Indian Affairs, *Annual Report*, 1824-1949. Included in U.S. Secretary of War, *Annual Report*, 1824-1848, and U.S. Secretary of the Interior, *Annual Report*, 1849-1949. LaCrosse, Wisconsin: Brookhaven Press, n.d. [1976-77]. A microfilm edition is available.

_____. *Statistical Supplement to the Annual Report of the Commissioner of Indian Affairs*, 1939-1945. Washington, D.C.: U.S. Department of the Interior, 1939-1945.

U.S. Congress, American Indian Policy Review Commission. *Final Report*, 2 vols. Washington, D.C.: U.S. Government Printing Office, 1977.

_____. *Report on Reservation Resource Development and Protection*, Final Report of Task Force 7. Washington, D.C.: U.S. Government Printing Office, 1976.

_____. *Report on Terminated and Nonfederally Recognized Tribes*, Final Report of Task Force 10. Washington, D.C.: U.S. Government Printing Office, 1976.

U.S. Congress, House of Representatives, Committee on Indian Affairs. "On Repealing the Act of 1819, for the Civilization of the Indians." June 10, 1842, 27th Congress, 2nd session, *House Reports*, no. 854, serial 410.

_____. "Regulating the Indian Department." May 20, 1834, 23rd Congress, 1st Session, *House Reports*, no. 474, serial 26.

U.S. Congress, House of Representatives, Committee on Interior and Insular Affairs. *Indian Heirship Land Study*, Committee Print no. 27, 2 vols. Washington, D.C.: U.S. Government Printing Office, 1961.

_____. *Investigation of the Bureau of Indian Affairs*. 82nd Congress, 2nd session, *House Reports*, no. 2503, serial 11582. Washington, D.C.: U.S. Government Printing Office, 1953.

U.S. Congress, House of Representatives, Committee on Public Lands. "Area, in Acres, of Lands in Federal Ownership." September 19, 1950, 81st Congress, 2nd session, *House Reports*, no. 3116, serial 11384.

U.S. Congress, Joint Economic Committee. *Toward Economic Development for Native American Communities*, 2 vols. Washington, D.C.: U.S. Government Printing Office, 1969.

U.S. Congress, Office of Technology Assessment. *Indian Health Care*, OTA-H-290. Washington, D.C.: U.S. Government Printing Office, 1986.

U.S. Congress, Senate, Committee on Labor and Public Welfare, Special Subcommittee on Indian Education. *Indian Education: A National Tragedy—A*

National Challenge. Washington, D.C.: U.S. Government Printing Office, 1969, 91st Congress, 1st session, *Senate Reports*, no. 501, serial 12836-1.

U.S. Department of Commerce. *Federal and State Indian Reservations and Indian Trust Areas.* Washington, D.C.: U.S. Government Printing Office, 1974.

U.S. Department of the Interior. *Register of Officers and Agents, Civil, Military, and Naval, in the Service of the United States on the Thirtieth of September, 1865.* Washington, D.C.: U.S. Government Printing Office, 1866.

————. *Register of Officers and Agents, 1869.* Washington, D.C.: U.S. Government Printing Office, 1870.

————. *Register of Officers and Agents, 1869.* Washington, D.C.: U.S. Government Printing Office, 1870.

————. *Register of Officers and Agents, 1871.* Washington, D.C.: U.S. Government Printing Office, 1872.

————. *Register of Officers and Agents, 1873.* Washington, D.C.: U.S. Government Printing Office, 1874.

————. *Register of Officers and Agents, 1875.* Washington, D.C.: U.S. Government Printing Office, 1876.

————. *Register of Officers and Agents, 1877.* Washington, D.C.: U.S. Government Printing Office, 1878.

————. *Official Register of the United States, Containing a List of Officers and Employes in the Civil, Military, and Naval Service on the Thirtieth of June, 1879.* Washington, D.C.: U.S. Government Printing Office, 1879.

————. *Official Register of the United States, 1881.* Washington, D.C.: U.S. Government Printing Office, 1881.

————. *Official Register of the United States, 1883.* Washington, D.C.: U.S. Government Printing Office, 1883.

————. *Official Register of the United States, 1885.* Washington, D.C.: U.S. Government Printing Office, 1885.

————. *Official Register of the United States, 1887.* Washington, D.C.: U.S. Government Printing Office, 1887.

————. *Official Register of the United States, 1889.* Washington, D.C.: U.S. Government Printing Office, 1889.

————. *Official Register of the United States, 1891.* Washington, D.C.: U.S. Government Printing Office, 1891.

————. *Offical Register of the United States, 1893.* Washington, D.C.: U.S. Government Printing Office, 1893.

————. *Official Register of the United States, 1895.* Washington, D.C.: U.S. Government Printing Office, 1895.

————. *Official Register of the United States, 1897.* Washington, D.C.: U.S. Government Printing Office, 1897.

U.S. Federal Trade Commission. *Staff Report on Mineral Leasing on Indian Lands.* Washington, D.C.: U.S. Government Printing Office, 1975.

U.S. Geological Survey. *Federal and Indian Lands: Coal, Phosphate, Potash, Sodium and Other Mineral Production, Royalty Income, and Related Statistics, 1920-1972.* Washington, D.C.: U.S. Government Printing Office, 1973.

U.S. Indian Health Service. *Chart Series Book, April 1986.* Washington, D.C.: U.S. Government Printing Office, 1986.

U.S. Minerals Management Service. *Mineral Revenues: The 1982 Report on Receipts from Federal and Indian Leases.* Washington, D.C.: U.S. Government Printing Office, 1983.

———. *Mineral Revenues: The 1983 Report on Receipts from Federal and Indian Leases.* Washington, D.C.: U.S. Government Printing Office, 1984.

———. *Mineral Revenues: The 1984 Report on Receipts from Federal and Indian Leases.* Washington, D.C.: Department of the Interior, n.d. [1985].

U.S. National Resources Board. *Indian Land Tenure, Economic Status, and Population Trends,* Report on Land Planning, Part X. Washington, D.C.: U.S. Government Printing Office, 1935.

———. *Report of the Land Planning Committee,* Report on National Planning and Public Works, Part II. Washington, D.C.: U.S. Government Printing Office, 1935.

U.S. Secretary of War. "Indians Removed to West Mississippi From 1789." February 5, 1839, 25th Congress, 3rd Session, *House Documents,* no. 147, serial 347.

U.S. Weather Bureau. *Climatic Survey of the United States.* Washington, D.C.: U.S. Government Printing Office, 1930-31.

Warren King and Associates, Inc. *Bureau of Indian Affairs Management Study,* Report to the American Indian Policy Review Commission. Washington, D.C.: U.S. Government Printing Office, 1976.

Washburn, Wilcomb E. *Red Man's Land/White Man's Law: A Study of the Past and Present Status of the American Indian.* New York: Charles Scribner's Sons, 1971.

Wilkie, James W., and Adam Perkal, eds. *Statistical Abstract of Latin America,* vol. 24. Los Angeles: UCLA Latin America Center Publications, University of California, 1985.

Index

About the Author

PAUL STUART is Associate Professor in the School of Social Work at the University of Alabama. He is author of *History of the Flandreau Santee Sioux Tribe* and *The Indian Office, 1865-1900*, as well as articles in social work and historical periodicals.